Poetics of Repair

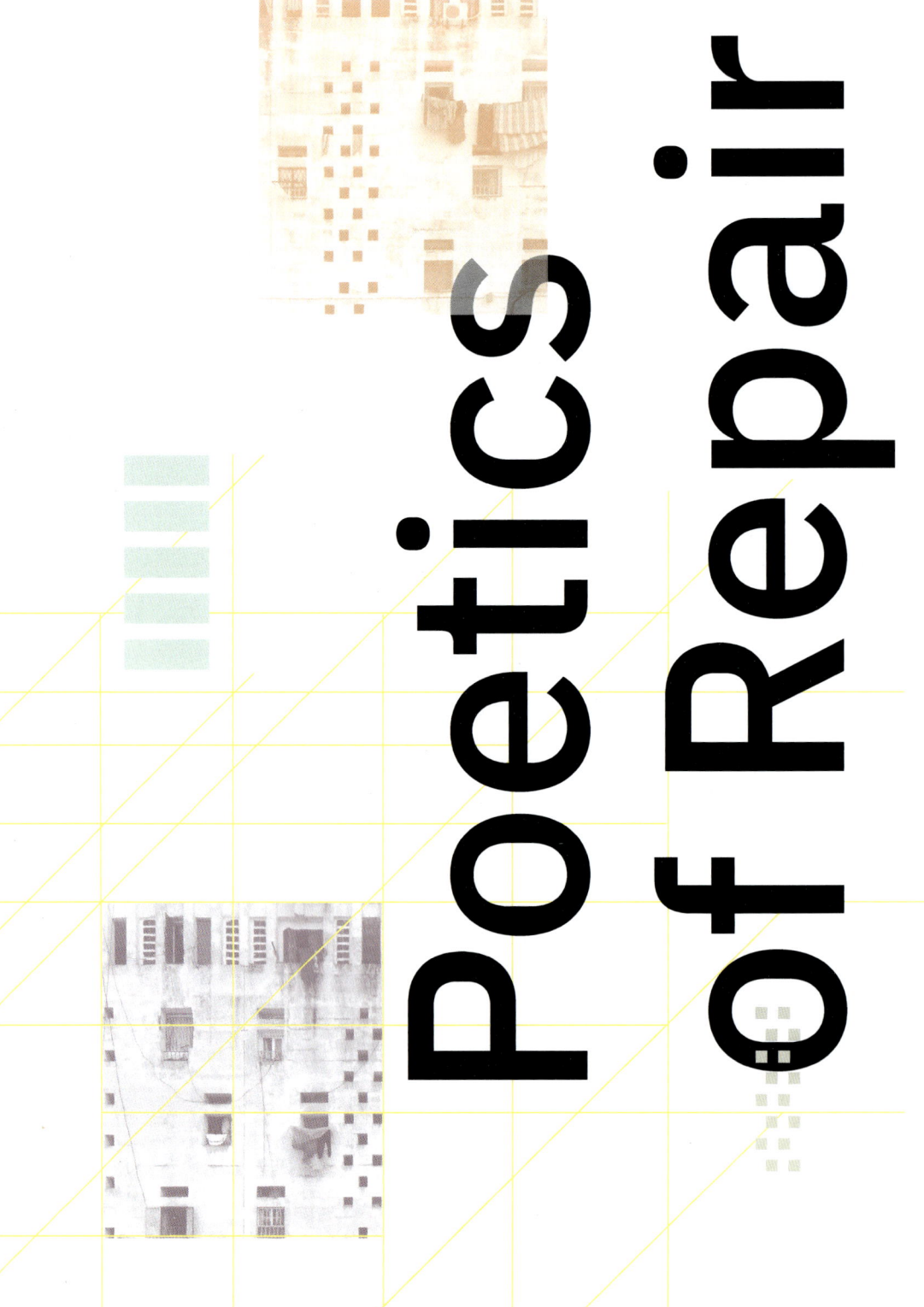

Poetics of Repair

Contemporary Arts and Afterlives of Colonial-Era Mass Housing in the Maghreb

Katarzyna Pieprzak

Duke University Press *Durham and London* 2025

© 2025 DUKE UNIVERSITY PRESS All rights reserved
Printed in the United States of America on acid-free paper ∞
Project Editor: Ihsan Taylor
Designed by Courtney Leigh Richardson
Typeset in Garamond Premier Pro and IBM Plex
by Westchester Publishing Services

Library of Congress Cataloging-in-Publication Data
Names: Pieprzak, Katarzyna, author.
Title: Poetics of repair : contemporary arts and afterlives of colonial-era mass housing in the Maghreb / Katarzyna Pieprzak.
Description: Durham : Duke University Press, 2025. | Includes bibliographical references and index.
Identifiers: LCCN 2024017403 (print)
LCCN 2024017404 (ebook)
ISBN 9781478031284 (paperback)
ISBN 9781478028055 (hardcover)
ISBN 9781478060277 (ebook)
Subjects: LCSH: Arts and society—Africa, North. | Arts, North African—Social aspects. | Arts, North African—Political aspects. | Public housing—Africa, North—History. | Human ecology in art. | Africa, North—Colonial influence. | BISAC: ART / Art & Politics | SOCIAL SCIENCE / Ethnic Studies / Middle Eastern Studies
Classification: LCC NX180.S6 P534 2025 (print) | LCC NX180.S6 (ebook) | DDC 700.1/030961—dc23/eng/20240820
LC record available at https://lccn.loc.gov/2024017403
LC ebook record available at https://lccn.loc.gov/2024017404

Cover art: (*Background and top/middle details*) Stéphane Couturier, *Alger—Cité "Climat de France" Façade #1*, 2011–12. Courtesy of the artist. (*Bottom left detail*) Wikimedia Commons.

For STELLA *and* MARGOT

CONTENTS

Note on Translations and Transliterations   ix

PREFACE
Unexpected Paths to Mass Housing   xi

Introduction
Mass Housing, Maghrebi Art, and the Poetics of Repair   1

1 ## Sonic Repairs to the Grid
Art Engages the Epistemology of Hay Mohammadi, Casablanca   27

2 ## Affecting Relation in Climat de France, Algiers
Decolonial Poetics and Embodied Ethics of Recognition   69

3 ## Remembering and Repairing Women's Homes
Nanterre, Bidonville de la Folie   115

Conclusion
Touching Feet and Moving Hands: Art's Repair from Affective Gesture to Capacious Home   165

Acknowledgments   173   Notes   175
Bibliography   195   Index   205

NOTE ON TRANSLATIONS AND TRANSLITERATIONS

Unless otherwise noted, all translations from French and Moroccan Arabic are mine. As common practice, I cite published English translations when they exist, but on a few occasions, I have altered those translations. Those instances are noted.

Transliteration of quotes from spoken Moroccan Arabic, Darija, follow the IJMES system for Modern Standard Arabic when possible. However, Moroccan and Algerian personal names and place names appear as they would most commonly figure in vernacular North African contexts.

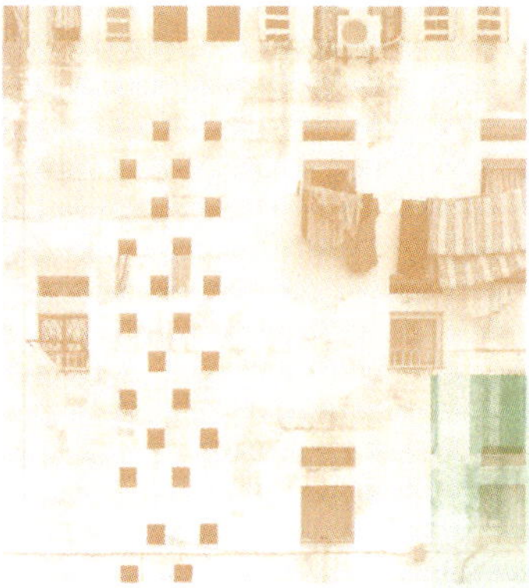

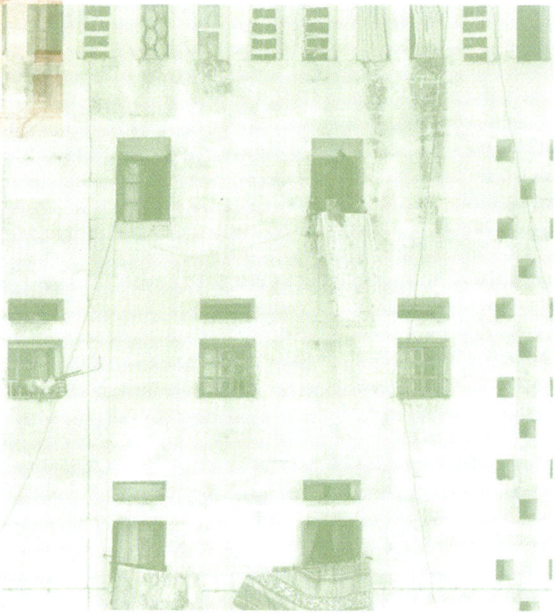

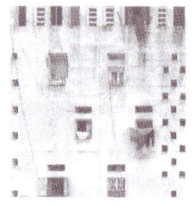

PREFACE: UNEXPECTED PATHS TO MASS HOUSING

Today Ben M'Sik is a bustling working-class neighborhood in eastern Casablanca. Dense low-rise concrete housing blocks with ground-floor shops and cafés line its wide central avenues and house its 131,883 residents.¹ At its origins in the 1920s, however, Ben M'Sik looked very different. A tightly knit settlement of small corrugated-metal-and-wood huts with no electricity or running water abutted factories and industrial sites. By 1953, this worker settlement, termed *bidonville* in French or *karian* in Arabic became the second-largest shantytown in Casablanca, housing over 50,000 people in a city of 713,000.² Home to workers from all over Morocco, Ben M'Sik also became a home to labor movements and political opposition. Claiming unsafe living conditions, the state started to dismantle the neighborhood, and in 1982, the process of rehousing its then 80,000 residents began. The political urban resettlement campaign turned into a drawn-out and fraught undertaking, and it wasn't until 2016 that the last homes were razed and their inhabitants evicted.³

Urban anthropologist Abdelmajid Arrif writes powerfully about the history and stories of this settlement neighborhood as well as the complexities of doing ethnographic research in a housing environment that has always been managed through state-maintained precarity.⁴ In one of Arrif's interviews, a then-resident who is facing resettlement repeatedly describes how no one takes the time to listen and understand him and his situation: "Tu sais, moi, si je pouvais tomber sur quelqu'un qui puisse me comprendre [*rwani*, lit. "me boire"] et que je le comprenne."⁵ (You know, if I could find someone who might understand me [*rwani*, lit. "drink me"] and who I understood.) Striking in his comments is his attention to understanding as an actively reciprocal process; not only does he want to be understood, he also wants to understand.

The Moroccan Arabic expression that he uses for understanding, *rwani*, can mean both "drink me" and "narrate me," and both meanings speak to a desire for a deep and fundamental incorporation. This demand for the incorporation of excluded people, stories, and experiences sets important ethical and methodological questions for mass housing in all its forms: How do we approach mass housing as a subject of study? How do we narrate the lives of its residents? What terms do we use? And what are the effects of that approach both on knowledge about buildings and on the people they house?

The path to this book about art and mass housing started in Ben M'Sik in 2011 when I first visited the Ben M'Sik Community Museum at Hassan II University. The Ben M'Sik Community Museum is small and modest with an oral history archive as the basis of its collection, an exhibit space with objects that speak to the neighborhood's history and cultures of rural migration, and a community meeting place for discussions of its present and future. The museum might be small and modest, but it is one of the most innovative museological spaces in Morocco in its work to remember a place, people, and built environment that many have ignored or would rather forget.[6] The oral history collection archives the many voices of the marginalized neighborhood in a reparative gesture to silences in the historical record, and its ongoing relationships with the present community chart paths to the future. In so doing, the museum both uplifts and responds to the methodological and ethical questions raised by Arrif's interview.

My visit to the museum came about through an invitation to talk with students at Hassan II University about my book *Imagined Museums* as part of a residency I was conducting with the Casablanca-based art collective La Source du Lion on the work of museums, marginalized memory, and participatory cultural actions in Morocco. Entering into the artistic ecology that is La Source du Lion became an entry point for me into the histories of mass housing and built environment in Casablanca. Led by artist Hassan Darsi and curator and art historian Florence Renault Darsi, La Source du Lion has changed shape over the almost thirty years of its existence, and its membership is both dynamic and elastic.[7] What hasn't changed however is its fundamental commitment to art practice as a form of participatory citizenship and relation building. The network of artists, writers, educators, and cultural actors that I met during the residency, as well as the artwork that I learned about during my stay with the collective, has fundamentally shaped how I approach the relationship between art and architecture, between art and people, between art and the city. It has also framed how I understand the potential of art to see and engage the lives and experiences of the people and stories around us. With gratitude for what I have and continue to learn from them, I make the argument in this book that art invites us to see and imagine mass housing and its residents in a way that architectural history, political science, and sociology cannot. Art has the potential to trigger unexpected sensations and attachments, and in so doing, illuminate connective fibers and create relationships between built environments and the people and histories they shape. This, I claim, is a poetics of repair: an art practice that conjoins, connects, or simply brings closer together broken materials, separated people, and severed timelines. Art doesn't just make connections felt and visible, however. It can fundamentally transform mass housing and in turn propose new forms, new histories, and new futures.

The visual, literary, and performance-based art that I have chosen to explore in this book—photography, installation and video art, theater, graphic novels, poetry, and dance—comes from multiple points and places, speaks different languages, and does many different types of work. Sometimes the artwork is produced by residents and former residents of the mass-housing projects. Sometimes, it comes from the outside. Sometimes, it quietly awakens interest. Sometimes, it is troublesome. Sometimes, it recognizes and reassures. Sometimes, it calls people to unite politically to fight for dignity and tangible justice. By exploring well-known and established artwork alongside lesser-known and amateur video, song, and dance, I hope to show that the relationship between artwork, buildings, residents, and knowledge is both complex and multidirectional and has the potential to affect everything and everyone it touches.

So let us then turn to Ben M'Sik again, this time through art. In 1981, the Moroccan poet Abdallah Zrika wrote the poem "Danse de Ben Msik" (Ben M'Sik's dance). The year 1981 was the year after Zrika was released from prison for writing and reading poems critical of the Moroccan state to audiences that "often numbered in the thousands."[8] The year 1981 was the year of what has been called the Casablanca bread riots, a social uprising to protest the price and conditions of life of the urban poor. The year 1981 was the year before the Moroccan state abandoned the NGO-led restructuralization project of the Ben M'Sik and adopted a resettlement program that would raze the neighborhood. In the poem "Danse de Ben Msik" (written in Arabic but to my knowledge accessible in published form only in the French translation by Moroccan poet Abdellatif Laâbi), we can see how poetic tension between shame and outrage about living conditions transform into an affirmation of worth and a direct call to action:

Ben Msik bois
la mort arrive aux lèvres avant l'eau
Ben Msik mange
entre toi et le pain une matraque
Ben Msik pieds-nus
sors et cherche des souliers
Ben Msik mets-toi en colère
les lettres qui te parviennent
passent au-dessus du feu
et s'embrasent
Ben Msik fou
imagine la voiture en flammes comme les arbres d'un jardin
Ben Msik échevelé
ton mal de tête
fait se dresser les cheveux
Ben Msik qui a saboté le téléphone
car ils t'ont oublié dans les tractations
Ben Msik qui a abattu les poteaux électriques
car ils t'ont oublié pour l'éclairage
Ben Msik l'obscurité
car une balle a éteint
la bougie dans ta tête
Ben Msik
tu es grand
car les balles sont petites
Ben Msik crie
tes morts ne sont pas partis
les oreilles bouchées
Ris
la vapeur de ton sang brûlant
tourne dans la tête
Chante
parmi les pieds de tes victimes
esclaffe-toi dans le chant de la mort
danse
car on ne danse vraiment bien que dans ta boue.[9]

(Ben Msik drink
death arrives to lips before water

Ben Msik eat
between you and bread, a bludgeon
Ben Msik barefoot
go out and find some shoes
Ben Msik get angry
the letters that reach you
pass over fire
and go up in flames
Ben Msik crazy
imagine the car in flames like the trees of a garden
Ben Msik disheveled
your headache
makes hair stand on end
Ben Msik that sabotaged the telephone
because they forgot you in the deals that were made
Ben Msik that knocked down electricity poles
because they forgot you for lighting
Ben Msik darkness
because a bullet has snuffed out
the candle in your head
Ben Msik
you are big
for bullets are small
Ben Msik scream
your dead have not left
ears clogged up
Laugh
the steam of your burning blood
turns in your head
Sing
amid the feet of your victims
burst out laughing during the anthem of death
dance
because we only dance well in your mud.)

This is not the first or only poem that Zrika devoted to Ben M'Sik. Though born in 1953 in the Carrières Centrales bidonville in Casablanca, Zrika spent his childhood in Ben M'Sik. Much of his poetry about Ben M'Sik speaks to the shame of poverty and the politics of exclusion; housing often figures in negative terms and reproduces negative discourse. Zrika writes of shame: the shame of having no access to education, the shame of having no access to standard sanitation and health care, the shame of letters lost in its mud when the postman's bag spills.[10] But in this poem, rather than primarily describing the neighborhood through the past and the memories and emotions it triggers, he instructs the neighborhood to act. The poet's series of commands ends with an exhortation to dance in the neighborhood mud: to find joy, belonging, and power through movement in the materials that have marked it with shame.

When Zrika wrote this poem in 1981, it was partly in response to the "bread riots" that had taken place earlier that year across Morocco and in which Ben M'Sik residents were active participants. We clearly see imagery of the protests and their suppression by the state: the bludgeon, the car in flames, bullets, and death. The death toll in Casablanca alone reached the hundreds. But the poem is not concerned with the dire economic conditions generally facing Moroccans across the country. It speaks specifically to a history of dispossession and resistance in the Ben M'Sik shantytown: a neighborhood without basic services, governed by the state through what Lamia Zaki has described as "management by absence." As Zaki writes: "By maintaining the inhabitants on the legal margin, the state creates a latent insecurity which sustains the shantytown dweller's fragility and limits the assertion of collective demands."[11] In this poem, Zrika refuses managed fragility and instead calls on the neighborhood to collectively assert its demands. Written against a shaming discourse of underdevelopment and poverty, during a time of potential political transformation, Zrika's poem shows how the very material of abjection is the material from which resistance and reparation emerge. And that insurrection takes the form of a life-affirming dance in the face of what Achille Mbembe terms "necropolitics": the "subjugating of life to the power of death."[12]

Dance as a form of protest and insurrection in the face of Middle East and North African political regimes has been powerfully theorized by curator and filmmaker Rasha Salti in her 2012 essay and series of talks "Shall We Dance? (Like It's Nobody's Business)." In that work, Salti observes how group dances, specifically the *dabkeh*, constituted a foundational insurrectional practice in 2011 Syria. She writes:

> One can easily observe the centrality of the body in the daily chronicles of street protests in Syria. . . . Syrian insurgents perform a version of the dabkeh in which dancers stand side by side, their arms stretched on the shoulders of one another, forming a chain of solidarity and moving

in synchrony.... Dancing as an insurrectional practice has deeper implications beyond this recentering of the body. Foremost is the choice to claim moral high ground using a pacifist, festive, joyous, and life-affirming language.[13]

How might we read the poem "Danse de Ben Msik" as a life-affirming dance with Zrika the poet as choreographer? The structure of the poem centers around a number of imperative directions. Ben M'Sik is told to drink, eat, get angry, imagine, scream, laugh, sing, dance. These actions speak to core bodily actions that define humanity—from physical needs (drink and eat) to emotional and psychological elements such as imagination, voice, community, and their expression in anger, laughter, and song. Dance is not only a life-affirming language, nor is it just a centralization of the body; it is also a powerful reclaiming and creating of communal space and time through movement. When Zrika writes that "we only dance well in your mud" he reclaims the public space to say that there is value in this neighborhood and its people. He disrupts negative state discourses and in so doing starts a reparative process of radical self-revision positing ownership of the space and neighborhood identity. The poem works to redefine the very materials of its built environment, and in so doing, it reconfigures the body's alienated relationship with the material conditions of its disavowal. It's an act and a call for repair.

The poem "Danse de Ben Msik" is an act of social and political recognition, an expression of and call for dignity in the face of injustice. By using poetry, an art form central to cultural patrimony in the Maghreb, Zrika also works to repair the transmission of memory and the future imagination of the neighborhood.[14] Moroccan poet Abdellatif Laâbi writes that "la poésie est tout ce qui reste à l'homme pour proclamer sa dignité" (poetry is all that is left for humanity to proclaim its dignity).[15] What does it mean for inhabitants of mass housing to have their homes and lives valued as a part of cultural patrimony? To have poems, songs, plays, films, and visual art engage their reality, advocate for their full potential, and imagine other futures? Art stages this poetics of repair.

This is a book about housing that I have primarily experienced through art and its various modalities: images, texts, performances, museum exhibits, sound, music, and conversation. I have not lived or spent significant time in these housing projects.[16] These housing projects are real. They are and were homes to many. The experience of living there changes across time and generations. And it matters. And yet, it is not my intent to test the veracity of artistic representations or evaluate their proposed repair work against real places.

What happens if we take artwork on its own terms? If we seek to understand the poetics that art builds? If we center the repair work of art and the worlds it makes and hopes to remake?

The image that hangs above my desk is a photocopy of a photograph featuring the paths that people make between buildings in housing projects, from a 2004 triptych entitled *Short Cuts* by Romanian-born artist Mircea Cantor. The image centers the well-trodden paths and sometimes surprising divergences from the asphalt walkways that building designers put in place. There is something about the texture of the dirt path as it emerges from the grass that resonates deeply with me. It triggers sensations and attachments that I can't quite name, perhaps emerging from incomplete memories of my early childhood in Poland living in these types of socialist housing landscapes. Perhaps more important though, Cantor's photograph speaks deeply to the pathways between buildings and their histories that I have centered in this project, well-trodden pathways of sound, image, and movement that produce powerful affects and kinships.

In an exploration of architecture and built environment, what does it mean to center the unexpected? Those ways of being and seeing that are created beyond the architect, planner, or even resident but also deeply in relation with them? Artwork has the potential to illuminate and create those pathways. Urban theorist AbdouMaliq Simone writes that "sometimes a politics of care is a matter of concretizing new lines of connection."[17] In illuminating and giving form to other pathways, artwork proposes a politics of care, a poetics that attempts to restructure broken relationships, conjoin severed histories, and concretize new lines for a habitable future.

This is a poetics of repair.

Introduction

Mass Housing, Maghrebi Art, and the Poetics of Repair

Dana Al Jouder, a Kuwaiti performance artist, architect, and novelist, dances through empty mass housing projects. In her 2013 video art pieces *Enfilade* and *Tiles*, she moves slowly on concrete and dirt, through hallways and courtyards, past mailboxes and toward elevator shafts. She is dressed in soft fabrics and shapes that both echo and disrupt the aesthetics of the buildings around her. Through choreography—the movement of her body through space and time— she creates a new space within, on top of, and in architectures of modernist housing. These apartment buildings could exist anywhere and in unmarked time, and at the same time, they are deeply sited. *Enfilade* is filmed in a forty-floor public housing development, the Tiong Bahru Estate HDB in Singapore.[1] *Tiles* is filmed in Kuwait in a "neglected expat housing complex in Hawalli."[2]

In both *Enfilade* and *Tiles*, when Al Jouder's moving costumed body comes into contact with mass housing, visions and affective intensities propose what might be different in and against these buildings. In *Enfilade*, she floats in richly colored and soft textiles across the hardness of white concrete and its seeming immobility. The title of the piece, *Enfilade*, references the architectural term used to describe a series of doors in alignment with each other, and Al Jouder describes the building's austere intersecting corridors as "poetic enfilades, as if purposely designed to be haunted."[3] Indeed, the flash of a cat running down the white concrete stairs is the only sign of life beyond her own, and Al Jouder asks what absence is revealed through her presence, what vibrant, moving, playful, or mournful life has disappeared. In *Tiles*, her dress reflects the rectangular tiles on the building's colonnades, and Al Jouder's attention to geometric forms reveals other structures of containment: containment of the body and of capacious migrant cultures and lives.[4] Both pieces are important interventions into gendered authorship and ownership of space; Al Jouder proposes female aesthetic agency and movement into an aesthetic environment conceived and built by men.

What do contemporary art interventions do to the architectural, political, and social histories of mass housing projects? What can they show us about past and future urban transformation? What feelings, emotions, and affects do they stir that make us look again, and differently? Artwork invites a different critical position on housing than that produced by the architect, resident, or academic researcher, even if the artist is one of the three.[5] For art can, and indeed does, build different structures that reposition our relationships to the world.

In her article "Three Tenses: Mass-Housing in Contemporary Art," Carmen Popescu proposes that European contemporary art that engages mass housing "poetically contemplates our recent history."[6] The words *poetic* and *contemplation* are important here. Art's primary engagement with mass housing is one of thoughtful looking and creative thinking over a sustained period of time, and Popescu defines time in three different tenses. Art that contemplates through a past tense shows how mass housing enters into the ruins of modernity and becomes an "architecture of unfulfilled promises."[7] Art that looks in the present tense seeks to depict "the living space of the present."[8] Art that thinks of mass housing with the future "takes time to see it differently" and asks, "What is to be done?"[9] Building on Popescu's articulation, I propose that in all of their tenses, these acts of poetic contemplation bear the possibility of repair.

What does and can it mean for contemporary art to *repair* mass housing? In this book, repair is an invitation from the present to the future through the past. Above all, repair brings people, histories, objects, buildings, feelings, and geographies out of isolation and into relation with one another. In so doing, the process of repair names what appears broken and rehearses the tensions, ambiguities, and paradoxes inherent to practices of imagination, constitution, and revision.

This book explores how different forms of artwork—visual, literary, and performance art—in and of the Maghreb practice repair in their engagements with mass housing, and how, in turn, these engagements propose reparative-centered epistemologies of architectural sites and built environments. In creating

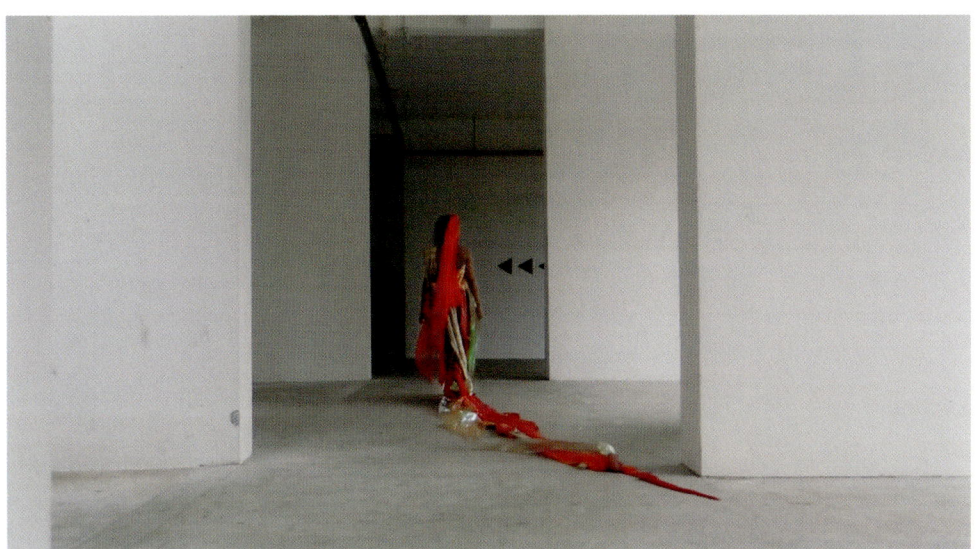

FIGURE I.I. Still from Dana Al Jouder, *Enfilade*, 2013. Video.

relationality through both temporary contact and more permanent scars, this artwork attends to registers of intensities and incipience and opens up the possibility of potential ontological reshapings and epistemological transformations. Practices of repair become sites of (fleeting) documentation, (temporary) archives of becoming, and (ephemeral) glimpses into what might be and what might be different. Artwork not only responds to historically, politically, and socially produced accounts of lives and built environments; it also produces new accounts of mass housing that have the potential to shift histories and futures.

Of course, not all artwork repairs, and not all repair work is the same. In fact, in its variations, limitations, and even failures, the artwork in this book is more often than not a "fragile yet potent experiment" in unsettling histories, envisioning different futures and mobilizing affect for transformative political work.[10] And these fragile experiments are of their time, becoming possible or claiming possibility in a specific moment. This introduction maps the terms, theories, and methodologies that structure the book and its attention to reparative experiments. Some frameworks emerge directly from Maghrebi art, while other concepts develop in conversation with a wide circle of thinkers engaged in understanding the relationship between built environments and life within containment and beyond capture.

What Mass Housing?

What worlds do we imagine when we think of mass housing? What shapes our understanding of this built environment? And if artwork proposes new accounts of mass housing, how does it shift established architectural histories, typologies, and their associated geographies and sociohistorical connotations?

In architectural history, the term *mass housing* typically refers to large-scale construction (usually repetitive/uniform, mass-produced, low-cost housing units) built to house large numbers of people (often as a way to address various housing crises, often focused on the urban poor and working class). While aesthetics and materials vary, the term *mass housing* is often shorthand for the concrete blocks of housing that started to emerge across the world in the 1940s and 1950s. When the term *modernist mass housing* is used, often the architect Le Corbusier and his large-scale modular constructions are evoked. In their edited volume, *Social Housing in the Middle East: Architecture, Urban Development and Transnational Modernity*, Kıvanç Kılınç and Mohammad Gharipour explore what they term the "marginalized histories of social housing" from Tunisia to Turkey to Iran. In so doing, they argue for a wider and more inclusive typology of mass housing that can recount "the diverse practices of social housing in the region" by "looking beyond elite pursuits of architecture" and paying attention to "spatial agency" and the ways in which "homeowners, tenants, and building contractors play a part in the production of the so-called modern vernacular, along with architects, planners, and economic patronages of authorities."[11] Their attention to how self-built vernacular housing typologies relate to large-scale government housing projects begins the work of deepening our understanding of a relational dynamic. If we look at Maghrebi cities today, we see cities that have and continue to build *in typological relation*.[12] In Algerian nomenclature, the word *cité* was often used to describe both shantytowns and housing projects. And as architectural historian Sheila Crane shows in her work, there is an important history that leads to the consolidation of mass housing terminology such as *bidonville*, *karian*, and *cité*. Crane charts how colonial-era rural ethnography and the industrial and extractive materials of colonial capitalism lead to these terms and definitions of built environment, and how they emerge almost simultaneously with elite architectural discourses on housing for the masses.[13]

These relational histories of type or material form are accompanied by a relational geography: the Maghreb. Traditional geopolitical definitions of the Maghreb have defined its borders as the land encompassed by Morocco, Algeria, Tunisia, Mauritania, and Libya. In this book, I take up the call of literary scholar Edwige Tamalet Talbayev to redefine "the Maghreb along new routes and roots" that are transcontinental in nature.[14] As such, in this book, the Maghreb is located both in parts of northern Africa and in the neighborhoods of major European cities: two sides of the Mediterranean deeply entwined in each other's histories and futures—mirrors of one another, fluid locations in sustained motion.

The sense of this Maghreb as a traveling crossroads of people, spaces, and forms is particularly resonant for the architectural history of colonial-era modernist mass housing. The pioneering work of scholars such as Crane, Zeynep Çelik, Tom Avermaete, Marion von Osten, Aziza Chaouni, Nancy Demerdash, and Samia Henni have shown how the emergence and then global boom in modernist mass housing from the 1920s through the 1960s occurred through Mediterranean crossings of architectural practices, materials, and workers, driven and facilitated by colonial capitalism and military operations.[15] Maghrebi cities, both in North Africa and on the borders of expanding French cities, became the frontiers of urban planning and architectural experimentation in mass housing. They also became frontiers in discriminatory housing practices and racially motivated marginalization.

When in the well-known opening of *Les damnés de la terre* (*The Wretched of the Earth*), Frantz Fanon described the compartmentalized racial order of colonial Algerian cities, he could just as well have been writing about migration and workers' housing in 1950s France. As Hannah Feldman writes:

> Living conditions in these [Parisian] bidonvilles were so stark that it would not surprise many if Frantz Fanon's famous claims about the compartmentalization of the colonial world had been written while looking out at one of these slums. In writing that "the colonial world is a world cut in two," Fanon could certainly have been thinking of Algiers, where he had lived for some time, but he could equally have been thinking of Paris, and this is precisely the point.[16]

Claiming Nanterre or Marseille as Maghrebi cities allows us to recognize the often-shared colonial grammars that managed both urban space and types of mass housing.[17]

The etymology of terms such as *bidonville* and *karian* give us insight into the colonial-era industrial materials that define these mass housing spaces—the barrel or jerrycan (*bidon*) and the quarry (*carrière, karia*). As Reda Benkirane describes, "These shacks borrow materials specific to the age of industrial production: planks of wood, zinc tiles, crenellated sheet metal, plastic drums."[18] Moreover, their sociolinguistic use shows us what value these neighborhoods and their residents are afforded in society, and furthers an understanding not only of relational typologies but social relations that are made and carried by mass housing. As Lamia Zaki argues, in the Moroccan urban imagination, the word *karian* is deeply associated with urban deviance, which in turn is seen as social deviance, and as such today the word is a marker of shame and class stigmatization.[19] Whether we link the idea of deviance to histories of rural migration that posit the unruly peasant from "lawless" rural areas known as *bled es-siba* against the erudite and sophisticated urban dwellers tied to structures of royal power called the *makzhen*, or more formally as architectural deviance in the shape and form of structures that bidonville residents create from a violent intersection between rural life and industrial materials, the important factor remains that since its appearance in the 1920s, the bidonville has been seen as simultaneously produced by and "outside" modern urban life. Both under the French Protectorate and in the contemporary political climate, residents of bidonvilles were and remain to this day routinely seen as marginal figures despite the fact that they come to the city as a labor force that helps run its economy, and often function as political voting blocs that support the state.[20] This perception of marginality and deviance is anchored in daily language used to describe its people. As Zaki and others explain, *kariani* is often used as an insult in Moroccan Arabic, and *walid* or *bent l-karian* (son or daughter of the shantytown) is used metaphorically to speak of people seen as outside societal norms of decency and honor.

Marginality, *deviance*, *exclusion*, and *crime* remain keywords in media representations of both shantytowns and large-scale social housing projects across the Maghreb (and one might argue, across the globe). The artwork that engages mass housing in this book rearticulates and reframes the question of societal norms and their implied morality. As we saw in the preface, poet Abdallah Zrika insists that joy and power exist in the very materials of abjection. And as artist and resident of the much-maligned mass housing project Climat de France Hamid Rahiche states most powerfully, his work photographing his neighbors is grounded in a commitment to "all the splendor of their dignity."[21]

Beyond their architectural history and social use, the terms *bidonville*, *karian* and *cité* have been highlighted in political theory as examples of urban structures of political exclusion, existential compartmentalization, and containment, but also potential liberation, self-constitution and self-revision. Reda Benkirane describes the dominant perceptual enclosures that characterize how shantytown residents are seen in this way: "official urban planning has long considered this area a 'ville en négatif' [a city in negative] and the average Casablancan has long seen his co-citizen as 'someone who lives behind the sun.'"[22] Benkirane's description evokes the type of political and existential marginalization—that Fanon would describe in *Les damnés de la terre* as the condition of a "sous-être" (less-than-being) and what he calls in *Peau noire, masques blancs* (*Black Skin, White Masks*) "zone du non-être" (zone of nonbeing)—that denies colonized people their humanity.[23] Africana political theorist Lewis R. Gordon discusses the image of living behind the sun, of being on the "dark side of thought," in relation to Fanon's zone of nonbeing.[24] Gordon, whose work focuses on "conditions of appearance" and "the lived reality of people hidden in plain sight,"[25] writes that the zone of nonbeing "could be a limbo ... or could simply mean the point of total absence, the place farthest from light, that in a theistic system, radiates reality."[26] The shantytown, as a zone of nonbeing, becomes the city's suspended, dark, or unreal other, an invisible other that is made to disappear in plain sight.

In addition to darkness, mud is the primary negative material of discourse on the shantytown as a captive space.[27] *Lghis* is the word in Moroccan Arabic used to refer to mud. It can carry negative connotations depending on the context. Because mud often forms from stagnant water, it refers to stench, and it can also refer to being stuck: *mghyes* means stuck and trapped in a situation.[28] As I discuss in chapter 3, mud is not only a structure of captivity that emerges from living conditions of poverty. In the context of migration, it also becomes an othering political discourse that subjugates identity and worth, and limits the possibility of self-constitution. Building on Fanon's articulations of zones of nonbeing, Ato Sekyi-Otu describes "closures and enclosures of the spaces of human being and human meaning" where "the challenge of our human temporality—our openness to the future and the possibility of self-constitution and self-revision that accompanies it ... withers away."[29] In this context, mud becomes a material that politically marks and encloses.

My theoretical reading on shantytowns and mass housing started with Fanon and frameworks of opposition and self-constitution. I have found, however, that Fanonian concepts of relation, further developed with care and at length by theorists such as Achille Mbembe and Giorgio Agamben, primarily take us to spaces of nonbeing, bare life, or social or political death. As such, the lives and environments of people in housing projects, termed zones of nonbeing and states of exception, become almost entirely subjugated to death-bound orders and logics. How might we simultaneously account for colonial mass housing as a space of subjugation and something else, something perhaps beyond capture?

In *Colonial Modern: Aesthetics of the Past, Rebellions of the Future* (2010), editors Avermaete, Karakayali, and von Osten take up the liberatory potential that Fanon also signaled when theorizing captive space and make the important point that architectures of colonial capitalism and containment in North Africa often become key structures in the decolonial process. In movements of liberation, these spaces of containment can transform into key architectures for rebellion.[30] Most recently, during the so-called Arab Spring of 2011, protesters from the Casablanca shantytown Sidi Moumen carried a small shack made of corrugated metal on a stretcher into the streets. On one side of the shack, the spray-painted words in Moroccan Arabic, "Is this a house for a human to live in?" critiqued Moroccan state practices of necropolitics and neglect. Concrete housing blocks are activated by their residents in movements of political self-constitution, brutalist office buildings turned into instruments of nation building, shacks instrumentalized as structures of critique.

The inhabitants rebel with the built environment and in relation to it, and as such the built environment itself becomes a companion in their claim making. AbdouMaliq Simone writes of this relationship of accompaniment between people and built environments in his 2022 book *The Surrounds: Urban Life within and beyond Capture*. Simone asks us to consider how "rather than seeing the built environment as the stage through which to exercise our privileges or as the concretization of aspirations, needs, and accomplishments, the built environment acts as an accompaniment to whatever we do. It pays attention to our practices; it bears witness to our travails and attainments."[31] This distinction between mass housing as a stage for rebellion and mass housing as a companion in rebellion is important for this book. The built environment accompanies both people and artwork. As artwork redraws relations and histories of mass housing, the built environment continues to exist and transform. Accompaniment suggests a nonreductive relationality between buildings, residents, political claims, and artwork.

Simone develops the concept of "the surrounds" to account for such spaces which exist within, between, and beyond capture. He writes that "the surrounds comes to embody a more generalized process of unsettlement, a maximizing of exposures, which like the apertures of cameras, fundamentally disturb the image of something that may otherwise been taken as 'for sure.'"[32] Simone's call to maximize exposures in order to unsettle logics of capture echoes Ariella Aïsha Azoulay's reparative charge in her 2019 book *Potential History: Unlearning Imperialism*. Like Simone, Azoulay asks what might be seen differently if the camera's shutter, a technology of archival violence, were to be held open. Azoulay insists that "to call for reparations is to hold the shutters open. To hold the shutters open is to see the full scale of reparations that need to be claimed."[33] By maximizing exposures, by holding the shutter open, what potential history might become visible?

In this book, I argue that artwork holds the ability to hold open the shutters and do the work of maximizing exposures beyond capture: unsettling fixed images, narratives, and time lines of colonial-era mass housing. Academic studies of mass housing projects in North Africa and France have been primarily written from a top-down history perspective that focuses on architects and their vision, state planning, and comparative colonial politics. Though fewer in number, studies by sociologists and anthropologists have been building a ground-up perspective that considers the lived experience of building residents and the lived reality of colonial policy and state planning.[34] Artwork has the potential to break, suspend, and reposition all of this fixed documentation, these different perceptual enclosures of mass housing. In that process, artwork sets up the possibility to name and practice repair.

Maghrebi Art and Its Reparative Potential

In order to maximize exposures of colonial-era mass housing, this book presents twenty-first-century Maghrebi artwork in its most capacious sense: photography, dance, video art, novels, music, graphic novels, poetry, and theater. I have chosen not to construct an argument about the limits and possibilities of different artistic genres to do this world building. Instead, I have taken an expansive approach to art, eagerly seeking out as many different professional and amateur aesthetic engagements with these buildings and neighborhoods. A song in Arabic builds differently than a photograph or French-language film, and that is precisely the point. Different genres in different verbal and visual languages create multiple entry points to the life and experience of these buildings and neighborhoods. Strikingly, I have found that many of the artworks that engage mass housing are deeply intermedial themselves: there are novels that stage filmmaking and acting, films about music, photography that functions as film, theater that uses photography, and poems that dance. Indeed, the artwork itself insists that we read it deeply, widely, and across genres, and as I will argue throughout this book, this intermedial or multigenre work is tied to its desire and potential for repair.

Furthermore, many of the artists whose work is featured in this book have deeply rooted and routed relationships to mass housing. A spectrum emerges where on one end some artists live in the local housing projects that they engage, while others live in a larger diaspora that extends to London and

New York. Again, heeding to multiple and expansive perspectives enables us to more fully name what the repair might mean. And attending to the poetics, the structures of the artwork, as a vocabulary for this repair allows us to see how specific forms of repair are articulated by those seeking reparation for and with specific built environments.

Maghrebi artists have long been practicing and articulating repair, whether in the context of colonial history, economies of extraction and environmental damage, race and slavery, gender identity, or urban space. A powerful example of visual artwork articulating the stakes of repair in terms of colonial history can be seen in Algerian artist Amina Menia's work *Enclosed* (2012–present) and Franco-Algerian artist Katia Kameli's *Trou de mémoire* (Memory gap, or hole) (2018). In both pieces, the artists take on a deep and sustained engagement with the colonial history and material structure of the Algiers *Memorial to the Liberation of Algeria*, formerly known as *Le Pavois*. Designed in 1922 by Paul Landowski and inaugurated in 1928 as a monument to the dead of World War I, the limestone monument was rehabilitated after Algerian independence by the artist M'hamed Issiakhem, who created what Menia calls a concrete "sarcophagus" around the original.[35] This encasing did not destroy Landowski's monument but rather embedded it into a new memorial dedicated to Algerians who died in the war for liberation. As Henry Grabar describes,

> Issiakhem encased the original monument in cement, and crowned it with a pair of fists breaking through chains. Issiakhem's work does not only preserve an artistic masterpiece beneath the cement, its layers also recall, rather than rewrite, the painful memory of the colonial period. Issiakhem's piece speaks to the deeper political truth of post-colonial identity: the past, however painful, must be acknowledged as the foundation of certain aspects of contemporary society.[36]

When the Issiakhem casing cracked in 2012, both Menia and Kameli saw the debate about its repair as an opening for artistic research and new propositions. Menia's *Enclosed* is a documentary installation, and when shown at the Sharjah Art Foundation Biennale 11 in 2013, it consisted of an eight-minute-and-fifty-three-second video, photographs, plans, postcards, coin, banknote, stamp, and documents.[37] Menia gathers an archive of the two monuments and also draws up an architectural plan that envisions the possibility of a new monument that opens communication and physically conjoins two interlinked histories of death and war (see figure I.2).

In describing Menia's artwork, Reeves-Evison and Rainey write that repair "has the ability to absorb, reflect and redirect history's lines of force, and . . .

even when chiseled from stone or cast from concrete, the results of repair are on-going, rather than one-off solutions to breakages or crises."[38] Menia's work is not only invested in history, however. It also proposes new lines of communication and relationality for the future. Menia writes: "As a representative of the third generation of artists to deal with this memorial, I have chosen to place the works of the two artists in dialogue. Issiakhem was obliged to cover the original monument, but he offered us the choice—or perhaps, the responsibility—to accept or reject it. Reflecting on this gesture, I highlight unseen details, creating links where only dots were left."[39] The act of "creating links where dots were left" is central to Menia's work, which as we will see in greater detail in chapter 2 builds nuanced relationality between fragments and remains of Algerian colonial housing, anticolonial liberation, and contemporary Algerian urban life. This relationality is not redemptive but rather processes the ambivalence of feeling when repair engages with damage and harm. Writing about anger, art, and repair, Susan Best argues, "The reparative position is not, then, simply about undoing or reversing damage; ambivalence precludes that wholly positive orientation. This way of thinking about repair should enable the incorporation of intense negative emotions and experiences such as the horror of annihilation, anger, and despair alongside positive feelings like tenderness, love and hope."[40] In her work, Menia connects the dots in a variety of ways: through love, rejection, appreciation, reflection, and critique.

Katia Kameli took a different but related approach in her reparative engagement with the monument. Her 2018 piece *Trou de mémoire* (Memory gap), made after the Algerian state sealed the 2012 crack, asks what is forgotten by this state repair and how the newly repaired monument might function as a hole that both swallows and expels memories and images. The piece consists of a photograph taken by Kameli of the repaired monument to which she attaches a cascading accordion of postcard images of the Landowski monument across time (see figure I.3). As witnessed in her larger work, especially in the series *The Algerian Novel* and *My History Book*, Kameli is deeply invested in the accessibility and circulation of colonial and postindependence images in Algerian society. Her reparative vocabulary is derived from images, primarily postcards and press photographs, and asks how the nation and its history are imagined and imaged: What archives exist in the public realm, and what might seeing, holding, and touching those images do for imagining a future?

Both Kameli's and Menia's work with archives is particularly powerful when one considers the history of Algerian archive destruction and the continuing colonial archive retention by the French state. Susan Slyomovics describes this history incisively in her article "Repairing Colonial Symmetry: Algerian

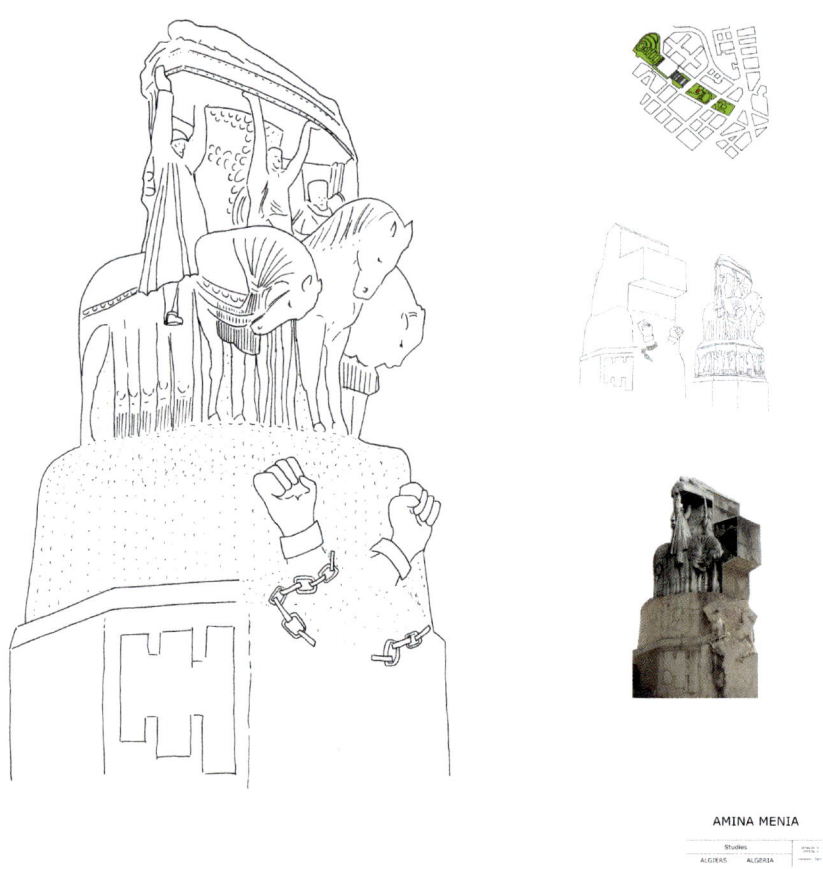

FIGURE I.2. Excerpted work from Amina Menia, *Enclosed*, 2012–ongoing. Installation. Courtesy of the artist.

Archive Restitution as Reparation for Crimes of Colonialism?" recounting how one of the first acts of archival violence by the French in Algeria was the simultaneous destruction of the local archives and production of new foundational documents:

> A significant proportion of archives, records, Arabic manuscripts, Ottoman Turkish bureaucratic paperwork, and land maps went up in flames at the same time that the new colony's first French newspaper made its inaugural appearance. In the heat of battle, colonial authorities both destroyed records and sought to erase their memories through acts of removal and replacement. In short order, new archives were organized to underwrite the paperwork needs of the new settler society.[41]

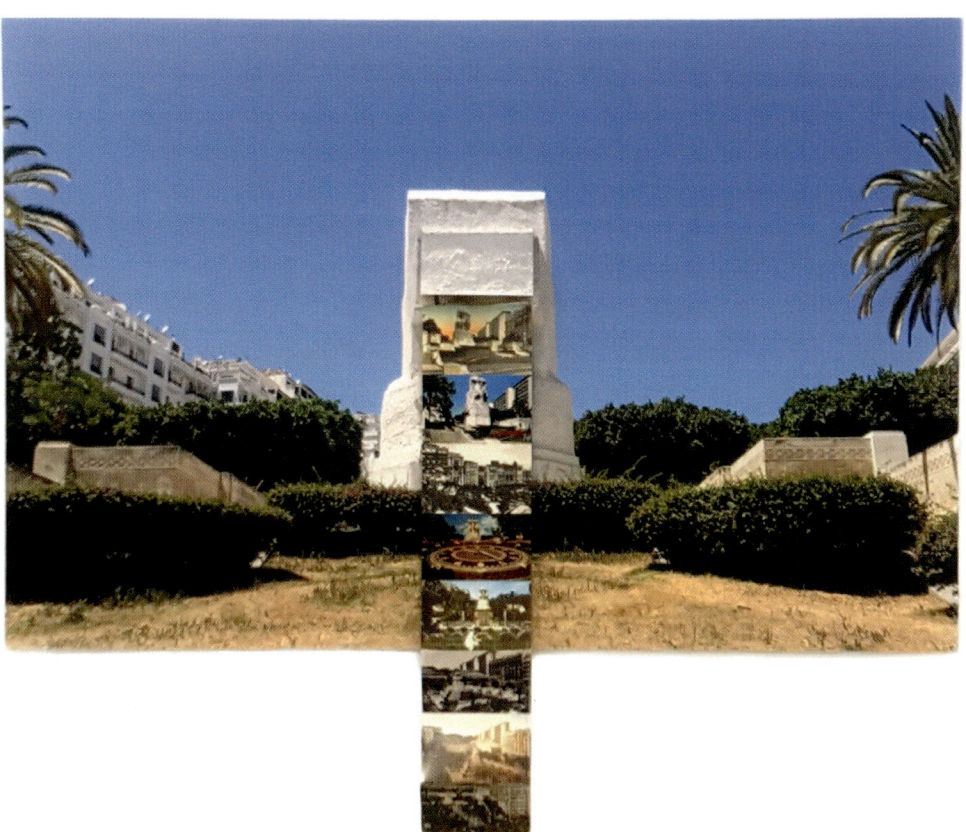

FIGURE 1.3. Katia Kameli, *Trou de mémoire (Memory Lapse)*, 2018. Photographic installation, inkjet print on Etching Rag 310g, mounted on aluminum, 120 × 80 cm © Katia Kameli, ADAGP. View of the work unfolded. Courtesy of the artist.

The production of new paperwork was accompanied by new imagery, as the remarkable rise of colonial photography can attest. In their work, Kameli and Menia are able to suspend and interrupt the representational logics of the colonial archive by dwelling in these images and widening how they are read and to what ends. Artwork here holds the shutter open and unsettles fixed documentation.

Artwork does more, however, than unsettle harmful histories through attention to widening representation. Through its ability to convey affect and create haptic and prelinguistic experiences, it also produces incipience—the fleeting emergence of an uncertain sense of possibility of other relations to the world. The work of Brian Massumi on affect and incipience has been a central undercurrent in my approach to reparative poetics. Reflecting on the transformative potential of affect, Massumi writes that affect

> is the force of thought, embodied. It comes before conscious rumination, alimenting it with the direct perceptual judgments that hit like fate in the incipience of every event, but already with a felt sense of potential alternatives.... Affect's force of thought also comes at the end, pressing beyond the given into the future, in the form of abductive leaps into a hypothetical course of action whose importance has yet to play out.[42]

Artwork has the ability to register, convey, trigger, and produce affects that carry in their force the possibility of different futures. Writing of art and affect, art historian Simon O'Sullivan states, "Art is something much more dangerous: a portal, an access point, to another world (our world experienced differently), a world of impermanence and interpretation, a molecular world of becoming."[43] These fleeting moments of possible becoming, presented in and through artwork, function as potential repair in the context of colonial built environments, again unsettling established representations—though this time through a deeply felt and embodied sense of something possibly becoming different.

Affect and incipience figure prominently in the work of Moroccan artist Hassan Darsi, and his artistic engagements with crumbling colonial architectures and neocolonial environments help us further understand the relationship between art, affect, and the built environment. With his art collective, La Source du Lion, Darsi has conducted long-term community-oriented projects since 1995, including a variety of interventions in and on the colonial-era Casablanca park L'Hermitage and a photo series entitled *Portraits de famille* in which he invited neighborhood residents to co-stage their family portraits by bringing an object of affection with them to his portable studio. His recent project, *Paradis perdu: Colonisation des paysages, destructions des eco-anthroposystèmes* has taken his attention to the rural Benslimane area and the Beni Aïssi village where he accompanied residents organizing against impending ecological damage from a planned quarry through a variety of civic and agricultural actions.

Darsi's 2014 eighteen-minute film entitled *Zone d'incertitude 1* (Uncertainty zone 1) is part of a larger project titled *Le square d'en bas* (The square down below)(2012–18) in which Darsi spent six years documenting and engaging with a decaying 1920s industrial woodworking showroom on Avenue Mers Sultan across the street from his then Casablanca studio.[44] This building, known as the Legal Frères building, served as a European-owned factory and showroom for the production of woodwork ranging from flooring to interior decoration from 1921 to 1932. When the company closed, the building was sold to a holding company owned by the Moroccan royal family and existed in a state of quasi abandon for many decades.

The film is one of the first artworks that Darsi produced linked to the building. In this piece, Darsi documents the labor of a worker hired to whitewash the facade of the building on the occasion of the street being included in a royal motorcade route through the city (see figure I.4). Darsi manipulates the film speed to slow the motion of the painter's work and the sound of the city. The slow whitewashing of the building pulls the viewer's attention to both the surface of the building and the body of the painter. At first, the successive layering of whitewash and the slowness of the gestures is almost painful to watch, as the underlying precarity of the worker's body causes tension and suspense to build. The soundscape is low and ominous. What will happen? Will the worker fall down? However, as the film continues, we are drawn out of speculation and into the surface and its present. The gestures become more dancelike and the repetition of movement meditative. The sound builds and falls. Sounds that we might recognize as jackhammers or construction work lengthen into almost human utterances—wails—and repetitive noise signals the pulse of the city. In writing about affect and architecture, Peter Kraftl and Peter Aday argue that a tension exists between "the concrete stability of architecture and its ephemerality, an ephemerality that easily exceeds the mutability of signification, and is a function of haptic, uncertain, performative, affective, perhaps noncognitive inhabitation and actualization."[45] It is the haptic, affective, and noncognitive moment that Darsi captures on film.

The title of the film, *Zone d'incertitude 1*, signals uncertainty and refers to a concept in organizational sociology developed by Jean Crozier in 1964. Crozier writes that "individuals or groups who control a source of uncertainty in a system of action where nearly everything is predictable, have at their disposal a significant amount of power over those whose situations are affected by this uncertainty."[46] Darsi slows the system of action to amplify its affects: the intensities, incipience, and uncertainties that emerge from it. A momentary possibility—of ontological shift, of the transformation of man and building and their mutual histories, of the creation of a city that might be—occurs through a slow attention to surface and to the moment of contact.

What do we see in two aging bodies touching and transforming each other upon a whitewash background? The (im)possibility of reshaping self and city? The joining of a lone man and abandoned building signaling a desire for reparation? And reparation from what? The temporary melding of a body and

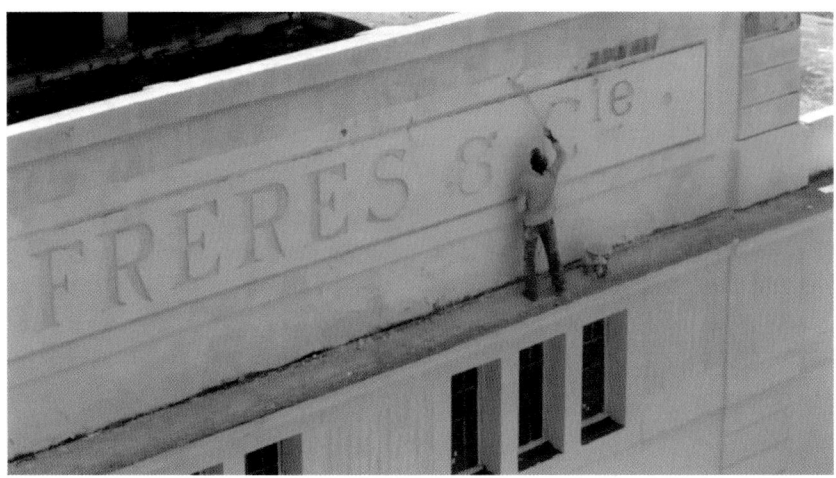

FIGURE 1.4. Still from Hassan Darsi, *Zone d'incertitude 1*, 2014. Video. Courtesy of the artist.

its environment reveal how the two enfold upon each other: the building's aesthetic beauty and structure, inextricably linked to a history of colonial violence, exists in relation with and through the body of the man who paints precariously, a man hired to uphold current structures of political power that deny him any protection of his humanity, a man whose slow movement appears to dance.

In my earlier writing, I saw Darsi's engagement with urban spaces in disrepair as one of "tactical museology": a way to engage the memory and history of objects and people excluded from the structures of a noninclusive museum. By paying attention to affect, I now understand more fully how this repair practice functions against the backdrop of threat, disaster, and their political administration. In researching, building, writing, and performing architectural models, Darsi and the Source du Lion have explored the relationship of what Jalal Toufic would call simultaneous material presence and immaterial withdrawal in the context and aftermath of disaster. What happens when objects, buildings, artifacts, and books which have not been "destroyed materially have nonetheless been immaterially withdrawn"?[47] Or as Finbarr Barry Flood describes Toufic's concept: "Seen but at the same time experienced and engaged with as if unavailable to vision"?[48] When we look at the maquettes of the Hermitage Park or the Legal Frères building, for example, and all of the multifaceted performances and workshops that are part of those larger projects, we see how material buildings, spaces, and objects that are still physically present but

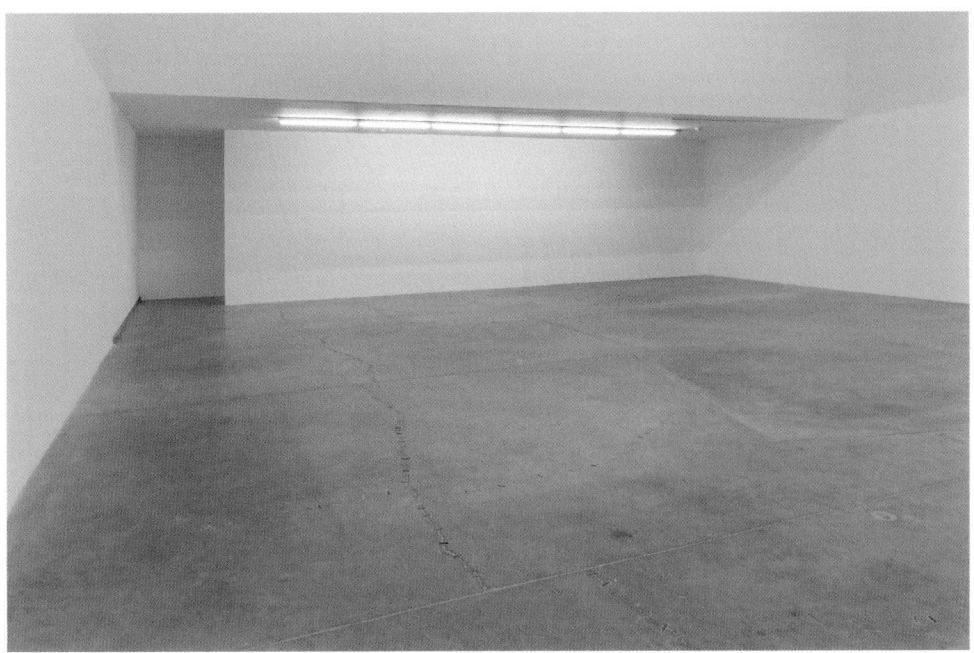

FIGURE I.5. Kader Attia, *Traditional Repair, Immaterial Injury*, 2014. In situ sculpture, metallic staples, concrete. Exhibition view, *The Field of Emotion*, The Power Plant, Toronto, 2018. Courtesy of the artist. Photo: Toni Hafkenscheid.

yet disappeared in plain sight are reactivated. Whether the threat or disaster is colonialism, neocolonial urbanism, neoliberal destructions of social fabrics, or ecological disaster, these art projects stage the reappearance of the immaterial: that feeling, emotion, essence, that memory, haunting, buried history, or sense of access and belonging that was evacuated or made to disappear.

The reappearance of the immaterial is a key practice of repair in the work of Franco-Algerian artist Kader Attia.[49] In his 2014/18 piece *Traditional Repair, Immaterial Injury*, Attia staples sutures across a cracked concrete gallery floor (see figure I.5). In this work, as in many of his others, the goal of repair is not to erase or cover the immaterial or material wound (psychic, historical, social, or physical) but rather to make immaterial injury visible as a demand for reparation. Attia describes how exhibit visitors to the 2018 installation of this piece in his solo show *The Field of Emotion* in Toronto would enter the gallery and be "desperately looking for an artwork" and how the piece called them to transform from their initial perception of emptiness to the sighting of the material scar that held both the wound and possible repair.[50]

Concrete is only one of many materials that Attia has engaged in this way. Over the course of his career he has sutured plates, patched fabrics, darned textiles, stapled wood, melded metal, and juxtaposed photographs of wounded and scarified bodies. This repair work is part of a large and iterative body of artwork and writing that explores the intertwined histories of colonialism, anthropology, science, and medicine and theorizes the potential of reappropriation, repair, and emotion. As Hannah Feldman writes, Attia's interest in bridging divides is tied to his commitment to "incorporating the unincorporated into a universalism that left them no room."[51] For Attia, the immaterial wound, the phantom limb, or that which has been made to disappear must be addressed. The act of incorporation, literally bringing something or someone back into a body, is an act of repair, and Attia emphasizes the scars that such a process produces.

Central to Attia's conceptualization of scars is the idea that the scar is a new aesthetic object that has the potential to create new realities and futures. Attia critiques Western practices that attempt to hide the repair as acts of erasing history and experience, writing:

> Whereas ancient societies from Africa to Japan repair while leaving the wound still visible (with kitsugi, for example, which consists in painting in gold the repaired crack in a ceramic object), the modern West applied to the letter the etymology of the word (from the Latin reparare which means "bringing back to the original state") by totally erasing the wound and claiming to return to the original state of the wounded thing. Keeping the wood's wounds visible, by repairing them with metal staples that allow the wound to look at you is to accept the real. What Western modernity denies by forever erasing the wound is history and therefore time.[52]

Attia's multimedia installation at dOCUMENTA (13) 2012, *The Repair: From Occidental to Extra-Occidental Cultures*, performed this move away from Occidental practices of erasure through the display of a large collection of reassembled or repaired objects. Bowls, textiles, masks, writing tablets, and toys from formerly colonized African communities sat on archival storage shelves and in wooden cabinets; photographs of scarification practices and images of mutilated European and African soldiers from World War I were juxtaposed in slideshow wall projections; books on African anthropology, African art, and the history of surgery were bolted down on shelves; and interspersed in between were sculpted busts that Attia commissioned from artisans in Bamako and Brazzaville modeled from the reconstructed faces of soldiers from the World War I photographs.[53]

The artwork that I have engaged up to this point has practiced various forms of repair that don't foreground mass housing. Attia's 2012 *Genealogy of the Modern* collage and installation series brings us back to housing. This paper collage series arranges photographs of French modernist mass housing projects with cut-out photographs of young minoritized men in the French suburbs and colonial-era postcards of West and North African architectural forms from world's fairs. The juxtaposition of such images presents a complex and deeply mediated genealogy that unsettles the images from their naturalized spaces of appearance (the architecture book, the colonial postcard, the ethnographic, and the journalistic). Likewise, it disrupts the naturalized history of modernist housing by revealing the multiple links between the dots (to return to Menia's articulation). For Attia there is no one original source or singular timeline: his genealogy of the modern emerges from a space of mediated flux, with people and forms in constant migration. Moreover, in this piece, by cutting different buildings out of their source texts, Attia actively reproduces (and hence also undoes) colonial planning actions of cutting through existing environments in order to build new buildings, neighborhoods, and even cities. Le Corbusier's 1942 proposal to cut through Algiers in order to create a new urban plan immediately comes to mind. Though that proposal failed, how many neighborhoods were razed under colonialism in North Africa? Attia takes severed cities, severed buildings, and severed people from across the Mediterranean and glues them back into relationships—genealogies that reveal their fragmented histories—that render visible memory loss and reveal structures of fragmentation that endure in the present. In this work, the glue, and the overlapping images, show the scar of repair.

In another iterative piece entitled *Kasbah* (2008–), Attia glues mass housing and the shantytown into relation. The project began with a set of corrugated tin bidonville roofs that filled up gallery spaces and, in some cases, required visitors to walk on them (see figure I.6). The bidonville was reduced here to its surface materials, denying the visitor access to the hidden space of life and possible economic mobility below. The impenetrability of what lies below and the literal walking on materials linked to the bidonville presents this form of mass housing as an aesthetic object seen from above, reproducing the gaze of European modernist architects and urban planners such as Roland Simounet, Michel Écochard, and Le Corbusier who studied such informal housing as they worked to develop formal mass housing projects.[54] In the Culturgest Fundação Caixa Geral de Depòsitos edition of the installation in Lisbon (*Kader Attia: Roots Also Grow in Concrete*, 2018), the bidonville rooftops and satellite antennas filled a gallery room while on one wall Attia projected his film *Normal City*

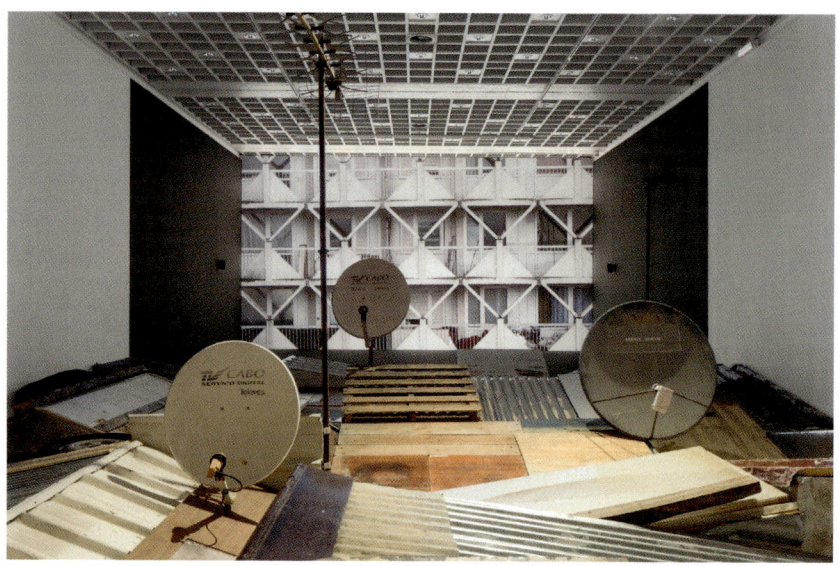

FIGURE 1.6. Kader Attia, *Kasbah*, 2008. In situ sculpture, wood, corrugated iron, TV antennas, satellite dishes, tires, found objects. Exhibition view, *Kader Attia. Roots Also Grow in Concrete*, Culturgest Fundação Caixa Geral de Depòsitos, Lisboa, Portugal, 2018. Courtesy of the artist. Photo: Bruno Lopes.

(Tour Robespierre), a slow-moving camera pan of a French housing project that focuses on the aesthetic qualities of its facade and unexpected breaks in the pattern of its windows and balconies.

As I argue throughout this book, shantytowns and housing projects are indeed two monumental architectures deeply intertwined in history and aesthetics—each always in the shadow or the mud of the other, inseparable not only historically but to this day. Indeed, new shantytowns continue to rise up in urban areas adjacent to new apartment buildings and construction across the world, despite national and international programs to create, as in Morocco, "Cities without Slums." By repairing the link between what has been (incorrectly) separated into informal and formal projects, we can see more clearly the visual and aesthetic objectification that both housing environments have endured and continue to endure, and speak more deeply to hegemonic perceptual enclosures and exclusions from self-representation of their inhabitants.[55] By paying attention to the uncertainty and precarity of these related environments, we can see more clearly shared formulations of self-constitution, practices of care, ethics of mutual recognition, and instances of solidarity and community building.

Reparative Epistemologies: Broken-World and Quakeful Thinking

Artwork that practices repair in turn invites, indeed demands, critical practices that create reparative epistemologies. When writing of technology and repair, Steven J. Jackson asks, "Can we identify anything like a standpoint epistemology of repair?"[56] His affirmative response lies in the concept of "broken-world thinking": the proposition to take "erosion, breakdown and decay, rather than novelty, growth and progress" as starting points for knowledge and technological innovation.[57] This type of broken-world thinking strongly echoes the possible collective repair work that can emerge from attention to affect. As Gabriel Winant writes, "Affect theory does not discover an authentic self buried by oppression; it constructs one anew from the wreckage of defeat. In doing so, it assembles collective knowledge."[58] Reparative epistemologies can emerge at sites of wreckage when we pay attention to affects: fleeting energies, shimmers, or atmospheres that are by definition prepersonal, that emerge from social spaces, structures, and institutions.[59] What epistemology of repair can emerge from starting points of erosion, breakdown, and decay in the Maghreb? What emerges from broken-world thinking? And how might broken-world thinking be linked to possibilities of collectively produced knowledge?

In a 2015 workshop, eleven women led by artist Katrin Ströbel and curator and cofounder of La Source du Lion Florence Renault-Darsi worked toward a reparative epistemology of Casablanca through attention to what was "broken" in the city. As documented in their 2016 edited book, *De l'espace autre* (Of another space), these women spoke and worked together and used the city as a screen upon which and through which they projected their thoughts, feelings, and bodies.[60] Unlike other collections of art, fiction, and poetry about Casablanca that seek to capture or represent the bustling city in time, this workshop created the time and space to begin identifying broken or otherwise unrecognized experiences of urban life.[61] Together they created a polyvalent exchange about power, gender, embodiment, colonialism, memory, and creativity. Collectively and individually, the women produced photographs, sketches, architectural drawings, and postcards and projected palimpsests onto the city itself. As Ströbel and Renault-Darsi put it, "Pendant que les uns détruisent, les autres construisent" (While some destroy, others build).[62] The most iconic images from the workshop are the black marker drawings on the window of the studio space that appear to redraw and repair the physical architecture outside (see figure I.7). From this reparative positionality and broken-world thinking, a different collectively produced knowledge of the city emerges. Elizabeth Freeman

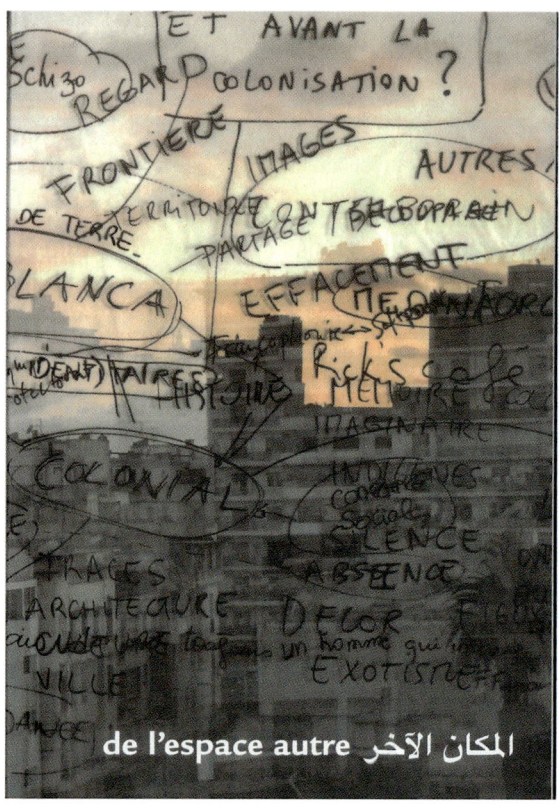

FIGURE I.7. Cover of Katrin Ströbel and La Source du Lion, *De l'espace autre* (Casablanca: Éditions La Source du Lion, 2016).

argues that affective critical practice disrupts linearity of space and time and "turns us backward to prior moments, forward to embarrassing utopias, sideways to forms of being and belonging that seem, on the face of it, completely banal."[63] This description of disruption in time and movement resonates with Ströbel and Renault-Darsi's project. In the workshop, the women literally created new space to engage with damaged histories, utopic futures, and banal presents, questioning not only from where but from when we produce knowledge and registers of experience.

In her 2017 novel *Climats de France*, Marie Richeux describes the destabilizing intensity of seeing the housing project Climat de France in Algiers for the first time. Touching the limestone, and feeling a tremor in her body, the narrator exclaims: "Entre les épaules et le ventre, à l'endroit que l'on dit être celui de l'attachement, se glissent la familiarité et l'étrangeté totale, l'excitation de la découverte et le coeur serré du retour."[64] (Between the shoulders and stomach, at the place that is said to be the site of attachment, familiarity and the complete unknown slip into each other, the excitement of discovery and the clenched heart of return.) She feels the incipience throughout her body, in her heart center, and while she senses that this reaction and feeling is coming from the stone of the building, at the moment it is happening, she resists analyzing or cognitively deciphering the experience:

> Je ne sais pas encore que cette cité a été dessinée par le même homme que celui qui pensa l'immeuble dans lequel j'ai grandi. Je ne sais pas encore qu'une pierre de taille, fameuse, me relie à cet endroit. Je ne sais pas encore que, pour aller d'un endroit à un autre, il ne suffira pas de traverser la mer, il faudra traverser la guerre, entendre la lutte et voir se déployer dans des textes et des voix une démente escalade de violence. Je ne sais pas encore que la drogue qui se vend dans la cour aux deux cents colonnes sur ces hauteurs d'Alger et rend méfiants les quelques jeunes attroupés tout à l'heure autour de nous, je l'ai croisée dans la Cité heureuse.[65]

> (I don't yet know that this housing project was designed by the same man who thought up the building in which I grew up. I don't yet know that a piece of cut stone, famous stone, connects me to this place. I don't yet know that to go from one place to another, it isn't enough to cross the sea. One must cross the war, hear the struggle, and see an insane escalation of violence deployed in texts and voices. I don't yet know that the drugs that are sold in the courtyard of two hundred columns, on these heights of Algiers, drugs that render the young people who gathered around us earlier mistrustful, that I crossed those same drugs in the Cité Heureuse [a name for the housing project where she grew up].)

As I discuss more fully in chapter 2, in this novel the movement toward knowledge comes first through an intensity that emerges from the buildings and is felt in the body. This movement toward knowledge starts with a sensing of something shared.

By paying attention to the affects of this scene, we can identify yet another type of reparative epistemology. What Richeux describes in the novel as a tremor, Edouard Glissant terms a *pensée du tremblement*, or "quakeful thinking": a trembling with the other, a trembling with difference, that has the potential to bring people and histories together into ongoing nonreductive relation.[66] Seismologically we tremble most at the crack or on the fault line that exists below a geological scar. In epistemological terms, quakeful thinking produces cracks in imbricated knowledge, and the ensuing trembling disrupts hegemonic narratives through the recognition and full acceptance of paradox, uncertainty, ambiguity, and inexplicability. As Glissant writes,

> Du tremblement lui-même à la pensée du tremblement, il y a toute la fragilité.... La pensée du tremblement nous éloigne des certitudes enracinées, nous supposons par exemple qu'elle inspire toute une partie de ces sciences actuelles, qu'on a donc appelées sciences du chaos, qui se méfient tant de la régie de l'universel et méconnaissent si fort la linéarité impérative.[67]

> (From trembling itself to quakeful thinking, there is all of fragility.... Quakeful thinking moves us away from rooted certainties, we can imagine for example that it inspires a whole area of current science, thus named the science of chaos, that mistrusts so much of the management of the universal and ignores imperative linearity.)

We see in this sentence many of the concepts found in the reparative impulse of affect theory: movement towards knowing that begins with affect and the body, a distancing of and from instilled cognitive knowledge, a rejection of linearity (Cartesian or otherwise) in time and space. Furthermore, according to Glissant, reparation occurs through the conjunction of this collective trembling with political and civic actions that do not tremble:

> Les actions qui ne tremblent pas resteraient stériles si la pensée de la totalité monde, qui est tremblement, ne les supportait. C'est là où la philosophie exerce, et aussi la pensée du poème. Nos poèmes, d'avoir à se souvenir du temps d'avant les consciences et d'avant la parole, quand la terre n'était étendue ni en continents, ni en archipels (pas encore enfantés par les sursauts et les divisions de la haute et grande mer, celle de l'Un), vacillent du rappel de cette indistinction.[68]

> (Actions that don't tremble would remain sterile if the thought of the complete world [this refers to Glissant's concept of a fully inclusive and irreducible *Tout-monde*], which is trembling, didn't support them. It's there where philosophy develops, and also poetic thought. Our poems, from having to remember time before consciousness and before speech, when the world hadn't spread into continents or archipelagos [not yet birthed by the bursts and the divides of the high and wide sea, sea of the One], teeter from the reminder of this indistinction/undifferentiation.)

Quakeful thinking awakens a poetic practice that, as Glissant describes, registers primarily affective tremors in order to recall a prelinguistic undifferentiated totality. But we don't have to start with an undifferentiated totality or move toward totality as a utopic goal in order to see the reparative utility of registering shared tremors as we deconstruct and then construct epistemologies. Quakeful thinking reinforces the idea in this book that repair is always a proposition of relation that is both hopeful and unstable.

The power of a Glissantian approach to repair is that it centers instability. Glissant was perhaps above all a poet committed to stirring up, disrupting, and dislocating processes of meaning making. Even when writing *Philosophie de la Relation* he was quick to undo the genre; the subtitle of the "philosophy" book is *poésie en étendue*: a poetry in/of scope, in/of expansiveness. Describing this dynamic of simultaneously making and undoing meaning that is at the center of Glissant's work, Michael Wiedorn writes: "At once present and absent, at once visible and invisible, saying something while not saying it, all the while saying it."[69] Glissant reminds us that poetry not only undoes, it also builds new structures and pathways to undo again; at once visible and invisible, it links the dots, the words, and the worlds that have been splintered and separated.

As the title of his more famous volume *Poétique de la Relation* (Poetics of relation) announces, Glissant was interested in not only the expansive and disruptive possibilities of thought through poetry, but also poetics. Most narrowly, poetics is both the art of writing and the study of literary technique and form and the effects they produce. In other words, poetics is a critical way of engaging texts "that is attentive to the specificity of their metaphors and their imaginative dimensions as well as a form of analysis that acknowledges the affective dimensions of knowledge."[70] In this book, poetics goes beyond the text to other objects, spaces, structures, and actions as a mode of analysis of the intersections of form, affect, imagination, and knowledge production. It is both analytical and creative, producing new pathways and paradigms for understanding; as Mayra Rivera writes, poetics can produce "modes of knowing, being, and acting in the world."[71] For this book, reparative poetics is the opposite of a poetics of isolation and containment, of closed systems of understanding, and, in political terms, of narrowly defined and defended concepts of nationality. Poetics can produce reparative epistemologies.

This book focuses on artwork and the possibility of reparative poetics and epistemologies in the context of three Maghrebi mass housing sites: the Carrières Centrales / Hay Mohammadi neighborhood in Casablanca (chapter 1), the Climat de France housing complex in Algiers (chapter 2), and the former shantytown La Folie in Nanterre (chapter 3). The book's movement from mass housing in Casablanca to Algiers to Nanterre functions organizationally in two ways. First, it is loosely chronological in terms of architectural history:

Carrière Centrales / Hay Mohammadi and its various forms of mass housing appear from around 1920 to 1953; the large mass housing complex Climat de France was completed in 1959; the Bidonville de la Folie in Nanterre appears in the mid-1950s and is razed in 1972 but is central to the story of the October 17, 1961, Algerian march and French state-sanctioned murders in Paris.[72] Secondly, all three housing projects have distinctly colonial-era origins, and this organization allows us to move through various aspects of decolonial movements and thought from different, but related, thematic and theoretical angles.

In chapter 1, I focus on sound and silence and approach Hay Mohammadi through artwork's sonic reparative disruptions of colonial modernist planning grids and ideologies. In chapter 2, Climat de France is read through artwork's creation of an affective anticolonial poetics of relation that attempts to rethink kinships and inheritances. Chapter 3 focuses on La Folie through artworks' attention to gender, transmission of memory, and the role of domestic space in anticolonial and antiracist movements. I attend to questions of gender and gendered spaces and representations throughout the book, but this chapter digs most deeply into the topic.

Finally, the book's conclusion, "Touching Feet and Moving Hands: Art's Repair from Affective Gesture to Capacious Home," takes a step back to reiterate how art's repair work bears the potential to unsettle histories of exclusion and redefine what is meant by *home*. Drawing again on examples from contemporary Maghrebi art on colonial-era mass housing, I theorize art's repair work as a gesture, an invitation that attempts (and sometimes fails) to bring people, histories, objects, buildings, feelings, and geographies into relation with one another.

What are the artistic afterlives of these mass housing projects? What can art build and imagine today on colonial structures from the past? How can art reveal what endures? What resists? What insists and asserts? What lives on? What is forgotten? And what unfinished business remains?[73] This book seeks to answer these questions by attending to the poetics of repair.

1

Sonic Repairs to the Grid
Art Engages the Epistemology of Hay Mohammadi, Casablanca

There is a sense of both joy and unease in Yto Barrada's 2013 photographs of the *cité horizontale* and *cité vérticale* housing blocks in the Hay Mohammadi neighborhood in Casablanca.[1] Joy emerges in the way Barrada playfully highlights repetitive colors and geometric patterns and forms: unexpected dashes of red, recurring small dark squares and rectangular windows on seemingly flat white walls, triangular crossings of electricity lines across red wall paint, and overwhelmingly rich greens and yellows of vegetation in communal spaces. In one set of photographs of the *cité verticale*, plants and flowers dominate Barrada's images, taking up the space of the frame and relegating the concrete housing blocks to the background. The lushness of the sunflowers and the fullness of the trees ooze life beyond the adaptive but crumbling structures of the Anthropocene. But as seemingly undisciplined greenery supplants and reclaims the housing grid, unease also emerges. The buildings appear distant, not as relevant. And where are the people? Unlike in Dana Al Jouder's films, Barrada's buildings are neither sterile nor empty. We see laundry hung to dry in windows and hallways, embroidered curtains, brooms, and satellite dishes. We see deeply lived spaces, with simply no residents in sight. The buildings are eerily quiet.

This series of photographs was commissioned by Tom Avermaete and Maristella Casciato as a "photographic mission" for the Canadian Centre for Architecture's 2013–14 exhibition *How Architects, Experts, Politicians, International*

Agencies, and Citizens Negotiate Modern Planning and the accompanying 2014 book, *Casablanca Chandigarh: A Report on Modernization*. Barrada and fellow photographer Takashi Homma were asked to photograph the modernist buildings under study in Casablanca and Chandigarh respectively in order to "introduce the variable of time in depicting a richly transformed and appropriated contemporary built environment."[2] Whereas Homma's photographs of Chandigarh feature human subjects in buildings and doorways, moving through and actively occupying buildings and spaces, Barrada provides only two glimpses of lone shopkeepers in her thirty-two photographs. Denying the viewer access to human subjects, or their faces, is a reoccurring practice for Barrada, who rose to prominence through her photography of migration entitled *A Life Full of Holes: The Strait Project* (1998–2004).[3] Her attention to the dignity and privacy of her subjects in that project has been carried over into her other work and features here as well. She catalogs human life in the housing blocks without essentializing people or totalizing a place. As Rasha Salti describes it, Barrada's "inventories produce visual ledgers, meticulous in detail, where the process of cataloging matters more than the ambition to represent the objective 'totality' of a situation, story, or location."[4]

In this photographic series on modernist housing, Barrada's abstraction of human life and space speaks to the deep engagement with modernism in her practice. Where other collections of photographs of Casablancan modernist housing blocks, such as in Sascha Roesler's *Habitat Marocain Documents*, chart the buildings' transformations over fifty years of use, Barrada's art encounter is less about representing the passage of time in relationship to built environment than it is about proposing a different poetics, a different way of seeing, and then cataloging time and space. In short, Barrada's photographs surpass the representational mission of their commission. Rather than "depicting" appropriated space, the photographs' creation of new forms plays with and appropriates the modernist history of the buildings and their conception, rearranging color and geometry into other schematics for understanding human life. This is as much a political as an aesthetic act. Engaging the work of the modernist architects and planners who conceived this housing, Barrada's photographs repair the formal frameworks that they created to understand Moroccan lives and housing. As Omar Berrada describes Barrada's practice: "Politics is inseparable from an attention to form and to the memory of forms. Consideration of political reality is mediated through an awareness of art and design history."[5] Engaging both form and the memory of forms, Barrada creates revised frameworks that speak to the possibility of a different history, a different register, and different futures.

At the same time, Barrada's attention to human life and futures occurs not only through the abstraction of form and creation of visual frameworks. The photographs also perform repair sonically, through strategic silences that in turn produce space for other affective registers. More specifically, by removing human subjects from the frame, Barrada creates a certain quiet that allows for other sounds, and other memories of sound, to emerge. As Tina Campt describes in *Listening to Images*: "Quiet is not an absence of articulation or utterance. Quiet is a modality that surrounds and infuses sound with impact and affect, which creates the possibility for it to register as meaningful."[6] Barrada's photographs are quiet and yet vibrate with real and imagined echoes of greeting, laughter, shouting, scolding, and sounds of work: construction, pots and pans clunking, water splashing. Memory sounds of life, and memory sounds of political resistance. And perhaps sounds that are not yet heard.

In this chapter, I pay attention to the sonic (repair) work of art in relation to the colonial modernist grid in Hay Mohammadi and the modernist mass housing that emerges from and within it: the former Carrière Centrales shantytown, the *cité verticale* and the *cité horizontale*, and the SOCICA housing project. From strategic quiet to vernacular articulations to the production of vibrant cacophonies, art's multiple sonic engagements with the modernist grid move us to consider different memories, stories, and futures of the built environment. Art engagement that focuses on sound asks us to shift our perspective from flat surfaces to the spaces of volume and amplification that the buildings create in between their walls. The sonic repair work of art—Yto Barrada's photography, Marion von Osten's video mapping project *This Was Tomorrow!*, Lahcen Zinoun's film *Le piano*, Fouad Souiba's novel *L'incompris de Hay Mohammadi*, and the poem/songs by the groups Nass El Ghiwane and Lemchaheb as shown in Sonia Terrab's documentary film *L7asla* (Lḥaṣla)—moves us from modernist buildings on the grid to the spaces in between—to streets, apartment interiors, and alleyways.[7] This sonic realignment gives "voice" to other stories and ways of knowing modernist mass housing and produces a different definition of ownership that mirrors how residents both use and remember the space.[8] In their work on concepts of functional heritage in Hay Mohammadi, Laurie De Vroey and Lize Nevens describe how residents don't necessarily speak about "certain buildings or sites, but about places, streets, neighbourhoods and the stories that unfold upon them."[9] By listening to art and its sonic engagements with the grid, how might monumental architectures give way to other constellations, movements, and voices that seek to repair fractured histories of the neighborhood?

SONIC REPAIRS TO THE GRID   29

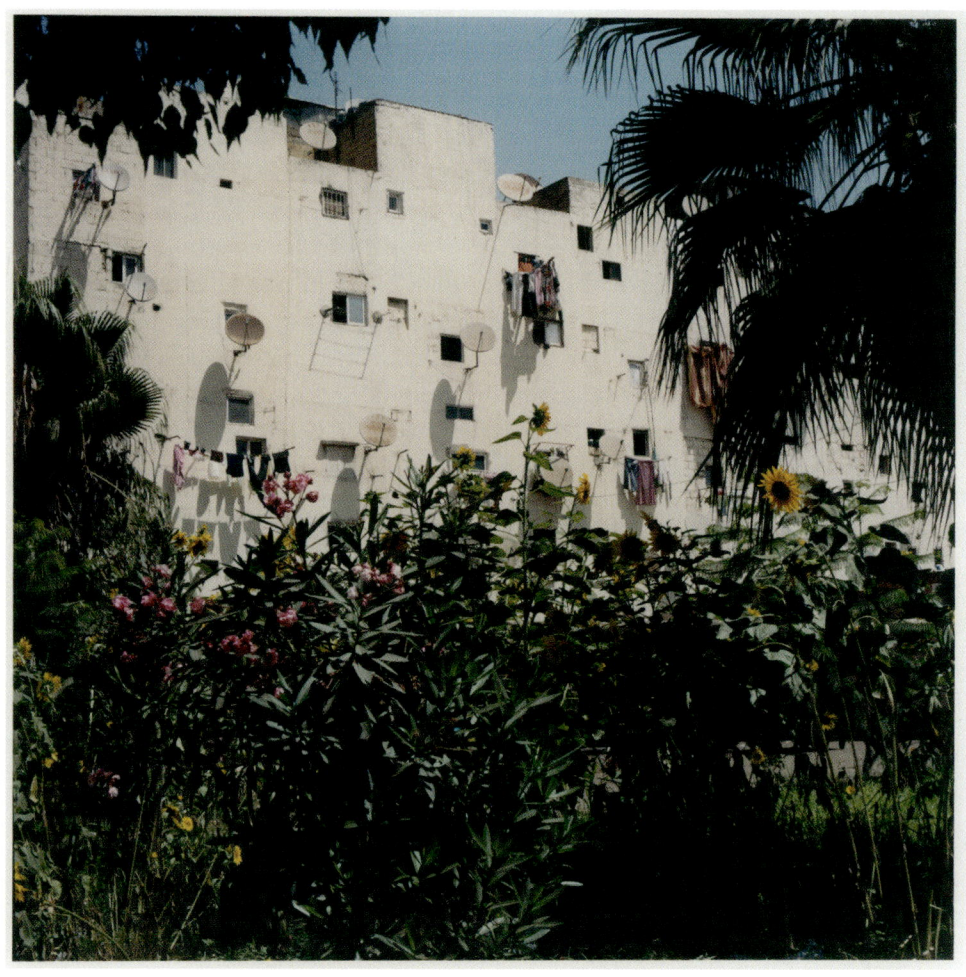

FIGURE 1.1. Yto Barrada, *Reprendre Casa*. Carrières Centrales, Casablanca, fig. 6, 2013. Chromogenic color print, 60 × 60 cm. Edition of 5 + 2AP. Courtesy of the artist.

Yto Barrada's Quiet Photographic Repairs to the Colonial Grid(s)

The Hay Mohammadi neighborhood, located near an industrial area in the eastern part of Casablanca, was first called Carrières Centrales, or Karian Centra, during the protectorate period in reference to its proximity to an industrial quarry. The neighborhood was officially renamed Hay Mohammadi in 1956 in reference to King Mohammad V, who visited the neighborhood upon his return from exile in 1955 and who in turn was named derisively by the procolonial party as the sultan of Carrières Centrales.[10] Like Ben M'Sik, the neighborhood began as a worker's settlement in the 1920s, housing men who migrated from rural areas in Morocco to work in quarries and factories. As described in the introduction, these workers brought building practices from their rural communities and built their own shacks using nearby industrial materials such as corrugated iron and tin barrels, creating bare-bones housing and giving birth to the term *bidonville*. While we might be tempted to think of the bidonville neighborhood as an informal settlement, it was a formally administered legal housing space.[11] The bidonville inhabitants were not squatters on public land but sanctioned inhabitants.

As the industrial labor population increased, private companies started building more permanent housing for their workers with joint funding from the French protectorate government. The 1940–42 SOCICA housing project, built near the Carrières Centrales bidonville was one of these *"cité ouvrières"* or otherwise termed industrialists' housing projects. SOCICA was designed by architect Edmond Brion for the Société pour la Construction de la Cité des Industriels de Casablanca, hence its name, and consisted of 368 small housing units, 353 of which had only one main room.[12]

As the need for housing continued to grow, the French protectorate director of urbanism Michel Écochard studied the Carrière Centrales bidonville intensely as part of his "housing for the masses" project and developed two modernist planning grids: the Groupe d'Architectes Modernes Marocains (GAMMA) analytical survey grid for urban planning, and the *"trame* Écochard"—a repeating grid of eight-by-eight-meter low-rise housing units which formed the basis of new construction.[13] Working from these grids and under Écochard's direction, in 1952, Atelier des Bâtisseurs (ATBAT) Afrique architects Georges Candilis, Shadrach Woods, and Alexis Josic designed a series of modernist housing projects with accompanying markets and educational and religious facilities to address housing the then 130,000 residents in the neighborhood.[14] The two most famous modernist housing buildings built in Carrières Centrales were the Nid D'Abeille and Semiramis, named for their visual references to honeycombs and the Hanging Gardens of Babylon respectively. These high-rise buildings became representative of the *cité verticale* concept, one of two building typologies on the grid. The other typology was termed the *cité horizontale* and consisted of low-rise modular housing based on the *trame* Écochard.

A lot has been written about the modernist grid, both at the time of its conceptualization and by architectural historians of modernism. In the Moroccan context, scholars recount the history of the GAMMA grid as a project initiated by Écochard and his office of urban planning and formalized in 1953 for a presentation to the ninth Congrès International d'Architectures Modernes

(CIAM). Le Corbusier had already systemized the grid as the primary CIAM analytical methodology for architectural research in 1947. Highly aesthetic and aestheticized, the grids were a template for

> graphically organizing information on new town planning projects. It is shaped as a matrix of basic cells (panels) of 21 × 31 cm with images and text. The columns represent nine analytical categories: environment, occupation of land, constructed volume, equipment, ethical and aesthetic problems, economic and social influences, legislation, finance and stages of realization. The rows represent the four urban design themes of the CIAM: living (green), work (red), cultivation of body and spirit (blue) and circulation (yellow).[15]

The GAMMA grid, entitled "Habitat for the Greatest Number Grid," was one of the first grids presented at CIAM to chronicle the work being done in bidonvilles.[16] Synthesizing architectural, economic, legal, and anthropological (cultural and social) research and visual documentation, the grid was proclaimed "a true 'tool for thinking,' an impressive frame of knowledge that shapes the contours of a new architecture."[17]

While Avermaete and Casciato laud the grid for its "exacting description of the actual terrain ... addressing ephemeral issues such as appropriation and the impact of collective and individual symbolism in the built environment," Marion von Osten questions its representational frameworks.[18] She writes:

> The two North African grids and their new categories not only misnamed the living patterns of the people who lived in the bidonvilles, but they also designed solutions for the shantytown dwellers that were far from answers to their living patterns and needs. The newness of the grids' approach was built on the tradition of colonial representation of the colonized, epistemological shortcomings, and violence.
>
> Thus, even though it was provocative to the older generation of CIAM architects, the GAMMA Grid study was not critically engaged in the political context in which it was conducted—that of colonial rule—and in the particular case of the Carrières Centrales, of the exploitation of phosphate and the workforce in Morocco. The GAMMA Grid did not show the toxic factories in which Moroccan day laborers toiled for low wages. It did not examine the perimeters allocated by the protectorate that designated where rural migrants could settle, far from the colonial city center. Instead, the grid propagated modernization, industrialization, and a new consumer society as a solution for the local population.[19]

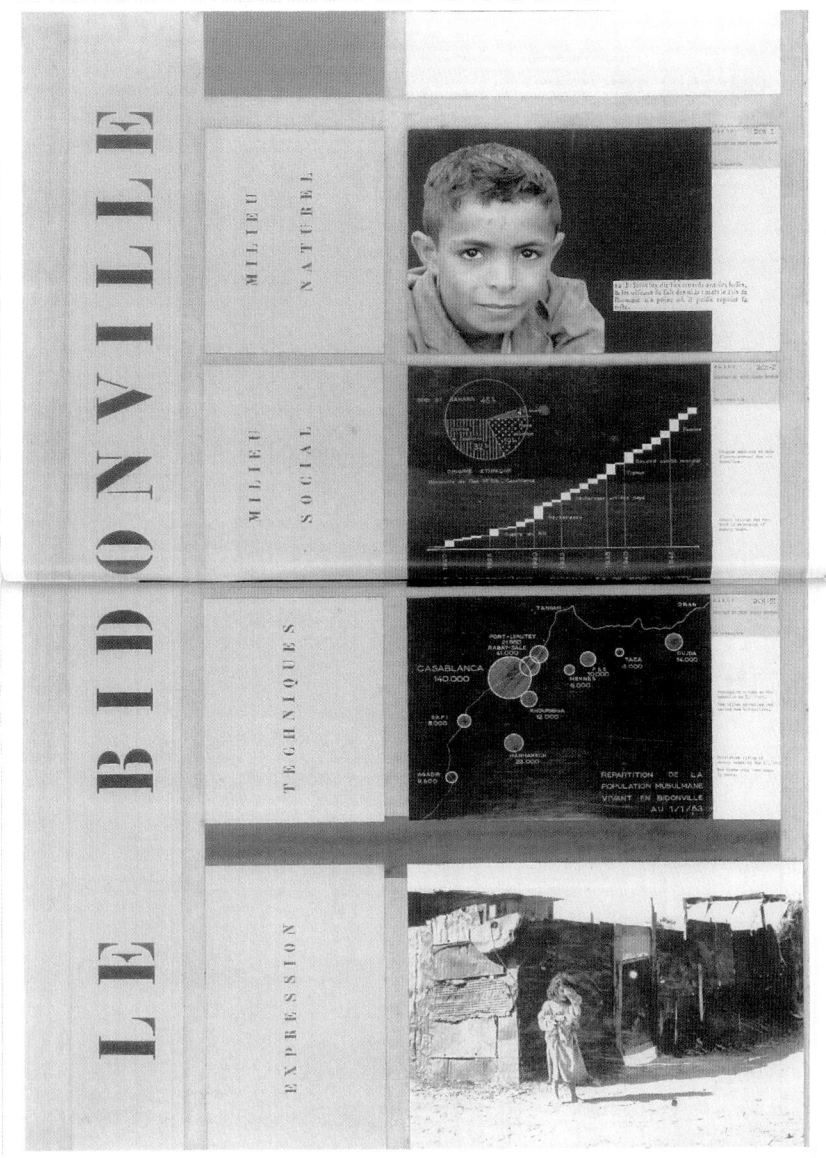

FIGURE 1.2. Section of one panel of the GAMMA grid presented at the 1953 Congrès International de l'Architecture Moderne (CIAM), Aix-en-Provence, France. Image reprinted from Marion von Osten, *In the Making*, 127. Original print at the National Library, Rabat, Morocco.

Yto Barrada's work engages both the visualization and erasure of life in Carrières Centrales, reframing voice in these modernist grids and the colonial and postcolonial epistemologies they produced through and by photography.

Photography played a key role in the documentation (and erasure) of the terrain that went into the urban planning grids. In fact, from the 1930s to the 1950s, there emerged a rich, one might even say obsessive, photographic record of bidonvilles and new modernist housing blocks across Casablanca. Carrières Centrales and Ben M'Sik were photographed and documented from all angles: from wide aerial shots of differing heights, to "street" and "alley" view, to the occasional interior shot. In addition to the buildings themselves, there is a rich visual record of people moving through the neighborhoods: on bikes, on foot, men, women, children. Écochard participated extensively in the creation of this photographic archive of buildings, building styles, and built environments. His most iconic photographs of Carrières Centrales are the 1949 sweeping aerial shots of the bidonville and the new housing construction being built under his direction. His photographs captured the patterns of both settlement housing and new construction from above, their attention to repetitive form creating remarkable aesthetic abstractions.[20]

These silent images of bidonvilles and new mass housing construction circulated widely in the press and on postcards on both sides of the Mediterranean and ultimately became loud and vociferous documents for and in colonial urban planning, helping to compose and amplify both the GAMMA grid for urban planning and the *trame* Écochard. Arguably, the sound of these grids presented to audiences worldwide in architecture conferences and magazines was discursively louder than the voices of the people that they aimed to house. Barrada's photography is a formal visual intervention into the form and history of these colonial analytical, visual, and physical frameworks and what they leave off the grid. By recasting the very forms of the grid, Barrada asks the viewer to think more deeply about history, photography, appropriation, traces of absence, and the very structures that constructed dominant ways of knowing these spaces.

At first sight, Barrada's engagement with the analytical grid is most evident in her visual play with the form of the grid as a matrix of rectangular and square cells. In the 2013–14 Centre for Canadian Architecture exhibit, Barrada's photographs were all printed at *almost* 30 × 30 centimeters (individual prints differ but most are 30.1 × 29.8 centimeters).[21] Out of the thirty-two photographs in Barrada's series for the book *Casablanca Chandigarh: A Report on Modernization*, twenty-six are printed on full pages in a square format with white borders. Barrada's choice to print the large majority of images in these almost 30-centimeter squares is perhaps the first formal nod to the matrix grids that defined the colonial history of Carrières Centrales. In the final pages of the book *Casablanca Chandigarh*, editors Avermaete and Casciato regroup Barrada's photographs into thumbnails across five columns and four rows. This editorial reproduction of her photographs into a physical grid amplifies Barrada's intervention into the grid's structure and reliance on photography.

More substantively, however, Barrada's photographs engage the grid through the production of new repetitive matrices and patterns within the images themselves. The repetition of rectangular windows or triangular wires that cross buildings asks the question: How can a new contemporary analytical grid invite the viewer into the history, present, and future of this neighborhood? What quiet new rhythm emerges from other repetitive forms?

Barrada's presentation of crossing of wires against building walls in several photographs is one example of how her work intervenes in the way we read visually across these spaces (see figure 1.3). In the GAMMA grid, knowledge was structured through vertical and horizontal comparisons, and the images signified meaning through both representational and metaphorical registers: the images presented buildings and people as anthropological documentation and served as a basis for policy by conferring judgment about social and economic conditions. In short, image leads to judgment which leads to policy. In Barrada's geometries, there is no one direction to knowing, and knowing doesn't necessarily emerge from representation. Whether following electrical wires, satellite dishes, or simply a washing line across a frame, Barrada's images highlight pathways made as appropriations to the built environment by building residents. Rather than imposing a GAMMA Cartesian structure, Barrada's camera highlights these vernacular grids and invites the viewer to follow the paths that residents themselves have made in order to better understand, and, I would argue, better sense, the space and its use. Indeed, in some photographs the repetitive forms might signify nothing more than their superficial geometry and produce solely formal "structures of feeling." But even purely formal restructuring produces a new relationality that can strategically engage or unsettle a deeper understanding of the buildings and their residents.

I have written at length about Barrada's play with surface and the superficial in my 2019 article "Whitewash as Affective Platform: Art and the Politics of Surface in the Work of Yto Barrada and Hassan Darsi."[22] In that article I read Barrada's 2011 artist book *A Guide to Trees for Governors and Gardeners* and her 2003 architectural model *Gran Royal Turismo* as affective registers of intensity and potentiality that reveal the performance of power through surface. In her photographic series of the Carrières Centrales buildings, she again highlights how photography of surfaces can produce fleeting documentation through

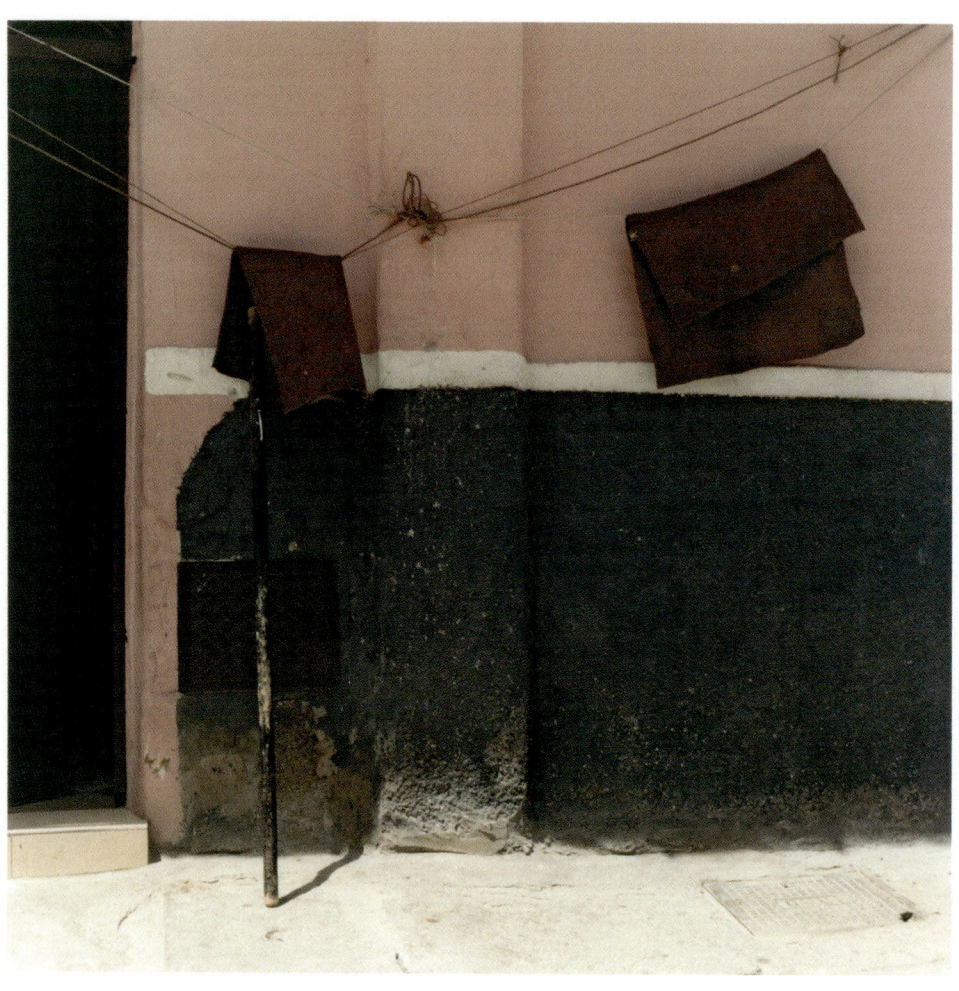

FIGURE 1.3. Yto Barrada, *Reprendre Casa*. Carrières Centrales, Casablanca, fig.18, 2013. Chromogenic color print, 60 × 60 cm. Edition of 5 + 2AP. Courtesy of the artist.

new geometries of presence and absence. Okui Enwezor has written about Barrada's practice of registering traces in an analysis of Barrada's 2002 photograph *Marks Left by a Football*: "The painterly ghostliness of the wall induces a kind of pictorial abstraction, yet the traces of the football marks amplify the whiteness of the wall as a space of presence rather than blankness."[23] In that photograph, as in the Carrières Centrales series, traces and marks amplify absence as a material presence.

In order to see this more fully, let us return to the absence of human bodies in these images. When compared with both the GAMMA grid and Takashi Homma's photography, there is a striking absence of people in Barrada's images. But as Barrada recounted in a panel discussion at the opening of the Centre for Canadian Architecture exhibit, "They [people] are very present to me." Rather than focusing on bodies, Barrada's photographs register the presence of people through the traces of their multiple adaptations of the physical environment. In this way, rather than focusing on their bodies (and objectifying them), Barrada is able to document the inhabitants' creativity and imagination through the traces they leave on the built environment: their ideas for transformation, their ways of living, and even their humor.

Barrada's centering and celebration of people as active creators of space contrasts with the ways in which colonial-era architects and urban planners bemoaned resident adaptations for occluding the original structures to an almost unrecognizable trace of their former selves.[24] Architectural historian Karim Rouissi writes that "in Casablanca more than elsewhere, modern architectural heritage was 'altered' by the inhabitants so what remains of that housing is simply a trace of the original horizontal '8 m × 8 m trame sanitaire.'"[25] Marion von Osten further describes how residents see this alteration of space as natural: "When I asked the man who guided us through Hentsch and Studer's Sidi Othman building how public spaces, architecture and interiors have been so thoroughly appropriated by the people, he responded that, 'We are all engineers, we are all architects. If we have a basic structure or some land, we just start to build.'"[26] While Écochard, Candilis, and other architects anticipated that housing would "evolve," they didn't realize to what extent their structures would be altered or how quickly it would happen. As Aziza Chaouni describes, "Evolving Housing (Habitat évolutif) [was] a concept which Candilis advocated in the Carrières Centrales project without fully resolving it. Evolving housing proposed single or double family units that could be enlarged by the owner when his budget allowed him to do so. In contrast, for Écochard the concept of Evolving Housing meant housing that evolves according to the user's civilizational level."[27] For Barrada, documenting the altered physical structures in a visual grammar of traces is thus not only a way to signal the presence of their inhabitants. It is also a way to show how inhabitants actively altered, or repaired, the ideological structures of colonialist or "civilizational" evolutionary narratives. In so doing, residents built space for other logics of life and civilization. Other logics that would also support potential uprisings. In her images, these quiet traces are in fact deeply resonant, creating a low hum of seismic vibration that has the potential to unsettle rigid conceptions about who builds, who designs, and who inherits the buildings. A reparative quaking.

In addition to taking on the GAMMA grid and its conceptual underpinnings, Barrada's quakeful repair also responds to the dynamics of spatial control imposed by the physical *trame* Écochard. After their initial exhibition in Montreal and publication in *Casablanca Chandigarh: A Report on Modernization*, Barrada retitled some of these photographs *Reprendre Casa* (taking back Casa) in the context of different exhibits (2015 Basel; Serralves). The new title plays with the idea of photography as an act of taking (*prendre une photo*), and by adding the prefix *re* Barrada announces a project of return and reappropriation. Indeed with the new title, *Reprendre Casa*, Barrada returns to an old text about spatial control: Écochard's 1955 memoir *Casablanca: Le roman d'une ville*, and she reappropriates Écochard's chapter 4 title, "Reprendre Casablanca," recasting the sprawling anonymous Casablanca into an intimate and relational *Casa* that takes back spatial and political control.

In order to understand this repair more fully, let's enter into Écochard's "broken" novel and its photographic illustrations. Subtitled a *roman*, or novel, *Casablanca: Le roman d'une ville* is part memoir, part planning treatise, and part historical record, with the city of Casablanca and Écochard himself as the primary characters in an evolving and antagonistic drama. The book starts with a description of the city's dynamic growth and a lament of its chaotic development. Écochard produces a number of images of the city, and in terms of mass housing, he includes four images of its bidonvilles before the construction of new mass housing: an aerial shot of the grid-like Ain' Diab bidonville; a landscape photograph of self-built housing with a small mosque in Carrière Centrales; an untitled photograph of a bidonville house constructed from a variety of materials including Shell oil barrels, barbed wire, crenellated metal, and woven materials (rear cover); and the decorated interior of a home in the bidonville of Ben M'Sik with the caption "Bidonville de Ben M'sik; interieur d'une habitation. (La pauvreté n'a pas tué le sens artistique)" (Ben M'Sik shantytown, shack interior [poverty has not killed artistic sensibility]). This last image (figure 1.4) shows painted geometric forms on wooden walls, the corner of a framed image, and several small photographs attached to the wall. The photograph unites handmade and reproduced images that emerge from the modernity of the space and also (literally) escape its frame. Écochard's parenthetical or throwaway comment regarding "artistic sensibility" reflects a larger colonial discourse on aesthetics in spaces of poverty such as the bidonville, a discourse that vacillates between a celebration of the ingenuity of people living in difficult conditions and a dismissal of the possibility of beauty amid poverty. Écochard's

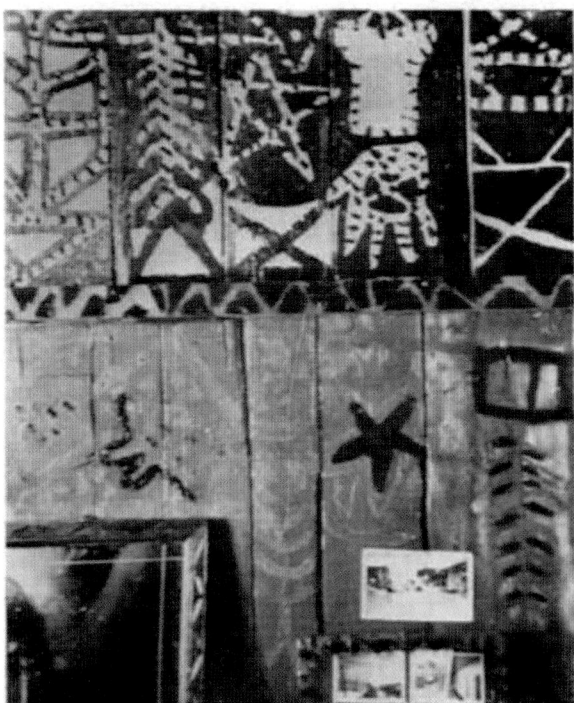

FIGURE 1.4. From Écochard, *Casablanca: Le roman d'une ville*, 29.

Bidonville de Ben M'sik ; intérieur d'une habitation. (*La pauvreté n'a pas tué le sens artistique.*)

photograph, unwittingly and momentarily perhaps, presents aesthetic forms escaping his grid, pushing the limits of colonial representations of shantytowns as disordered urban forms without aesthetic value.

Toward the end of the book as he details his urban development plans, new photographs of architectural models and construction sites appear that realize the formal 8 × 8 meter grid structure that Écochard would propose and build as a solution for "housing for the greatest number": aerial photographs of the Sidi Othman housing block "Habitat Marocain" designed by Jean Hentsch and André Studer, and the south and north sections of Carrières Centrales's *cité horizontale*. The final photograph in the book is an aerial shot of the new Carrières Centrales horizontal and vertical housing blocks in their almost shiningly white 8 × 8 meter unit grid formation (see figure 1.5). This white grid was a fitting conclusion to Écochard's aspirational "story" of the city, a novel that started with the dynamism of disorder and ended with the hope of ordered

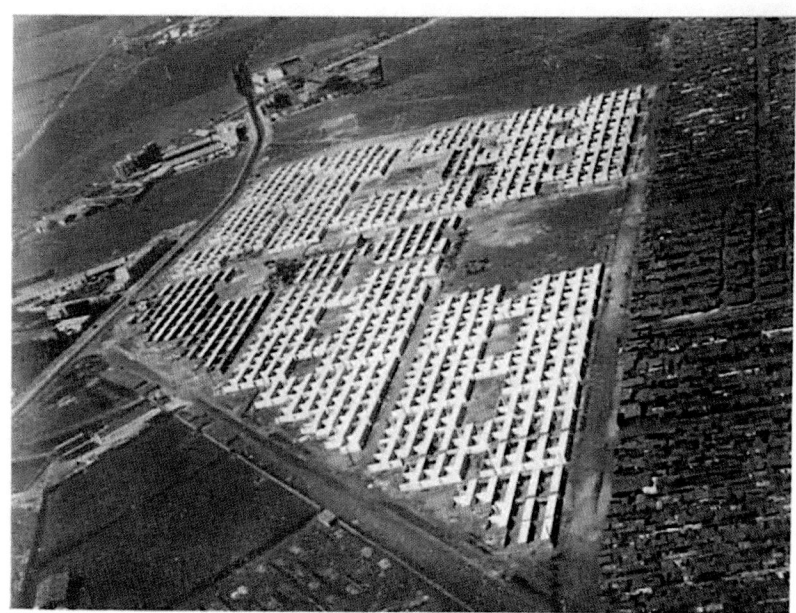

FIGURE 1.5. From Écochard, *Casablanca: Le roman d'une ville*, 142.

frameworks. While the "story" focuses on the built environment, it is also a tale of political control through urban space.

As architectural historian Karim Rouissi has shown, the shiny, ordered grid lauded by colonial officials as a solution to social and political instability was seen differently by anticolonial nationalists. Rouissi quotes at length a conversation between architect Georges Candilis and some (unnamed) Moroccan nationalist leaders:

> Nationalist leaders in particular resented the different way of constructing "native" as opposed to European housing. George Candilis (2012, 191–192) said, "I had before me outraged nationalist leaders. As if in an interrogation, one of them said to me, 'Why are you constructing housing [for us] that is different from the rest?' [I replied,] 'Because I am looking for solutions that can be adapted to our living conditions and to our current economic conditions. These solutions demand a different architecture than what is currently being made.' [The nationalist replies,] 'That's why we called you. We knew you were looking for something else [than the colonial style]. Well, you are completely wrong.'" Candilis: "I

am wrong?" Nationalist: "Why don't you make us the same houses as for the Europeans, the same houses as in France?" Candilis: "I am looking to find your identity." Nationalist: "That's neo-colonialism, a form of paternalism that is even more dangerous than all the threats that come to us from declared enemies."[28]

This exchange is silenced in Écochard's narrative but engaged through Barrada's spoken statements about the grid as a spatial structure of control that sought to quell political unrest and contain building inhabitants in acceptable evolutionary narratives.

During the 2013 panel discussion that occurred on the occasion of the exhibit opening of *How Architects, Experts, Politicians, International Agencies, and Citizens Negotiate Modern Planning*, Barrada described her exhibit photographs as incomplete, stating, "What I see in these images, those that I made, that are incomplete, is the absence of violence."[29] She recounts how when she was researching the documentation on Carrières Centrales, she noted the nationalist flags in the bidonville, the 1952 anticolonial strikes and brutal suppression by French forces, and the pride and celebration around the visit of King Mohamed V upon his return from exile.[30] As scholars such as Jim House, Sheila Crane, Léopold Lambert, and Susan Slyomovics have shown, bidonvilles and housing projects across Morocco, Algeria, and France were vibrant centers of anticolonial political action and resistance. In terms of Carrières Centrales specifically, in December 1952, five thousand residents of the Carrières Centrales protested in front of police stations upon news of the assassination of Tunisian union leader Ferhat Hached, and in 1953, according to Slyomovics, the most militant clandestine groups for the Moroccan independence movement formed in the shantytowns Carrières Centrales and Ben M'Sik.[31] It is interesting, then, that on the surface Barrada's photographs of Hay Mohammadi do not reference this history explicitly. When speaking of that political absence, Barrada noted that the photographic series for the Canadian Centre for Architecture were, in her words, "incomplete." But by later renaming the photographs and displaying them in exhibits with other works that speak more directly to histories of colonialism, Barrada takes a step toward rendering that political history and violence more present and also more intimate. Like for Kader Attia's work, the iterative aspect of remixing artwork and installations draws out elements of artwork that were differently resonant or perhaps incomplete. In this sense a piece that is strategically quiet in one iteration holds embedded sound that can resonate when placed into a new matrix of relation at another time.

This is particularly important when faced with the fragile tolerance of the Moroccan state toward its postcolonial history of repression. Against this background of evolving levels of state censorship, we would do well to return to the critical potential of seemingly quiet photography articulated by Tina Campt. Campt encourages us to "challenge the equation of vision with knowledge by engaging photography through ... sound."[32] By creating strategic visual silences in her representation of human forms and activities, Barrada's photographs draw the viewer to listen to life *around* the buildings and resist a representational mode of power (both colonial and postcolonial). Moving away from a monumentalization of built form toward the complexities of human voice, life, and rhythms in the neighborhood, Barrada's photographs enter into multiple moments and histories of taking something back and thus perform several repairs, even if (necessarily) incomplete. In terms of form, Barrada's contemporary photography takes on and takes back the structures and representations produced by colonial photography. In terms of politics, strategic silence clears space for imagined sounds, memories of sound, and future sound, activated by Barrada's repetitive grids. In both cases, *reprendre* is a political act mediated through form and sound. Barrada's play with the form and function of the grid opens new paths or poetics of knowing and invites us to rethink epistemologies of these mass housing projects.

Marion von Osten Curating New Vernacular Grids

Artist and curator Marion von Osten's 2008 project *This Was Tomorrow!* also engages the form and function of the Moroccan colonial modernist grid through visuals and sound. Reproducing the geometric form of the modernist grid as a structure of collection but emptying it of its colonial data, *This Was Tomorrow!* amplifies contemporary vernacular expressions of life in Hay Mohammadi and other mass housing projects. Where the GAMMA grid relied on the silence of photography to support colonial ideologies, von Osten and her art collective Labor k3000 turned to amateur video and all of its potential to lift up multiple and marginalized voices.

Marion von Osten (1963–2020) was a German artist, theorist, curator, and professor deeply engaged with the history and practice of colonial modernism.[33] Her practice as a collaborative visual artist became a key methodology in her scholarly and curatorial engagement with modernist architecture in Casablanca, especially in the *In the Desert of Modernity: Colonial Planning and After* project and exhibition (2008–9), which resulted in the seminal publication *Colonial Modern: Aesthetics of the Past, Rebellions of the Future* (2010), and

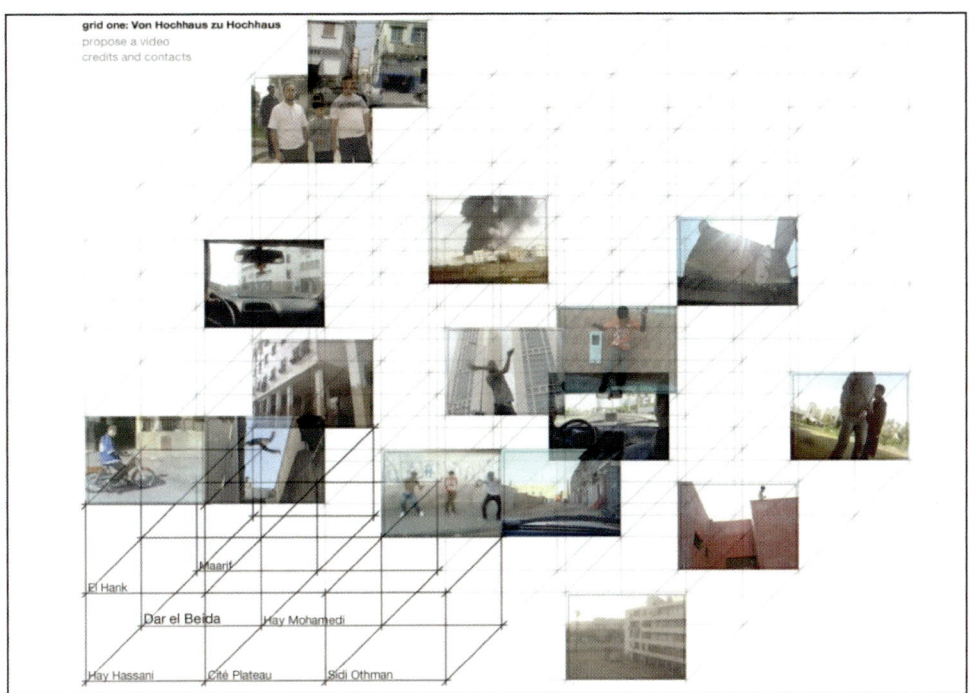

FIGURE 1.6. Screenshot from www.this-was-tomorrow.net. Online project and film archive by Labor k3000 (Marion von Osten, Peter Spillmann, Michael Vögeli). From Marion von Osten, *In the Making*, 97.

then later in rethinking the history of Bauhaus from a decolonial perspective in the global *Bauhaus Imaginista* project (2018–19).[34]

This Was Tomorrow! was a collaborative online mapping project created by von Osten's art collective Labor k3000 (cofounded with Peter Spillmann in the late 1990s) and contained "an archive of over 100 video and film clips that were made by residents of 1950–1980s housing projects across Europe and northern Africa."[35] Video clips collected or submitted by housing residents were embedded in the online website this-was-tomorrow.net that presented the clips in schematic grids, the interstices marked with neighborhood names and cubes filled with video stills that linked to clips (see figure 1.6).[36]

As von Osten describes, "The website . . . reflects the principle of the grid that was popular in modernist and colonial city planning, considered to be an infrastructure that allows for an integrated, joint usage of mostly geographically separated, autonomous resources."[37] If Yto Barrada's photographic mission to Carrières Centrales enters into the colonial visual ledger and invites reparative engagement with the GAMMA Écochard grids, Labor k3000 plays with the grids to create a new structure whose entirely vernacular content is populated by residents of modernist mass housing in Casablanca and beyond. In its incorporation of amateur videos, the new grid not only speaks but also gives voice to the building's residents in the languages of their choice.

Furthermore, by mapping the grid beyond Casablanca, von Osten et al. opened a comparative participatory infrastructure that generated both shared and disparate experiences of mass housing residents in North Africa and Europe. This integration of what might be considered "geographically separated, autonomous resources" thus produced a different set of engagements. First of all, the new grid arose through self-representation as opposed to exterior visual perception or sociological study. And as such, this new grid surfaced dynamics and structures of feeling that the colonial grids implicitly embraced, assumed, ignored, or buried: joy, laughter, dance amid and despite containment, and most notably "the ongoing struggle of residents and young migrants against discrimination, deportation and social inequality."[38] In a sense, the new grid also entered into a dynamic of reparative relation and created what Manthia Diawara calls a Glissantian *lieux-commun*: "sites where calls are made about one condition of the world to the other sites of the world, so that they too may relate it to their own conditions and relay it to all the corners of the world."[39]

Von Osten describes the genesis of the project as an informal activity in which she "searched for videos by inhabitants depicting high-rise estates posted on YouTube from 2008 to 2011. The everyday life of people and their daily creative approaches to tactically or strategically deal with the living conditions and negative representation of their homes became accessible due to the new distribution channel."[40] As the project started to take shape, von Osten and Spillmann started to focus specifically on

> non-commercial posts by residents of mass housing settlements in France, Morocco, and Germany to see how the buildings were depicted, used, and interpreted in everyday actions, including posing, dancing, and meeting in the spaces, as well as shooting features on site or telling stories about the buildings. These types of activities of dwellers living in such neighborhoods are usually not taken into account when thinking about architecture discourse.[41]

Indeed, when colonial urban planners and architects built mass housing, even though they were deeply immersed in modernist aesthetics and their production, they were not thinking about housing as a place for dance, music, and art. When Moroccan families built onto and into those housing structures, dance and music probably weren't priorities either. However, their artistic and creative practices, constrained or expansive, took (their) place in the buildings every day, showcasing relationships and relational perspectives with housing and releasing affects and emotions through art: song, dance, and storytelling.⁴² As von Osten describes:

> These everyday forms of creative production alter the existing visual culture discourse on postwar modernist neighborhoods, as they do not speak in an attitude of failure or indicate problems to be solved (as an urban planner does) but rather speak with an empathy and identification as a dweller who relates to her or his home. This perspective taken by the YouTube posts also alters the understanding of who might be called or become a cultural producer beyond the existing institutional frame of art, film, and design schools.⁴³

I would like to take a moment to discuss the idea of self-representation central to *This Was Tomorrow!* and highlight a phrase in one of von Osten's project descriptions above. Von Osten writes that the videos that she and Spillmann looked for, found, or were given presented residents' "daily creative approaches to tactically or strategically deal with the living conditions and negative representation of their homes." Like von Osten, I have not dwelled on the negative representations of Hay Mohammadi in this chapter, though I could have easily started from that point. Instead, I wished to highlight and amplify (self-) representations and artworks that were tactically, strategically, and affectively generative in the context of the negative ontology of containment to which mass housing is often relegated. There are novels and pieces of art that certainly replicate this dominant discourse. My article "Zones of Perceptual Enclosure: The Aesthetics of Immobility in Casablanca's Literary Bidonvilles" digs more deeply into negative perceptions and the struggle of literary representations of bidonvilles in Casablanca as they relate to the possibilities of self-constitution and self-revision by their residents. In that piece, I argue that certain texts, like Mahi Binebine's *Etoiles de Sidi Moumen*, engage in an aesthetics of immobility that subsumes any agency (from the everyday to the political) in a reductive mud-bound representation that limits the possibility of human being and becoming. As Richard Pithouse argues, representations of the urban poor are "often incapable of recognizing the independent agency of poor people, who are reduced to their material situation and show up as suffering bodies, not as people who always think and sometime organize in the midst of material deprivation."⁴⁴ Von Osten refuses this aesthetics and adamantly insists on the possibility of thought, organization, and self-representation in Casablanca's mass housing.

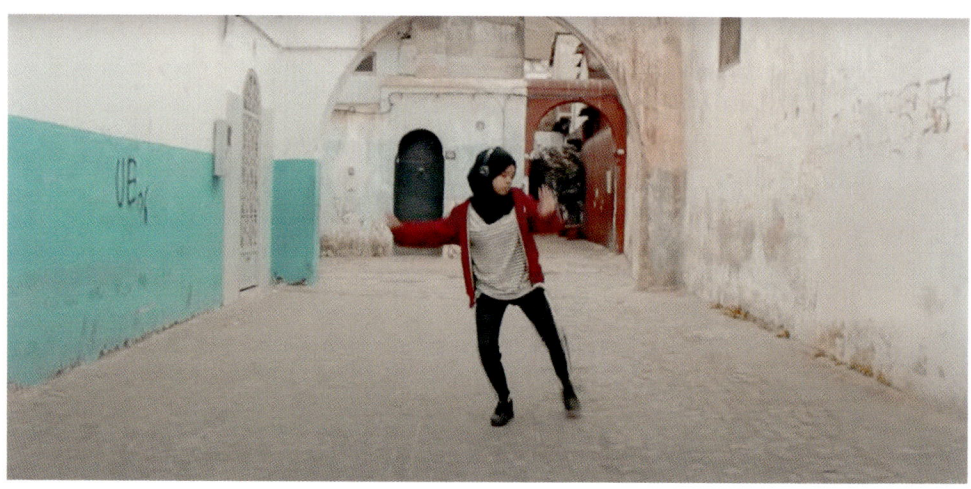

FIGURE 1.7. Screenshot from YouTube video of kids dancing to Hamza Namira's song "Al Ayta" in the SOCICA housing project. Abderrahman Janyen, dir., *Hamza Namira Al Ayta (cover video)*, Izla Production, 2019, accessed November 24, 2020.

While von Osten's project is no longer accessible online, her methodology certainly is. What might we find if we commit to such a search? When in November 2020, amid the global COVID pandemic, I conducted such internet explorations, the most popular amateur videos to reference Hay Mohammadi were videos of the neighborhood streets from moving cars (called "car ride" videos) or of traffic from an apartment window. It was almost as though the pandemic lockdown had turned cameras outward to document signs of movement. But there were also many pre-COVID videos of young men rapping in the neighborhood, some of whom, like "Ach Man," shot videos such as "Calme-toi" with millions of views.[45] In "Calme-toi," Ach Man stands in the street and sings about being told by everyone (father, mother, society, police) to calm down. In a reparative response that speaks of self-determination and self-constitution, he raps: "We needed medicine, but we healed ourselves."[46] Another rap video, "Psyco-9—ZÉRO4-HAY MOHEMADI ft Polini," shows young men singing and dancing in front of social housing.[47] Documentaries have also emerged such as *Sons of the Hay and Proud of It*, and Abderrahman Janyen has made music videos with adolescent boys and girls posing and dancing in the streets of the Hay Mohammadi and the SOCICA housing project.[48] In the SOCICA video in particular, the workers' housing development is more than just a background: it participates in the joyous dance of youth with the dancers keenly aware of how they are engaging with the space.

Unlike the dynamics of haunting, absence, and isolation that we see in Al Jouder's work with dance and modernist housing, these dance videos project affirming connections between housing and its residents. The young people appropriate the passageways fully. While the music that they dance to is contained within the headphones on their heads and does not bounce across walls, their energy does, and it invites the curiosity of passersby. In this instance it is not so much about the music but its embodiment, and how that joyous body relates to and fills the space around it.

Marion von Osten and Labor k3000's *This Was Tomorrow!*'s video grid mapped not only self-representation but an affective topography of place. Through the curation of a new vernacular grid, both viewers and producers see and feel the joy, community, fatigue, anger, and frustration, the structures of feeling that inhabit and create this place. The vernacular grid that speaks the neighborhood thus performs a sonic repair. The visual silence of the colonial grid that was instrumental in speaking to/for the modernist housing project is replaced by people speaking and singing their relationship to the space. Again, the buildings are reconfigured in relation to their residents as the social spaces in between the interstices of the grid become stages for self-representation.

Zinoun Making Room for Music in SOCICA

The 2021 videos of young people dancing with joy on the SOCICA grid exist in remarkable contrast to earlier representations of constrained music and dance in the neighborhood. Indeed, constraint and limitation dominate the 2002 film *Piano* by Moroccan dancer, choreographer, filmmaker, and child of Hay Mohammadi, Lahcen Zinoun.[49] Born in 1944 in Hay Mohammadi, Zinoun is considered Morocco's most established contemporary choreographer. After winning the top prize in dance at the Conservatoire de Casablanca in 1964, Zinoun left Morocco for Brussels for further training and eventually became a star dancer for the Ballet Royal de Wallonie. He returned to Morocco in 1973 with his wife Michèle Barette, and both taught dance at the Conservatoire de Rabat. In 1979 he settled definitively in Morocco and founded the Ecole Ballet Théâtre Zinoun in Casablanca, and in 1985 he created a national dance troupe to study and interpret traditional Moroccan dances that were disappearing from practice. As Hélène Tissières describes it, "Il part avec sa troupe découvrir les pas et rythmes encore pratiqués dans les villages pour les incorporer à sa chorégraphie."[50] (He left with his dance company to discover the steps and rhythms that were still practiced in villages in order to incorporate them into his choreography.) This reparative action not only sought to document older dance forms but also, in transforming their elements into contemporary art, produced a new cultural object. His sixteen-minute semiautobiographical Arabic-language film proposes another type of cultural repair by staging the possibility of reparative relationships between art, social class, and physical space of the SOCICA housing grid.

As I described earlier in this chapter, the SOCICA housing development was built in Hay Mohammadi in 1940–42 as a workers' mass housing project. As Cohen and Eleb describe, "The dwellings were conceived as single- or two-story dwellings (the latter incorporating a steep staircase) and were delivered with a kitchen and lavatory, as well as a 'hidden' patio, though this was always converted into extra living space once the residents moved in."[51] Edmond Brion "put himself forward for designing the arcades and the Moroccan detailing of twin windows and wrought-iron grills"; however, due to an increasing lack of resources during World War II, numerous other decorative features were not included.[52] The resulting workers' development was judged as more plain and bare-bones in comparison with Brion's other projects such as the Habous neighborhood or the Cosuma housing project. In a sense Zinoun's film indirectly builds off Écochard's caption about poverty and art: How can what is deemed a reduced and aesthetically limited workers' housing development contain and produce expansive art?

In an April 21, 2018, interview for the Connect Institute in Agadir, Zinoun talks briefly about his childhood in Hay Mohammadi. He describes the neighborhood in mainly negative terms. It was a dangerous space, an isolating space, a space that presented interdictions: "J'ai commencé à fuir, à m'isoler, c'était extraordinaire, et ça m'a servi d'être isolé, à force de m'isoler, j'ai trouvé mon chemin par la suite grâce à l'indépendance et la découverte du Conservatoire."[53] (I started to flee, to isolate myself, it was extraordinary, and this isolation served me. Forced into isolation I found my path, thanks to independence and the discovery of the Conservatory.) Zinoun would attend every possible performance at the conservatory theater and then return many kilometers by foot to Hay Mohammadi. The discovery of classical ballet as an artistic calling led to an argument with his father, who saw dance as promiscuous, packed Zinoun's belongings into a suitcase, and asked him to leave. Zinoun says he chose dance over his family. In this interview Zinoun posits isolation and containment as the starting points for a journey of self-constitution through short- and long-term departure(s) from the neighborhood. The neighborhood is the negative space that pushes him away in order for him to create.

The film *Piano* however returns to the neighborhood and its housing. In contrast to his interview, Zinoun's film shifts from flight and departure, and asks what happens, or what could happen, when art from an outside space is brought into the housing development and the home. The central plot of the film centers on the desire of teenager Ali to rent a piano that he can play in his house. This is not just a whim but a necessity: in order to continue his studies at the conservatory where he is seen as a rising talent, Ali must be able to practice and train for the Chopin concerto competition. But how can he overcome the refusal of his father, the cost of renting a piano, and finally, the space it will need in an already small and modest home?

Zinoun starts the film with a black screen upon which an epigraph from French composer Hector Berlioz, "Le pire ennemi, c'est la résignation" (The worst enemy is resignation), appears in white. The next shot announces the setting in Arabic and French as 1959 Casablanca, and the first scenes present the bustling SOCICA housing development, with children running in one direction and Ali's father walking his bicycle home through the alley near one of the neighborhood's iconic white arches. From there, subsequent scenes take us from housing exterior to interior. The second scene shows Ali's mother on a rooftop taking down the laundry while Ali reclines behind a sheet, looking through a musical score and playing the piece with his fingers on a small table. The next shot takes the viewer into the house, the interior of which is presented as modest, clean, and sparsely furnished. The house has oil lamps, and as he settles in for dinner, the father tells Ali to ask the neighbor to share their electricity so that he can switch on the radio. Though his father has a job and his maternal uncle runs a neighborhood furnace, on multiple occasions the mother reminds Ali that they are poor. When Ali brings up the issue of renting a piano, his mother replies that "Shābk ya waldī lqadiyya sahla! Shūf a 'Alī . . . nta waldi 'zīz 'liyya . . . u katqtr lī mn l'īnn, walākin khask ta'rf b-llī f hād ddnyā, kayn shi ḥwāyj nqdro 'lihūm, u kayn shi ḥwāyj lā, u hād piyānū dyālk . . . mn l-ḥwāyj llī manqadrūsh 'lihum."⁵⁴ (In life there are things that we can do and other things that we can't, and this piano of yours is among the things that we can't.) A minute later she explains: "Ḥna rāh nas ḍ'āf" (We are poor people).⁵⁵ Indeed, later in the film, one of the delivery men says that the piano is worth more than the entire house.

Despite this, she asks Ali how much room he would need in the house. He replies, twice the size of her kitchen, and as she leaves the kitchen, Ali touches the wall with his fingers. In this scene Zinoun's camera focuses on the walls of the house as a metaphor for the constricted possibilities for creativity. Restricted

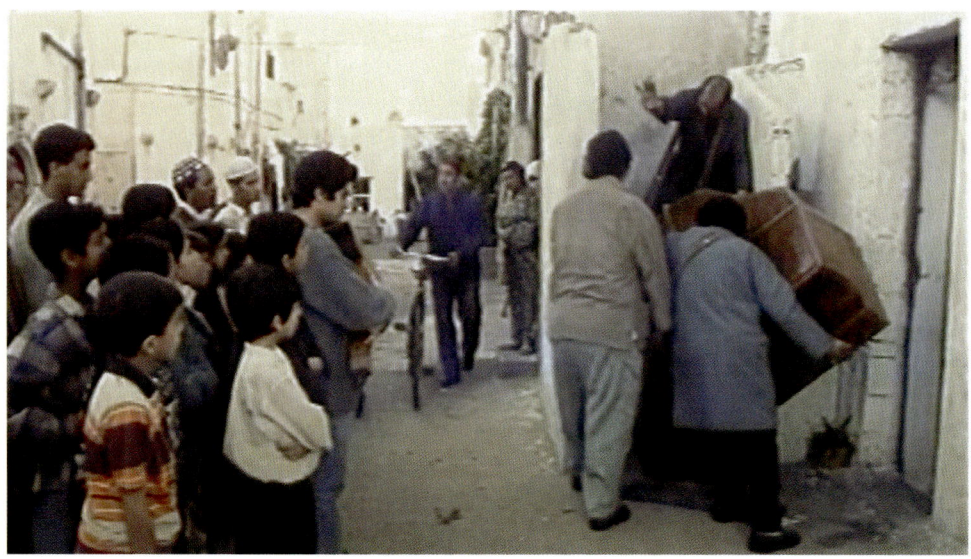

FIGURE 1.8. Still from Lahcen Zinoun, *Piano*, 2002. Short film.

artistic production is presented again during the scene in which Ali meets with his maternal uncle. The uncle explains how he has always loved music and how at Ali's age, his own father caught him playing the *guembri* and struck him, breaking his skull and leaving a scar that he shows Ali. Discordant music plays in the background as the uncle speaks, and the camera reveals a record player that is playing such badly scratched and warped records that it is hard to identify the music. But despite the broken nature of this music, and his broken body, the uncle still loves music and gives Ali the money he needs: a first reparative gesture in a family history of artistic repression.

At the end of the film, Zinoun's camera once again returns its attention to the walls of the housing. We see the workers struggling to lift the grand piano up the short set of stairs to the main room, and in the final scene the camera shows damaged walls, with broken bricks and plaster still lying on the steps. The image of the damaged staircase begins the final scene of the film, with a slow sweeping camera pan up the stairs and into the house as Ali is heard playing a concerto.

The music that Zinoun chooses for Ali to play is by Frederic Chopin, the *larghetto* movement of the Concerto for Piano and Orchestra no. 2, op. 21, a sweepingly romantic repertoire that speaks to revolution and grand gestures of freedom.[56] The damage to the built environment, to mass housing, was necessary in order to allow space for music and creativity. The "severe" father who

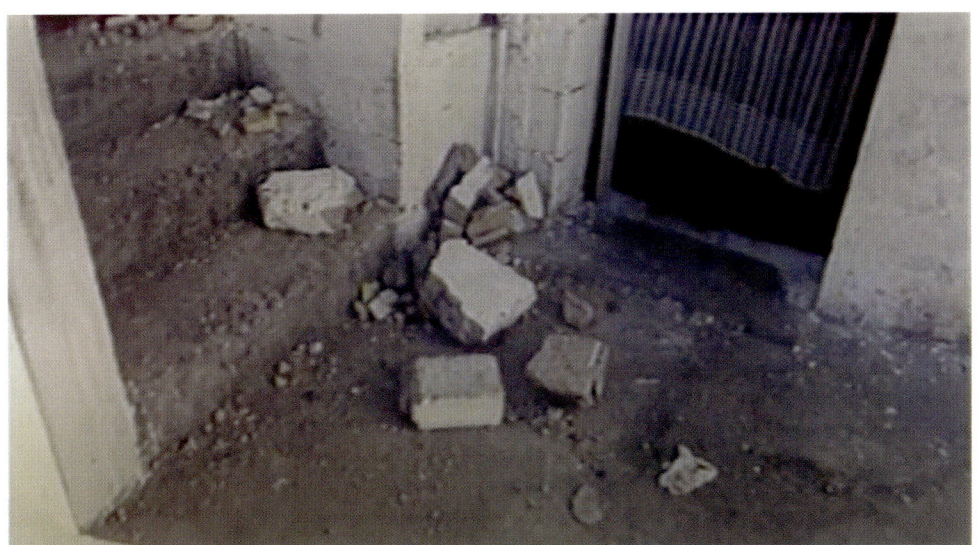

FIGURE 1.9. Still from Lahcen Zinoun, *Piano*, 2002. Short film.

had threatened violence has walked away, and windows both in the interior of the house and outside in neighboring units burst open in rhythm with the music that Ali is playing.

Writing on the film in 2017 for the Moroccan French-language newspaper *Libération*, Yasmine Bouchfar describes the scene: "Le héros joue de la musique: la joie règne et les fenêtres s'ouvrent en guise de soulagement."[57] (The hero plays music: Joy reigns and the windows open themselves in a sign of relief.) Zinoun's film floods the streets with a music that undoes the spatial and social constraints presented in workers' mass housing. The final scenes of interior windows opening in joy and relief contrast with the broken steps and plaster (see figure 1.9) that led to the installation of the piano into the small house. In this ending Zinoun affirms the place of a European art judged as ill-fitting in the neighborhood, one that appears to exceed its limits: in physical, cultural, and colonially ideological terms.

Bouchfar argues that Zinoun wishes to transmit the message that

> la musique est à la portée de tout le monde, et n'est pas l'apanage d'une seule catégorie sociale. Il suffit d'avoir une passion et d'aimer ce qu'on fait et surtout croire en soi.... Tant qu'il y a la vie, il y a de l'espoir. Alors, il ne faut jamais baisser les bras et se résigner. Tout être humain est capable de faire des miracles. Lahcen Zinoun a réalisé un film jalonné

SONIC REPAIRS TO THE GRID   51

de valeurs humaines et principes, vu l'époque de l'histoire et la date de la sortie du film, il y a un grand écart aux niveaux sociologique, culturel, idéologique. Mais les principes et les valeurs traversent les époques. Tout art est beau, tout être humain a le droit de goûter cette beauté quelle que soit sa condition. Sans beauté, on ne peut pas vivre et continuer d'exister; on a tous besoin des arts et des sciences humaines pour faire face à la réalité faite de souffrances, de problèmes et d'interdictions. L'art, en général, est une thérapie et une échappatoire.[58]

(Music is available to everyone and is not the privilege of one social group. It suffices to have passion and to love what one does and above all believe in oneself. As long as there is life, there is hope. So, one should never give up and resign oneself. Every human being is capable of making miracles. Lahcen Zinoun created a film defined by humane values and principles, considering the historical period and when the film came out, there is a large gap between sociological, cultural, and ideological levels. But principles and values traverse time. All art is beautiful, every human being has the right to taste this beauty, whatever its condition. Without beauty, one can't live and continue to exist; we all need arts and humanities to confront a reality made of suffering, problems and interdictions. Art, in general, is a therapy and a way out.)

I cite this article at length because the argument the journalist makes to a middle-class Moroccan readership for art as therapeutic repair and escape from enclosed structures in Moroccan society shares Zinoun's perspective. Like Zinoun, she argues that art is universal and has the ability to transcend societal structures and restrictions and heal multigenerational wounds. If given a chance, music creates boundless space and social possibilities even in the tightest quarters. However, this sense of art's universality and its aspirations is not shared by all, as we will see in the next section.

Souiba Centering Sounds of Opposition in the Grid

Novelist Fouad Souiba presents a more derisive view of "universal" European music and its ability to repair Moroccan societal wounds when he rewrites Zinoun's triumphant piano story in his 2012 novel *L'incompris de Hay Mohammadi* (title of the Moroccan edition) also known as *L'Homme qui voulait être comédien* (title of the 2016 French edition). The narrator describes an extraordinary figure named Sakkouti, a composite character who loosely resembles Lahcen Zinoun and Tayeb Saddiki:[59]

Le troisième défi qui n'était pas le plus simple était de contraindre le quartier tout entier, y compris son imam de père, à subir le camouflet du siècle. Il comptait tout bêtement planter un piano dans le gîte familial. La totale, quoi! Aucune défiance ne trahissait la conviction du jeune Sakkouti, totalement investi dans son labeur et disposé à en découdre, y compris à faire face à toutes les formes d'opposition qui se manifesteraient.[60]

(The third challenge, which wasn't the simplest, was to force the entire neighborhood, including his father the Imam, to submit to the humiliation of the century. Quite foolishly, he intended to dump a piano into the family den. Can you imagine? A total disaster! But no disapproval, including every form of opposition that appeared, could sway young Sakkouti's conviction, totally invested in his project and willing to rip the house apart at the seams.)

Rather than a liberatory and self-actualizing gesture, the introduction of Zinoun/Sakkouti's piano into social housing is seen by Souiba's narrator as an outrageous cultural challenge to the neighborhood, the "humiliation of the century." Souiba's account of the neighbors' reactions to the piano gives voice to the perspectives of a suspicious neighborhood and a stubborn and single-minded artist.

Where Zinoun's film ends with welcome relief and acceptance of Chopin's concerto, Souiba continues the story and highlights how the effects of Sakkouti's constant practicing at all hours deeply disturbs the neighborhood:

En réalité, Sakkouti poussait le bouchon trop loin. Il avait tort de mettre en avant ses devoirs musicaux à domicile à des heures impossibles. L'embêtement des voisins était le cadet de ses soucis. A leur tour, ils ne comprenaient pas pourquoi on voulait à tout prix leur imposer une musique qu'ils ne connaissaient ni d'Eve ni d'Adam. Ce qui est en soi: manquer de respect à autrui! Une erreur monumentale de jugement! Il aurait mieux valu les tuer que de leur faire subir des séances de cacophonie absolue.[61]

(In truth, Sakkouti went too far. He was wrong to give precedence to his music homework at impossible hours. His neighbors' irritation was the least of his worries. On their end, they didn't understand why he wanted to impose on them at all cost a music that they didn't know from Adam or Eve. Which is in itself: a lack of respect for others! A monumental error of judgment! It would have been better had he wanted to kill them than make them submit to these performances of absolute cacophony.)

Calming music to some, cacophony to others. Instead of reproducing sounds of presumed universal freedom, in this scene Souiba centers music as a site of complex if vociferous opposition. And so, where both Barrada and Zinoun make sonic repairs to the existing form and formal qualities of the grid, Souiba's novel works to repair colonial and postcolonial structures of oppression by amplifying all sounds of opposition emerging from the grid. From the start of the novel, Hay Mohammadi and its forms of mass housing are presented as spaces of uprising against and resistance to domination by both political and aesthetic regimes. In this, Souiba makes the quiet traces of uprising that Barrada references obliquely in her work loudly central to his.

Writing with humor, derision, and a large amount of creative license, Souiba creates a cast of composite characters that evoke real historical figures and a series of episodes that gesture to historical events. What does it mean to write a history of twentieth-century Morocco with Carrière Centrales / Hay Mohammadi at its center? And what advantage is there to making that story fictional, generalized, and often elusive? By playing with and revealing the limits of historical representation, Souiba draws his readers' attention to the limits of official Moroccan history while highlighting the intensity of felt history and lived experience. In an interview with Khalil Rais in the Moroccan newspaper *L'Opinion*, Souiba states, "Nous ne connaissons qu'une infime partie de notre Histoire" (We only know a minuscule part of our History), and describes his intervention into the historical record as "plus qu'une simple technique de mise en condition ou de remise en forme, c'est une véritable tentative de se dénoncer, de reconnaître sa culpabilité et de s'impliquer volontairement dans l'histoire de ces gens qui ont peiné et peinent toujours à vivre décemment" (more than the simple techniques of recounting or reshaping, it is a veritable attempt to denounce oneself, to recognize one's guilt, and to implicate oneself in the history of those people who struggled and continue to struggle to live decently).[62] Souiba's literary approach to history works to transcend a *"mise en forme"* (shaping of history); rather, he hopes to forge a pathway of consciousness, of accountability, and of engagement and action. This literary act is in line with Brahim El Guabli's argument for the centrality of literature in producing both historical archives and interventions.[63] Souiba produces ledgers of oppositional voices that blur univocal history and claims of innocence and offer multiple entry points into the built environment.

Chapter 2 of the novel is perhaps the most striking example of this approach. After an initial chapter which describes the struggle of the young protagonist Sbaâ-Ellayl to enter into a career in the theater, Souiba turns his attention to both the titular neighborhood and Sbaâ-Ellayl's origin story through the murder of his mother in an anticolonial uprising in Carrières Centrales while he, an innocent infant, is strapped to her back. The chapter begins with a powerful scene of police and military violence in mass housing. Critics have argued that Souiba's literary style is cinematographic, blurring the boundaries between media.[64] Indeed, the first paragraphs of chapter 2 describe a neighborhood under military siege in images that could easily have been taken from Hollywood films. Bombs, napalm, bullets, and shrapnel rain down on the shantytown:

> Métamorphosé en un véritable champ de tirs, le quartier *Hay Mohammadi* croulait sous les bombes. La carrière centrale de *Dar Beida* s'exposait à un embrasement d'enfer qui n'épargnait ni coin ni recoin. Moitié en dur, moitié en tôle, ses habitants, n'avaient aucune chance d'échapper à la puissance de feu du contingent militaire du Protectorat....
>
> Pendant ce temps-là, le napalm brûlait tout sur son passage. Aux bombes incendiaires, s'ajoutait une panoplie de projectiles crachée par les canons de mitraillettes laissant résonner une violente cacophonie.[65]

(Transformed into a veritable firing range, the Hay Mohammadi neighborhood crumbled under the bombs. The central quarry of Dar Beida [Arabic for Casablanca] was laid open to a hellish blaze that spared no nook or corner. Housed half in concrete, half in sheet metal, its inhabitants had no chance to escape the powerful fire of the military contingent of the Protectorate....

During this time, napalm burned everything in its way. In addition to firebombs, an array of projectiles spewed by machine gun barrels rang out a violent cacophony.)

A different type of sound—violent cacophony—enters into the picture as Souiba describes the built environment of mass housing as both victim and product of colonial violence. Interspersed in this hellscape imagery of war, the narrator creates a connection between the shantytown and modernist buildings. The shantytown is presented as "mille et une baraques, sorties d'une terre mi-noirâtre mi-bleuâtre trônaient tristement sur les lieux" (a thousand and one shacks that emerged from the half-blackish, half-blueish earth reigned sadly on the premises).[66] They are "de monstreuses boîtes de conserve ... fabriquées à la base de matériau fait de plaques d'acier craquelant, rouillé. Four en été et glacière en hiver" (monstrous tin cans ... fabricated from a material made of brittle and rusted steel. Oven in summer and icebox in winter).[67] The modernist housing blocks are not described as much better: "L'autre versant du quartier construit en dur ne montrait aucun signe d'opulence démesurée. Seulement de minuscules unités d'habitation d'un à deux étages ne dérogeant pas à la règle d'être abritées par un quartier peu enclin à confier tous ses secrets."[68] (The other side of the neighborhood that was built in concrete showed no sign of excessive opulence. Only minuscule housing units with one or two floors, that did not depart from the rule of being housed in a neighborhood uninclined to hand over its secrets.) There is little shelter in either from the daily violence of colonial life and poverty.

Souiba's neighborhood geography is not limited to these two types of mass housing structures, however; the third element that is equally present and is a constitutive factor in a history of violence in the neighborhood is the Derb Moulay Cherif police station: "Bâti en dur par les militaires" (Built in concrete by the military).[69] When Moroccans hear the name of the Derb Moulay Cherif police station today, it is not primarily associated with the colonial period but rather with the infamous torture center from the Years of Lead. Souiba will take the reader to that place and time later in the novel, but first he names the police station in the context of colonial-era built environment, colonial violence, and repression.

While Souiba doesn't give a date, the military violence that opens chapter 2 is a reference to the French military retaliation to the December 24, 1953, bombing of the Marché Central by Moroccan nationalists.[70] After the initial and unrelenting soundscape of a neighborhood under fire described above, the narrator presents a united and vociferous neighborhood marching in opposition in the early morning to the police station to protest the bombing of their homes and the imposed curfew. At the head of the crowd, the reader finds Mmy Aïcha and her infant:

> Sortie de nulle part, surgissait une dame qui portait son enfant. Attaché, il était enveloppé dans une étoffe qui le fixait au dos de sa mère, avançant fièrement au beau milieu de la chaussée. Marquant un arrêt au cœur de l'artère centrale, elle faisait maintenant face au plus gros des troupes de l'armée coloniale.[71]

> (Coming out of nowhere, a lady carrying her young child suddenly appeared. He was wrapped in a cloth that attached him to his mother's back, advancing bravely right into the middle of the pathway. Creating a stoppage in the heart of the central artery, she now confronted the largest of the colonial troops.)

Souiba positions Aïcha in relation to the physical and symbolic space of the neighborhood around her, first appearing from "nowhere," then in the "middle of the roadway," then at the "heart of the central artery." He fully incorporates her into the city and likewise gives bodily form to the neighborhood.

Mmy Aïcha incarnates the neighborhood's opposition: opposition to the French military, colonial grids of oppression, and to the degradation of dignity and life in Hay Mohammadi. Souiba stresses that Mmy Aïcha speaks freely, "sans réserve" (without reserve), articulating a list of demands that primarily focus on the return from exile of Mohamed V and the expulsion of the French from Morocco.[72] The strength of her words, her principles and values, radiates from her body. As Souiba writes: "L'éclat du regard de Mmy Aïcha était totalement épris des valeurs de liberté et de droit. Valeurs qui finissaient de la remplir du courage et d'abnégation d'une égérie montant en puissance et prête à faire face à toutes les épreuves de la vie."[73] (The radiance of Mmy Aïcha's expression was totally infused with the values of liberty and justice. Values that in the end filled her with courage and selflessness, with a growing energy, ready to confront all the hardships of life.) This power of opposition is swiftly met with brutal repression; her body and her words silenced by two shots in the head:

> Le poing levé vers le ciel, Mmy Aïcha eut à peine le temps de faire entendre sa voix qu'elle recevait aussitôt deux balles en pleine tempe. Tombée par terre le front contre le sol, elle saignait. Le gamin toujours attaché à son dos éclatait en sanglots. Il s'était fait mal à l'impact de la chute. Du sang rouge écarlate chaud coulait tendrement du cadavre, sous les yeux du môme incapable de comprendre la tournure des choses.[74]

(Her fist raised to the sky, Mmy Aïcha barely had time to make her voice heard when she received two bullets straight to her forehead. Fallen to the ground, her forehead against the earth, she bled. The little child, still attached to her back, burst into tears. He was hurt from the impact of the fall. Bright-red warm blood flowed tenderly from the body, in full view of a kid incapable of understanding the turn of events.)

While many accounts detail the asymmetrical violence exerted by the French military against Moroccan civilians, the shooting of a young woman with an infant on her back does not figure in the historical record. However, historian Mohamed Sakib, considered by many as the living memory of Hay Mohammadi, confirms this story among the many atrocities he remembers.[75]

Having emerged from the space of colonial mass housing, Mmy Aïcha's body returns to it. When the military officers aren't paying attention, two young men pick up her body and pull her back into the shantytown, back to the "structures métalliques rouillées faisant office d'habitation" (rusted metallic structures that act as housing).[76] The child, Sbaâ-Ellayl, is still attached to her back and has fallen asleep. When neighbors help to carefully extract him, he awakens screaming. In this scene, the death of his mother symbolically becomes a rebirth for Sbaâ-Ellayl. Incapable of understanding what is happening, the child screams the intensity of the moment to a crowd of onlookers. Where his mother articulated her opposition through words, the child can only communicate affectively, his body registering his terror and incomprehension. This scream is a quakeful moment—an unsettling of colonial domination of sound but also an unsettling of anticolonial heroism. In popular histories of Moroccan nationalism, the December 24 bombing of the Marché Central is often considered the birth of the war for independence. Souiba links Sbaâ-Ellayl to this history, but not by the child's choice—he is a victim, not an actor.

As the novel later reveals, Sbaâ-Ellayl's implication in politics always appears by accident and as unwanted: an implicated bystander in a history and built environment of opposition. This dynamic comes to a head in chapter 20, when Sbaâ-Ellayl is arrested and detained in Derb Moulay Cherif as a result of a series of comically tragic entanglements that turn him into a presumed enemy of the state. His incarceration in Derb Moulay Cherif is also a return to the neighborhood. Speaking to the character Mouriziz, fashioned after Abdelaziz Mouride, he says: "Au fait, je suis emprisonné dans mon propre quartier! Toute mon enfance et mon adolescence, je les ai passées à courir le long de ce commissariat."[77] (Incidentally, I'm imprisoned in my own neighbhorhood! I spent all my childhood and adolescence running up and down the side of this police station.) Then identifying himself to the guard, he gives yet a deeper genealogy: "Fils de Bassou, héros nationaliste de l'indépendance et petit-fils de Mmy Aïcha: martyre, décédée sur le champ d'honneur sous les feux du colon ici même au quartier Hay Mohammadi!"[78] (Son of Bassou, nationalist hero of independence and little son of Mmy Aïcha: a martyr, killed on the battlefield by the fire of the colonist, here in this very neighborhood of Hay Mohammadi!) Rather than be acknowledged as the renowned theater actor he has become, Sbaâ-Ellayl is now identified as foremost a son of the neighborhood and one of its marginalized peoples. Sbaâ-Ellayl is tortured, and when he finally emerges from prison, his life falls apart.

Architectural historian Karim Rouissi writes:

> During the French occupation, the Carrières Centrales housing development was the site of social mobilisation and political resistance against exclusion; this activism continued even after independence. The Justice and Reconciliation Commission of 2004 even designated that neigh-

bourhood as one that should receive community reparations because it housed a population that had suffered collectively from government oppression.[79]

Indeed, since 2004, the testimonies of neighborhood residents continue to be gathered and published in collaborations with numerous neighborhood and human-rights associations. In 2011 the neighborhood organization Initiative Urbaine published a booklet of resident stories and testimonies in collaboration with the Conseil National des Droits de L'Homme (CNDH) and with texts by activist and writer Fatna El Bouih, CNDH member Mohammed Soual, and historian Najib Taki entitled *Cariane Central, Hay Mohammadi: Mémoire et dignité*. The volume, published in French and Arabic, collected the stories of thirteen residents and former residents who recount their memories of life in the neighborhood and hopes for the future. In October 2019, another bilingual booklet gathering stories and histories of the neighborhood by its residents was published as a collaborative project between the Initiative Urbaine association and Manon Troux (an architect and PhD student in the Laboratoire Architecture, Ville, Urbanisme et Environnement at the University of Paris, Nanterre), the Musée Collectif de Casablanca and the art collective Atelier de l'Observatoire. This booklet conducted ethnographic research in tandem with art practice as research. The forthcoming documentary project *Casamantes* directed by Hélène Harder and Karima El Kharraze draws on a multiyear educational collaboration that brought together teenagers from Hay Mohammadi and Mantes (France) "to understand their environment through writing, photography and film and to conceive each according to their own imaginary, a virtual landscape: Casamantes."[80] One powerful clip from the film's trailer entitled "Keltoum: The Ghosts of the Commissariat" speaks to the ongoing presence of specters of human-rights abuse history in the urban landscape. The camera follows a young girl walking toward the former Derb Moulay Cherif police station building in silence, her hand gently touching neighboring walls before standing in front of the closed door. Her touch is both an act of memory and mourning.

Souiba's novel emerges at the same time as these numerous testimonials and resident histories but differs in its goal and methodology of representation. The novel works to register the intensity of collective pain and violence experienced in the neighborhood—from the colonial period through the Years of Lead. But it also registers something else: the chance and randomness by which people are pulled into this history and perhaps a lack of moral clarity when faced with a history of opposition, violence, and pain. The character Sbaâ

Ellayl, who claimed an apolitical position and sought shelter in the arts, cannot maintain his innocence and is presented as a victim, an outraged bystander, an unwilling participant, and a casually complicit agent all at once. Souiba's voicing of history of the neighborhood, its residents, and Morocco at large is deeply nuanced and complex and allows for competing emotions to exist simultaneously. Repair is not redemptive here.

Songs from and across the Grid: Nass El Ghiwane, Lemchaheb, and Raja Ultras

In his novel, Souiba uses the word *cacophonie* to describe both the sounds of colonial gunfire and the sounds of Debussy's *Douze études pour le piano* on Sakkouti's piano.[81] In this final section, I would like to take a moment to talk more deeply about sound as music in Hay Mohammadi and how music engages and transforms the housing grid. Resident descriptions of mass housing across its different typologies refer to the steady sound of neighbors living in close proximity: talking, fighting, laughing, loving, and singing. The Musée Collectif de Casablanca has even produced *Radio de mon quartier—Hay Mohammadi*, a program in which residents talk about the neighborhood and listeners hear music and sounds from the streets.[82] The relationship between the neighborhood and popular music is a particularly rich one, with two famous musical groups emerging from Hay Mohammadi housing: Nass El Ghiwane and Lemchaheb. Both bands turned away from the musical currents of their time, the popularity of *Sharqui* music (music from Egypt and the eastern Middle East), to embrace and popularize Maghrebi forms of music. In describing the music of Nass El Ghiwane, Elias Muhanna writes:

> The plaintive melodies and chants brought to mind 'aita, a popular style associated with the shikhat-independent women of sometimes ill repute—but also melhoun, a medieval Moroccan oral tradition with roots in the courtly arts of Moorish Spain. The group's hypnotic rhythms borrowed from the mystagogic cadences of the Sufi brotherhoods, especially the Gnawa—descendants of West African slaves, whose ritual exorcisms entailed what might be the original trance music. The banjo—a grittier African alternative to the Arab zither—reinforced the sense that this music, which was unlike anything ever heard in Morocco, was in its own reckless way a summation of everything ever heard in Morocco.[83]

In terms of lyrics, the bands sang about dignity, loss, migration, and societal injustice. In many ways, these musical and lyrical interests were a reflection of the deeply diverse populations of Hay Mohammadi, where since the 1930s people from all over Morocco, especially the rural south, migrated to Casablanca and brought their local histories, stories, and music with them. As their worlds rapidly changed, people were eager to hear themselves and their lives reflected both in musical styles and in Moroccan-spoken Arabic.

The music group Nass El Ghiwane was established in 1971, and with four members of the group from the neighborhood, the band regularly met at the Dar Chabab, a community arts center in Hay Mohammadi where they participated in a theater program led by Tayeb Saddiki.[84] Dar Chabab was a sociocultural architecture that existed on the other side of the same coin as Derb Moulay Cherif: both born out of colonial violence. As Jaouad Mdidech describes,

> Dar Chabab a une histoire, que les habitants du Hay se transmettent, de génération en génération. En effet, dans les années 1950, une tuerie eut lieu aux abords du marché central, perpétrée par les irréductibles du protectorat. Plusieurs victimes étaient des habitants du Hay. Considérant qu'ils avaient une dette vis-à-vis de ces victimes, les libéraux français, dont Jacques Lemaigre Dubreuil (assassiné par les fachistes d'Action Française), construisirent alors Dar Chabab de Hay Mohammadi, un complexe socioculturel, le premier de son genre à Casablanca, qui servait à la fois de bibliothèque, d'école de théâtre et de musique, et de lieu de divertissement pour les enfants le dimanche matin.[85]

(Dar Chabab has a history that the residents of the Hay transmit from generation to generation. In essence, during the 1950s a massacre occurred in the surrounding area of the central market, perpetuated by colonial hardliners. Several victims were inhabitants from the Hay. Realizing that they had a debt to these victims, French liberals, including Jacques Lemaigre Dubreil [assassinated by the fascists of Action Française], would build Dar Chabab of Hay Mohammadi, a sociocultural complex, the first of its kind in Casablanca, that would serve at once as a library, a theater and music school, and an activity space for children on Sunday mornings.)

Ahmed El Maanouni's 1981 film *Trances* shows archival footage of members of Nass El Ghiwane participating in the theater program, as well as band member Allal Yaala giving oud lessons to neighborhood adolescents.

For the band members who grew up in the neighborhood, both their singing and political practices emerged from within the walls of the housing itself.

In one testimony in the *Cariane central Hay Mohammadi: Mémoire et dignité* booklet, a resident named Rachida recounts her relationship to Boujmii, one of the band's founding members:

> Lorsqu'ils ont déménagé de Kariane Khlifa, Boujmii et sa famille ont habité chez nous au rez-de-chaussée. Nous avions un lien de parenté, Boujmii était mon cousin. J'ai grandi dans une ambiance de chants sahraouis et de rires. Ma tante, la mère de Boujmii, avait une voix agréable et Boujmii et son père l'accompagnaient souvent dans ses chants. C'est dans ces lieux que Boujmii a découvert sa vocation de chanteur, parolier et musicien.[86]

> (When they moved from the Khlifa shantytown, Boujmii and his family lived with us on the ground floor. We were related, Boujmii was my cousin. I grew up in an atmosphere of Sahraoui songs and laughter. My aunt, Boujmii's mother, had a pleasant voice and Boujmii and his father would accompany her in her singing. It is in this space that Boujmii discovered his calling to be a singer, songwriter, and musician.)

The housing is described as an ambient container of Sahraoui song and of laughter, and Rachida stresses that this space is where Boujmii found his artistic calling, giving credit not only to the family but perhaps most importantly to his mother and her voice. Rachida continues her testimony to describe how Boujmii never forgot where he came from: "Boujmii est un enfant des pauvres et il est resté pauvre, il nous a toujours invités à venir dans ses concerts où il obligeait les organisateurs à nous accueillir comme des personnalités importantes."[87] (Boujmii is the child of poor people and he remained poor. He always invited us to come to his concerts where he obliged the organizers to welcome us as VIPs.) She talks about how he and bandmate Laarbi Batma attended her wedding, played music over the seven-day event, and helped pay for the costs of welcoming the hundreds of guests who came to hear them: "C'était un homme généreux et fier de ces racines."[88] (He was a generous man, proud of his roots.)

Journalist Mona Badri writes that "the band contributed to the shaping of a conscious and politically aware generation. Their songs had stinging criticism of society and the spread of corruption within its institutions."[89] But band member Omar Sayyed insists that they weren't a political band with a political agenda, and that their songs weren't political interventions, but rather humanist interventions and representations of changing life in Morocco: "Look, we were street kids from the poorest part of Casablanca, and we sang from that perspective. It's not an elevated perspective, you see. It's not a perspective from which somebody can criticize the people who have power, in order to take it for himself. Because the man of the street, the beggar, doesn't have any hope of getting power, so he can be honest about what he truly feels."[90] Perhaps the reason that so many critics have read the band as a political group is precisely this ability to reflect Moroccan reality affectively. Songs about death and loss could be felt as either or both personal and political, simultaneously reflective meditations and societal critique.

While Nass El Ghiwane wrote many songs that referenced the human condition and deep values of dignity and solidarity among Casablanca's urban poor, the 1993 song/poem "Essemta" is the only song to my knowledge that names mass housing directly. The chorus of the song—"I am neither lonely nor exiled / I am a shackled citizen / Injured by the sharp knife"—speaks of the conditions for North African migration, both rural and across the Mediterranean.[91] The shackled citizen, or city dweller, lives in an environment of dispossession and a widening class divide between the wealthy and poor: "my people live in the dark." And the high-rise is inseparable from the shacks of the bidonville: "High-rise buildings go up / Shanties are buried / hidden." In the repetitive nature of the chorus, words repeat, build up, and commit to memory the message that Moroccans are all shackled citizens until there is greater equality, dignity, and justice.[92]

Nass El Ghiwane's song invites the listener to sing along, and indeed, hundreds of thousands of Moroccans knew their songs by heart. The band seemed everywhere: "They played before thousands of fans at packed arenas, in country and abroad, and released dozens of recordings. Their songs played on every radio station, their logos emblazoned on T-shirts, bumper stickers, and window decals. . . . Everybody knew every word, the music tied us all together."[93] The music performed a reparative relationality, reconfiguring the possibility of kinship across generations, class lines, and neighborhood borders.

Hay Mohammadi is presented as such a world—a world of song and a world where people sing along—in the 2020 documentary *L7asla* by novelist and filmmaker Sonia Terrab, coproduced by the Moroccan TV channel 2M and Ali'N.[94] The film opens with the famous song "L7asla" (Impasse or Dead-End) by the 1970s band Lemchaheb and shows how one generational musical universe is eventually replaced by another, that of the songs of the ultras supporters of the Casablanca soccer team Raja.[95] The film traces the shift in neighborhood culture from art to sport, but the thread that ties both together are songs seeking justice and dignity.

Lemchaheb was founded in 1974 and members of the band came from two Hay Mohammadis: the Hay Mohammadi in Casablanca and the Hay

Mohammadi of Marrakech. Like Nass El Ghiwane, the group dived deeply into popular forms of music from across the country and wrote songs that spoke of life and loss for Moroccans of modest means. Sonia Terrab's film starts with a video of Lemchaheb from the late 1970s singing their song "L7asla" on a concert stage. The song asks:

> Wīn humā shllā nās zmānī?
> Kulhum ghābū duk lusūd
> Āsh hād l-ḥaṣla?
> Bin qūm al-maʿmiyya
> Jmaʿa jāfla u gāfla malhiyya? [96]
>
> (Where are the people of my past?
> These lions have disappeared
> What is this dead-end?
> Amongst the one-eyed?
> The unschooled and the distracted?)

This lyric becomes a repetitive refrain in the film. Terrab films both young and old people singing these words in different spaces across the neighborhood: in front of apartment doors, in the streets, and in cafés. And the lyrics become the entry point for discussions of the neighborhood: its past and future. One young man exclaims: "Lḥaṣla hiyya llā ḥaslin hna ya khtī " (the dead-end, we are stuck here sister).[97] An older man explains: "Lḥaṣla ulla lbṣla? ḥna ḥaslin f lbṣla (Dead-end or dirt? It's both, and we are all stuck in the dirt).[98] Another man states: "Gha ngūl lik ḥaja wḥda baqa zwina f l-ḥay, tārīkh. Lmāḍī llī bāqī zwīnn" (I'll tell you the only good thing left in the Hay is its history. The past is all the good we have left).[99]

However, not everyone is nostalgic for the past and for its cultural forms. One young man exclaims that everyone talks about Nass El Ghiwane but that they are dead. They sang sad songs while high. But he and his friends are not interested in culture, they are "*sportifs*," interested in sports and soccer in particular.

The shift from the Dar Chabab as the central neighborhood space for young people to the space of soccer (the streets and neighborhood cafés that broadcast soccer matches) as the main site of cultural identity becomes the central dynamic that Terrab follows in the rest of the film.[100] Over the course of a year, she traces the lives of young men from the neighborhood who are supporters of the Casablanca soccer team Raja: filming them hanging out together, talking about their team, talking about their hopes and lives, showing them studying and working. One young man is shown studying hard for the baccalaureate

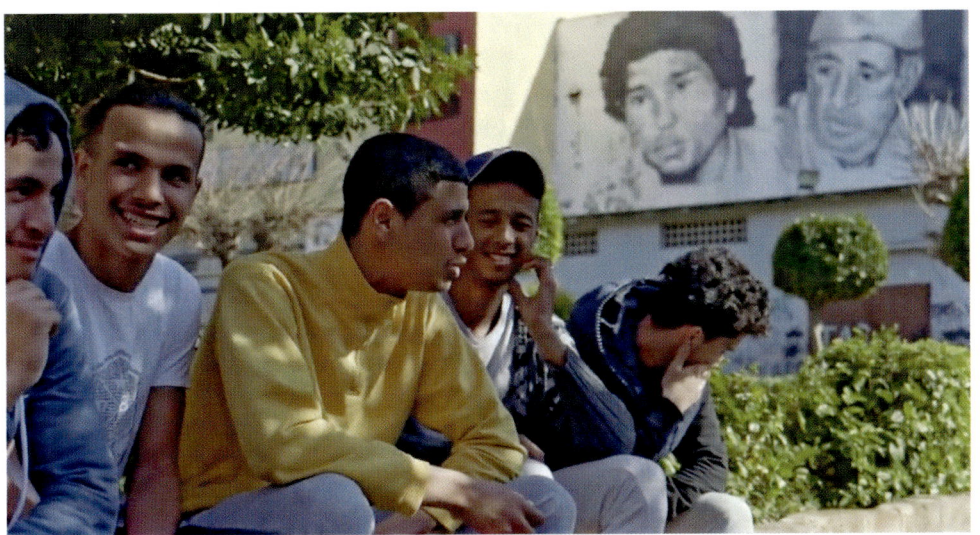

FIGURE 1.10. Still from Sonia Terrab, *L7asla*, 2020. Short film. Neighborhood adolescent boys in front of a mural of Nass El Ghiwane on the Dar Chabab.

exam; another is working, first selling socks and other Raja branded items and then opening his own snack stand as he decides to establish himself more securely after his family adopts a baby boy. In many of the scenes, Terrab shows the young men singing with joy and passion, and the songs they sing are Raja ultras fan songs.

These songs sung by crowds of young male fans in stadiums, in cafés, and in the streets are primarily chants sometimes accompanied by percussion, and their lyrics are deeply critical of living conditions in Morocco. In one YouTube video, a stadium full of fans sings:

> In this country, we live in an allusion and a hell
> And we hope that God will help us
> They drowned us with drugs
> They made us orphans
> God will avenge us from them.
> . . .
> You lost an entire generation
> You killed enthusiasm.[101]

This chant, entitled "Fī blādī ẓlmūnī" (In my country, they've done me wrong), speaks to the fans' anger at then-recent laws such as Law 09-09 (June 2011)

SONIC REPAIRS TO THE GRID 65

that legislate behavior at sporting events. But beyond the immediate issue, the chant also expresses their deep disillusion with a state and society that is seen as having failed them in their lives. In her documentary, Terrab captures both the emotional intensity of song performance and the tension of watching the soccer game itself as if the young men were watching the possible success or failure of their lives.

In the film, the streets of Hay Mohammadi and its housing grids are filled with these chants. While different from the sung poetry of Nass El Ghiwane and Lemchaheb, they express and perform a shared emotional intensity about the struggles of life in the neighborhood and by extension in the country. Cacophony to some; to others, a reparative act that brings relief, beauty, and an expression of dignity.

Conclusion

The sonic repair of art in this chapter brings together mass housing architectures and the in-between spaces in the built environment of Hay Mohammadi and ultimately shortens what De Vroey and Nevens describe as "a somewhat odd distance between stories, histories and memories (immaterial heritage) on the one hand, and spaces, buildings and objects (material heritage)."[102] From strategic silences that clear space for sound on the grid to an insistence on song and its ability to render more audible the lives and dreams of residents, the artwork examined in this chapter engages mass housing in both its material and immaterial heritage, creating links between the two, new scars that reparatively bring the two together.

De Vroey and Nevens describe local Hay Mohammadi historian Mohamed Sakib's idea for building a *halqa* (storytelling) garden on the former site of the last shantytown in Hay Mohammadi as a remarkable example of bringing together "the perceived oppositions between spaces and stories, the colonial and the indigenous, the static and the dynamic, with a most elegant ease."[103] They write:

> Remarkably, the focus is not on the remembered legacy of past halqa-spectacles in the quarter as such, but on the construction of a space that allows a similar social dynamic—be it literally as *halqa*, or as a reinterpretation of the concept. Spatially then, the project is not obliged to carry references to the bidonville that it replaces, but again is hoped to re-enact the social coherence and feeling of unity the place stood for. The project looks back, but equally projects into the future.[104]

Sakib's *halqa* garden, which would invite people to speak about their past and hopes for the future, again brings sound into a reparative relationship with the built environment. The audible and inaudible melds with the visible and invisible and forms a new spatial dynamic between existing buildings and traces of their past. Might this matrix that emerges from sound be similar to what AbdouMaliq Simone calls a "rhythm of endurance"—a back and forth movement between "attempts to reach beyond the confines of limited places and routines" while "retaining a microscope's view of the constantly surprising details about places that could be left behind"?[105]

Urban historian Diana Wylie describes yet another example of an artist creating possibilities to sonically move across the Hay Mohammadi grid and bridge physical space with embodied histories and stories. Myriam Zidi, whose family once lived in Hay Mohammadi, designed a large-scale board game that she played with children at the Initiative Urbaine social center in the neighborhood. As Wylie describes the game:

> On each block she had drawn a site with local resonance: a former factory, the new tramway, the "Bees' Nest" social housing, worker housing—SOCICA and Cosuma—built by the French, and a notorious local prison (the former Centre de détention Derb Moulay Cherif) where protesters were held and tortured in the 1970s and 1980s. When a child lands on a particular site, he is obliged to tell its history in order to move on around the board.[106]

Children are not only "obliged" to learn the histories of these buildings; their bodies and voices move between and across the physical grid, playing creatively with the construction of knowledge and putting the construction of knowledge into sonic and embodied play.

Perhaps this is one important insight we can glean from this chapter and its focus on artwork and its sonic interventions in the history and representation of mass housing. From photography to film to literature to song, video, and play, artwork stages the relations between built home space and creativity, what it means to build something in and among dominant, oppressive, or inhabitable architectural grids. Art's sonic reparative engagement creates new forms, new sounds, and new space in and on the physical and conceptual grid(s) of mass housing. This artwork, both professional and amateur, constantly builds new structures and creates new ledgers and catalogs of life in order to both look back in history and also attempt to imagine the future into something more livable.

2

Affecting Relation in Climat de France, Algiers
Decolonial Poetics and Embodied Ethics of Recognition

Grim representations of the afterlife of Climat de France litter the French and Algerian press. Most often, the monumental housing project that is home to fifty thousand residents is depicted as a site of lawlessness, drugs, and social exclusion. Articles have called the housing project "an Algerian wound," a "ghetto," and "a crumbled utopia" that "is a concentration of all that is bad in Algerian society."[1] Images on the news frequently show the buildings and their surroundings as stages of protest amid conflict with the police. In March 2011, Climat de France made headlines in Algerian newspapers for the "riots" that broke out in response to the government razing informal housing structures built in the neighborhood.[2] Later that same year, journalist Mohamed Benchicou published his novel *Mensonge de Dieu* (God's lie). While stuck in traffic as he and his family attempt to leave Algiers, the character Samy describes the monumental housing complex as a theatrical stage of misfortune and woe, with an ironically poetic name:

> Comment, en effet, ne pas rire encore et toujours de l'insoutenable désolation du quartier quand une étrange ironie du sort et un usage insidieux de la métaphore avaient osé le baptiser du joli nom de Climat de France? Vivre à Climat de France, c'est pourtant habiter de miteuses cités surpeuplées, mais la litote fut définitivement adoptée pour ce qu'elle contribuait

à théâtraliser le malheur. On vécut alors de pain sec et d'honorabilité ressuscitée, celle-là providentielle, qu'octroyait le prestige factice de l'enseigne trompeuse: "Je réside à Climat de France, près d'Alger." Le simulacre de l'écriteau masquant si parfaitement l'immonde réalité des ghettos, on en généralisa l'usage jusqu'à donner un nom poétique à chacune des "cités d'urgence," ces affreux baraquements en dur construits à la hâte par l'administration française pour y entasser les milliers d'indigènes que le dénuement poussait à penser aux armes.[3]

(How, indeed, can one not laugh again and again at the unbearable desolation of the neighborhood when a strange irony of fate and an insidious use of metaphor dared to baptize it with the pretty name Climat de France? To live in Climat de France is to live in shabby overpopulated housing projects but a rhetorical language was adopted for its understated ability to stage misfortune. We lived thus on dry bread and a resurrected sense of honor. An honor that was fortuitous, granted by the false prestige of the misleading sign: "I live in Climat de France, near Algiers." The sham billboard so perfectly masked the filthy reality of the ghetto that it became widespread in its usage and gave poetic names to each of these "emergency housing projects," those horrid concrete shacks built in haste by the French administration in order to cram thousands of Algerian natives that destitution was pushing to consider taking up arms.)

No one can deny the economic precarity and social exclusion that Climat de France perpetuates despite its foundational narratives of dignity in housing. But is there another way of looking at the housing and what it produces beyond narratives of destitution and the false advertising of construction billboards? How do accounts of lawlessness and unrest conceal a spectrum of other histories and codes of self-rule from self-constituted moral norms and proletarian engagement for social and political change? What other possible relations form within and outside its walls? And how does art imagine and amplify them?

Where the last chapter looked at artwork that engages the grids of two modernist mass housing projects built on a former shantytown in Casablanca, this chapter explores how art interactions with the 1959 housing project Climat de France in Algiers produce a "poetics of relation" often articulated through an affective and embodied lens. Édouard Glissant famously theorized poetics of relation as an open-ended transformative process of creolization and *métissage* (hybridization), a processing of foundational spaces and histories of contact, and the radical imagination of interaction and exchange with an irreducible Other. As he writes, "Relation diversifies forms of humanity according to infinite strings of models infinitely brought into contact and relayed" and "its work always changes all the elements composing it, and consequently, the resulting relationship, which then changes them all over again."[4] This maximalist approach to figuring and refiguring relation beyond capture resonates with Simone and Azoulay's call for maximal exposures and open shutters that don't foreclose possibility, as discussed in this book's introduction. Poetics of relation is the opposite of a poetics of isolation and containment, of closed and fixed systems of understanding, and in political terms, of narrowly defined and defended concepts of nationality.

Inspired by Glissant, my reading of relational poetics in art encounters with Climat de France explores the idea of relation as a reparative process that dynamically transforms colonial history through new definitions and possibilities of kinship. Staged through affective and embodied encounter, these emergent relations redefine scale, perspective, and legacies of inheritance, and redraw pathways toward knowledge, understanding, and imagination. Reparative art in this chapter connects the dots between segregated histories and peoples, and in so doing attempts to register a decolonial practice of recognition.

This chapter begins with the proposition of relationality made by Marie Richeux in her 2017 novel *Climats de France* where Climat de France is rendered plural in the title and written from multiple cross-Mediterranean perspectives. Richeux's invocation of plurality moves us from the monumentality of the singular—one massive social housing development, designed by one architect, Fernand Pouillon, with one downward social history—into the relationality of the many, the multiple experiences of the building, and the many climates and futures (emotional, social, political) that it produces. Amina Menia's 2012 artwork, the video piece *A Peculiar Family Album / Un Album de famille bien particulier*, produces relation by placing archival colonial footage of the building's construction into a contemporary and decolonial narration of the city's history and future. This peculiar family album reveals new encounters and interpretations of both family and history. Photographer Stéphane Couturier's 2011–15 series of photographs and films of Climat de France, and Couturier's professional relationship with Abdelhamid Rahiche, a building resident and emerging photographer, open another powerful poetics of self-representation and reciprocal recognition in Climat de France. Both artists approach the building and its residents carefully, with dignity and respect. As Rahiche powerfully states, his work photographing his neighbors is grounded in a commitment to "all the splendor of their dignity."[5] Repairing dignity, repairing connection, repairing ownership, the artworks in this chapter attempt to reconfigure Climat de France, its history and future, from a housing site of social exclusion into a home space of reciprocal attachments and self-constitution.

Between Affect, Apprehension, and Innocence in the Plural
Climats de France

Designed in 1954 by the French architect Fernand Pouillon upon the request of then mayor of Algiers Jacques Chevallier, the Climat de France housing complex was commissioned to rehouse Muslim Algerians living in bidonvilles in the city as part of a social housing policy with political aims for pacification as the city entered more fully into the war for independence. Located in what is now called the Oued Koriche neighborhood in the heights above Bab El Oued, Climat de France was completed in 1959 and consisted of 6,500 apartments distributed across 40 buildings, housing a total of approximately 30,000 residents. Arguably the largest housing project in Algeria with shops, post offices, dispensaries, a mosque, a hammam, and 180 classrooms, the complex was seen and is still seen as a sort of city within the city. The center or heart of the housing project is its large 233 × 38 meter central courtyard building named Deux Cents Colonnes that conjoins and straddles the apartment buildings that descend the hill. Zeynep Çelik describes the courtyard as "a monumental agora ... the similarity of its size to the Palais Royal in Paris was a matter of pride. The courtyard was surrounded by a three-story-high colonnade made up of two hundred square columns that gave the project its name."[6] The apartments in the Deux Cents Colonnes were built for residents with the lowest incomes, and Pouillon famously declared that "pour la première fois peut-être dans les temps modernes, nous avions installé des hommes dans un monument ... ces hommes étaient les plus pauvres de l'Algérie pauvre" (for perhaps the first time in modern history, we have moved residents into a monument ... these men were the poorest of Algeria's poor).[7] Today the population of the housing complex has risen to close to fifty thousand residents, and additional informal housing has been built on its terraces and adjacent buildings.

When the main character of Marie Richeux's novel *Climats de France* first visits the Climat de France housing project in the spring of 2009, the encounter is deeply felt throughout her body. It stirs emotions and intensities that she cannot yet name but that appear to emerge from the sight of the building's stone material. The character, Marie, describes the sensation and its location in this way:

Entre les épaules et le ventre, à l'endroit que l'on dit être celui de l'attachement, se glissent la familiarité et l'étrangeté totale, l'excitation de la découverte et le cœur serré du retour. . . .

J'enregistre tout. C'est de cette vision et de l'émotion profonde qu'elle provoque en moi que tout part. C'est l'orage que déclenchent ces perspectives, la démarcation de la pierre presque jaune sur la colline derrière, qui sont le début de tout.[8]

(Between the shoulders and stomach, at the place that is said to be the site of attachment, familiarity and the complete unknown slip into each other, the excitement of discovery and the clenched heart of return. . . .

I register everything. It's from this vision and the deep emotion it stirs in me that everything starts. It's the storm triggered by these views, the dividing line of the almost yellow stone from the hill behind it, that are the beginning of it all.)

Marie's body is the primary register of this precognitive moment. She feels the incipience throughout her body, in her heart center, and as I noted in the introduction, while she senses that this reaction and emotion is coming from the stone of the building, at the moment it is happening, she resists analyzing or cognitively deciphering the experience.

This description of Marie's deeply affective encounter occurs in the second chapter of the novel but has an important antecedent in the text. In a lean preface, entitled *Chante avant que le jour se lève* (Sing before the day breaks), two paragraphs in italics recount an experience of feeling and hearing but not knowing:

Mon oreille touche le mur. Je distingue plusieurs voix et les harmonies puissantes que créent leurs chants m'arrivent par salves. Avec le temps et les déformations de la mémoire, tout a certainement gagné en volume, mais le chant résonnait avec force dans la cage d'escalier cette nuit-là. Comme tout ce que l'on entend sans en connaître la source, il avait une part égale de monstruosité et de merveille.[9]

(My ear touches the wall. I make out several voices, and the powerful harmonies that their song creates come to me in bursts. With time and the distortion of memory, everything has surely increased in volume, but that night the chant reverberated with force throughout the stairwell. Like everything that one hears without knowing its source, there was an equal sense of monstrosity and of marvel.)

Emerging from an ephemeral moment of touch between her body and the building, between her ear and the wall, Marie describes the affective experience that precedes knowing as equally monstrous and marvelous. Indeed, the trope of the monster and the marvelous has a long discursive history in Europe, emerging from epistemologies that range from Greek mythology and early Christianity and that are further cemented in the Renaissance with the age of discovery and exploration. As Cécile Tresfels argues, in sixteenth-century France, the act of apprehension straddled this fine line between monstrosity and marvel and led to the definition of apprehension as an understanding or recognition that emerges from fear, anxiety, and their perception.[10] The powerful chant that reverberates and is amplified by the building stairway is a quakeful moment of unsettling: unsettling her sense of space, sight, and knowledge. Incipient, this unsettling is simultaneously monstrous and marvelous; it carries the possibility of apprehension and transformation.

What is heard and felt is identified and explained later in the first chapter of the novel. There the reader learns that the initial account is from 1997, when a young Marie overhears prayers for the dead chanted in Arabic coming from the apartment across the hall in her housing block in Meudon-la-Forêt. But in the moment of first reading the preface, we do not know this. We are only presented with a poetic title asking someone, perhaps the reader, to sing in the darkness. This staging of the precognitive affective encounter for the reader is a central dynamic for the novel as it follows Marie in a journey from vague feeling that emerges from sound to form, from sensation to knowledge.

Published in 2017, *Climats de France* is Marie Richeux's first novel following an earlier collection of short stories entitled *Polaroids* (2013) and a *récit personnel, Achille* (2015).[11] *Climats de France* takes a kaleidoscopic form of short chapters that jump around in time and perspective from 1955 to 2016.[12] The book is structured through the perspectives of two main characters, Marie and Malek, but the novel also includes chapters that engage the points of view of architect Fernand Pouillon, the former mayor of Algiers Jacques Chevallier, to a lesser degree French ethnologist Germaine Tillion, and an unidentified Algerian friend of Marie's identified as "S." living in Algiers. Marie is a young journalist/writer who grew up in Meudon-la-Forêt, and Malek is a retired taxi driver who left Algeria for France in 1955 and created a life and family in the Parisian region. They are separated by a generation and a hallway. As the novel unfurls, Marie digs deeper into Malek's story through a series of conversations with him and an exploration of her childhood memories in Meudon-la-Forêt. In the course of their conversations, Marie learns about Malek's life, his experience of the Algerian war for independence, and the loss of his son Abdelkader to a drug overdose. At the same time, inspired by the recurrent conversations with Malek, Marie also engages in research to learn more about the Algerian war, the Pouillon buildings, and the political mission of Chevallier. Her path is through both archival research (reading letters, memoirs, and files) and site visits to Algiers to tour various buildings from the colonial period, including an initial visit and then hesitant return to Climat de France. In this sense the character Marie comes close to the author Richeux, and in one scholarly article Isabelle Bernard writes about the "recherches bibliophiliques" and "egogéographies" of the author, using quotes from the book about Marie as references to Richeux's actual research and writing process.[13]

The two starting points of the novel, the overheard prayers and the first visit to Climat de France, are deeply affective personal experiences that function as points of departure in a reparative research process that moves through language and history, from the micro/personal to the macro/political. When Marie starts to process her experience at Climat de France, she recollects that at the moment of encounter:

> Je ne sais pas encore que cette cité a été dessinée par le même homme que celui qui pensa l'immeuble dans lequel j'ai grandi. Je ne sais pas encore qu'une pierre de taille, fameuse, me relie à cet endroit. Je ne sais pas encore que, pour aller d'un endroit à un autre, il ne suffira pas de traverser la mer, il faudra traverser la guerre, entendre la lutte et voir se déployer dans des textes et des voix une démente escalade de violence.[14]

> (I don't yet know that this housing project was designed by the same man who thought up the building where I grew up. I don't yet know that a piece of cut stone, famous stone, connects me to this place. I don't yet know that to go from one place to another, it isn't enough to cross the sea. One must cross the war, hear the struggle, and see an insane escalation of violence deployed in texts and voices.)

She is tied to this Algerian building not only through architectural *liens de parenté* (both the housing project of her childhood and *Climat de France* are designed by architect Fernand Pouillon), but also through a longer history of colonial violence that she must work to uncover. In an interview, Richeux states that the process of apprehending a history that is present but not yet entirely known to her is the central methodology of the book. She states,

> C'est très important pour moi de dire combien ce livre a à voir avec la manière dont on dialogue avec les silences, que ce soient des silences d'état, des silences politiques, des silences intimes. Sur ce palier d'immeuble,

quelque chose se tisse qui vient sinon remplacer le silence ou parler dans le silence, en tout cas le chatouiller ce silence, ne pas le laisser tranquille. C'est vraiment un livre qui essaie de ne pas laisser tranquille le silence.[15]

(It was very important to me to say how much this book is about the ways in which we dialogue with silences, whether those are state silences, political silences, or intimate silences. In an apartment building hallway/landing, something weaves together that comes to either replace silence or speak in the silence, in any case, tickle/titillate this silence, not leaving it alone. This is really a book that tries not to leave silence alone.)

In order to unsettle the silence, to rub against it, to refuse to leave it alone, the novel posits a relational dynamic, centering movements and dialogues between buildings, between people, and between time periods, and asking the central questions: What relationship do we have with our neighbors? What do we know and what do we imagine? And how do we understand and break imprinted silences from painful histories? How do we "hear through the architecture"?[16] And yet, as we will see, while the novel aims to create and repair relationality between people, buildings, and histories, due to its insistence on personal innocence, it struggles to disrupt the colonial structures that have dictated the terms of relation and understanding in the first place.

This innocence functions in both senses of the word: as an expression of "not knowing" and as an abdication of personal responsibility or guilt. In the text, innocence is articulated through definitive negations such as *rien, jamais, point,* and *personne* (nothing, never, not, no one) that claim personal innocence in the context of the failure of French society or state negligence. When Malek asks her what she wants to write, Marie says:

Je voudrais raconter que je ne connais personne qui soit allé faire la guerre là-bas. Je ne connais personne qui ait été tenu de revenir. Je ne connais personne qui m'ait dit quoi que ce soit sur ce pays. Je voudrais raconter que je ne me souviens pas de l'avoir étudié à l'école. Ni de la violence. Je voudrais raconter comment cet immeuble s'élève pourtant entre autres sur la guerre d'Algérie et l'exil. Et dire que j'y ai passé vingt ans, sur le même palier que toi. Je voudrais dire la puissance d'un palier, qui me fait découvrir un jour que tu es né là-bas.[17]

(I would like to say that I don't know anyone who might have gone to war over there. I don't know anyone who might have returned. I don't know anyone who might have said anything about that country. I would like to say that I don't remember having studied it in school. Nor the violence. I would like to tell the story, however, of how this apartment building was built, among other things, upon the Algerian war and exile. And to say that I spent twenty years there, on the same landing as you. I would like to narrate the power of the landing, which made me discover one day that you were born over there.)

The repetitive conditional form of the verb *vouloir* ("voudrais") is an important choice here. Signaling a polite distancing from more direct expressions of wanting, it also posits the question of conditionality: What *are* the conditions that would allow for the story to be told? For silences to be disturbed and broken? Moreover, the verbal form also almost points to an incapacity to do so: After several "I would like to say" sentences, will a "but" that signals failure follow? In describing her first arrival in Algiers in order to learn about the stories she claims not to know, Marie again uses terms that insist on an innocent personal positionality. She writes:

> Retour vers quoi? Je ne connais rien ni personne ici. Je ne viens pas sur des traces. Des lettres cachées au grenier, point. Des services militaires, mauvaises années, mauvais endroit, point. Des maisons d'enfance, des souvenirs de figues, quelques mots d'arabe dans une berceuse, rien.... Retour vers rien. J'arrive.[18]

> (A return to what? I don't know anything or anyone here. I am not coming here with any traces of the past. Letters hidden in the attic, none. Childhood houses, memories of figs, a few words in Arabic in the cradle, nothing.... A return toward nothing. I'm coming.)

In this passage, Marie insists on no familial or intimate connections to Algeria, even hidden ones. But what about Malek, her primary interlocutor? Is he included in the "personne" and "rien"? If the process of apprehension reveals both perception and fear of the unknown, perhaps it also reveals perception and fear of guilt and responsibility. The exclamation of personal innocence in relation to personal ties to and responsibility for French colonial history is still a powerfully present position for whiteness in twenty-first-century France.[19] Even in its desire to articulate the move from not knowing to knowing history, neighbors, and buildings, the novel reproduces that exculpatory dynamic and ultimately reveals the limits of its reparative potential.

With this larger dynamic of apprehension and partial reparation in mind, let's turn to mass housing. While the primary relationship in the novel is between Marie and Malek, Richeux centers mass housing in the networks of relationality that emerge. Indeed, when Marie is asked what she is writing about, she answers: "'J'écris sur deux bâtiments.' Silence. 'Des bâtiments?—Je ne sais pas comment être plus claire.—Non, c'est juste qu'on dirait que tu parles d'êtres quand tu dis ça.—Mais je parle d'êtres.'"[20] ("I'm writing about two buildings" Silence. "Buildings?—I don't know how to be more clear.—No, it's just that it seems like you are talking about beings when you say that.—But I am talking about beings.") Marie adopts an expansive sense of buildings and beings here. For her, a building includes relations between the building residents, between the architect and the mayor, between the architect and the workers—and this relational kaleidoscope spirals out even further to include the relationships between the cities Marseille and Algiers and even the relationship between stone and skin. As I will show, however, this most expansive relationality is simultaneously exclusive. While the novel's attention to the buildings allows for a deeper fictional register of the architect's and mayor's emotions and thoughts, such deep attention to textual and embodied archives of these men obscures other, indigenous perspectives about Algiers and housing at the time.

In the novel, architect Fernand Pouillon is depicted as a man of extreme personal ambition who maintains singular focus on his building project despite the violence that is erupting throughout the city. In the chapter titled "Fernand Pouillon, Alger, 1957," Richeux first describes the overarching violence that has taken over the city: "Qui dort vraiment en 1957, quand la violence s'est répandue dans les veines de la ville plus vite que le sang ou l'air?"[21] (Who is really sleeping in 1957 when violence has spread through the veins of the city more quickly than blood or air?) Richeux then places Pouillon at the Climat de France construction site at night:

> Un soir de printemps, Fernand Pouillon visite le site. Il est le seul Européen à la ronde. On le reconnaît, bien entendu. On chuchote sur son passage. Il a chaud. On chuchote encore sur son passage. Il traverse l'espace. C'est lui qui a pensé cela, ces grandeurs, ces ouvertures, la future fenêtre, le nombre de pas, les colonnes. Il marche, on le regarde. Il a sculpté cela pour le marcheur, pour celui et celle qui, après lui, marcheront là chaque jour. Il voit leurs corps, il sent leurs yeux, les habitants sont déjà là, depuis le premier dessin, jusqu'au dernier ajustement. Les habitants, Fernand Pouillon veut leur offrir des sensations plus que des logements.[22]

> (One spring evening, Fernand Pouillon visits the site. He is the only European around. He is recognized of course. There are whispers as he walks by. He feels hot. They whisper again as he goes by. He crosses the space. He is the one that thought up all this, this scale and grandeur, these openings, the future window, the number of steps, the columns.

He walks, he is watched. He sculpted this space for the pedestrian, for the man or woman who would walk there every day after him. He sees their bodies, he feels their eyes, the residents are already there, from the first drawing to the last adjustment. Even more than lodging, Fernand Pouillon wants to offer the residents feelings and sensations.)

Pouillon continues his walk around the building feeling more and more ill at ease from both the heat and a mounting fear, and finally leaves in his jeep. The chapter ends: "Il accélère, secoue la tête. Alger se désagrège, ça pue."[23] (He accelerates, shakes his head. Algiers is falling apart, it smells bad.)

In these passages, Pouillon is represented as the sole European walking through an eerily quiet worksite of Arab men, identified by the singular pronoun *on*. As we will see later in this chapter, in contrast to this solitary walk, the archival footage in Amina Menia's film shows that most site visits to Pouillon's construction sites bustled with European officials and dignitaries. But in the novel, he is a European alone. Occluded by nightfall, Arab men appear to whisper in the shadows, and Pouillon is markedly not in conversation with them. Rather, he is talking to a different imagined resident population that is not yet there. Richeux's depiction of Pouillon's philosophy of building for the future resident lines up with accounts in biographies of the architect and in his own 1968 autobiography *Mémoires d'un architecte*.[24] What the novel offers additionally however is deep sensorial attention to the somewhat contradictory dynamics of this relationality. The fictional Pouillon feels discomfort and then fear around the whispering but unseen Algerian worker all the while imagining and "feeling" the eyes of future Algerian residents of his buildings and wishing to offer them a sensorial environment. This Pouillon keenly feels the Algiers that is "falling apart," and in subsequent chapters devoted to him, Richeux deepens her descriptions of the problematic relationality between what is seen and the intensity of what is felt. Pouillon feels pressure from both himself and Chevallier to build more and build faster, to repair the city, but at the same time, the novel questions what is fundamentally being built:

> Tout est trop lent pour Pouillon.... D'un côté l'on rase des bidonvilles, de l'autre on construit des baraques qui s'effondrent sous la pluie. Les sols glissent, on déplace de la terre, des milliers de mètres cubes de terre, on regarde les plans, qui regarde les plans? On envisage la suite, le futur, le confort. Qui envisage quel futur?[25]
>
> Everything is too slow for Pouillon.... On the one hand, they are razing the shantytowns, on the other they are constructing shacks that are

crumbling in the rain. The ground is slipping, they are moving earth, thousands of cubic meters of earth, they are looking at the plans, who is looking at the plans? They are envisioning what follows, the future, comfort. Who is envisioning what future?

The almost breathless prose of this passage conveys an architectural situation on the brink of failure, a feeling of control slipping away. But it is obviously much more than that. The question of who and what future posed by Pouillon's interior voice arises from a morally ambivalent feeling at the height of the Algerian war for Independence: "Who is envisioning what future?"

This questioning of control and ownership is shared by the character of Jacques Chevallier, mayor of Algiers. In the novel, Chevallier is shown as a man desperate to do the right thing for the city and all of its inhabitants in order to bring peace.[26] In the seven chapters devoted to him, Richeux presents Chevallier as the ultimate liberal humanist caught in a colonial project. In one chapter, she presents a fictional speech that Chevallier gives in which he argues for "un urbanisme plus rationnel et plus humain: faire éclater la ville sur les hauteurs pour que chacun puisse profiter de l'air, de la vue, de l'ensoleillement et de la verdure" (a more rational and human urbanism: make the city burst/explode upon its heights so that everyone can take advantage of the air, the view, the sun and the greenery).[27] In this quote "chacun" signifies all of Algiers's inhabitants, not just the European and French. In another chapter titled "Chevallier, Inauguration du chantier de Climat de France, Alger, 4 août 1954," Chevallier is quoted as saying: "On ne gère pas une ville pour quelques-uns, on la gère pour tous, sans exception aucune."[28] (One doesn't manage a city for some, one manages it for all, with no exceptions.) Through the figure of Chevallier, presented in his most positive light, Richeux depicts the war for Algerian independence relationally and places the people of Algiers into three camps: those for independence, those against it, and those for humanity, caught in between. In two passages of a letter that the real Chevallier wrote and that Richeux quotes directly, Chevallier signals his position above the political lines, ready to work for peace and critiquing both sides of the independence struggle for their disregard of human life: "Nous vivons une révolution, donc un imbroglio où toutes les vengeances personelles sont permises, tous les coups bas justifiables. La vie humaine ne compte guère, de sorte qu'on n'est pas enclin à la comptabiliser."[29] (We are living a revolution, an embroilment in which all personal vengeances are permitted, all low blows are justified. Human life doesn't count for anything, to the point where we are not inclined to keep count.) There is a problem with this dynamic, however, a problem that echoes Marie's positionality. Does being a humanist imply innocence? This dynamic points to the problematic heart of French liberal approaches to the war that position a French-defined universal humanity above freedom and equitable access to resources. In the final chapter devoted to Chevallier, Richeux stages a conversation between Chevallier and an American student journalist based on a scene from Chevallier's 1958 memoir *Nous, Algériens*. Richeux writes, "Jacques Chevallier se laisse enregistrer ce soir, mais si on l'écoute, il ne dit vraiment rien" (Jacques Chevallier lets himself be recorded that evening, but if you listen to him, he really says nothing).[30] The recitation of humanist principles and articulations of hopes for an end to violence seem empty and without hope.

Richeux's hope for a relational dynamics that would bring people together hits a dead end here: both within the plot of the novel, where the narrator Marie acknowledges the limits of what Chevallier sees as relational understanding, and in the structure of the novel itself whose kaleidoscopic form now concludes with chapters that focus primarily on Malek and Marie but are written mostly from Marie's perspective.[31] In so doing, Richeux's novel self-consciously and purposefully reveals the limits of using French archives and French-centered networks to answer the questions about history and the personal and state silences that she wished to disturb. But rather than repairing the archive by interrogating, undoing, and rethinking it from another, perhaps Algerian, perspective, Richeux returns inward to emotion and speculation.

In the penultimate chapter that focuses on Marie's trip to Algiers in December 2016, Marie asks herself what life was really like in the Climat de France housing blocks and is subsequently asked by a nameless voice (later revealed as two elderly women):

> "Vous allez parler de Climat de France, mais vous allez dire que cela a raté, n'est-ce pas? Vous ne pouvez pas vous arrêter au chantier. Il faut absolument dire que ça a raté! Les gens n'ont pas été heureux dans cet endroit. Le projet, c'était de changer les vies. Je crois qu'il faut dire que cela n'a pas eu lieu, les vies n'ont pas changé!" J'écoute et je pense aux bidonvilles bâtis sur les hauteurs de la cour des deux cents colonnes. Coquillages sur coquillage rectangle blanc. Je pense à ces baraquements qui rappellent, soixante ans plus tard, les baraquements qui avaient été rasés pour bâtir la cité à la place. J'ai lu tant de fois que Pouillon songeait au bonheur des gens qui habitent les endroits qu'il dessinait. . . . Je continue d'écouter ces deux femmes âgées qui connaissent Alger pour y avoir passé leur vie, je me dis que le bonheur des uns et des autres est une mesure bien difficile.[32]

("You are going to talk about Climat de France, but you are going to say that it failed, aren't you? You cannot stop the story with the construction. It is absolutely necessary to say that it failed. The people there were not happy. The project was meant to change lives. I think you must say that this didn't happen. Lives did not change!" I listen and I think of the shantytowns built on the roofs of the 200 Colonnes courtyard. Shells on a white rectangular shell. I think of these shacks that recall sixty years later, the shacks that had been razed to build this housing project in their place. I read many times that Pouillon considered the happiness of the people who lived in the places he designed.... I continue to listen to these two older women who know Algiers having lived their lives there. I tell myself that calculating the happiness of some and that of others is very difficult.)

Did Pouillon's buildings make the inhabitants happy like he intended? How does one measure happiness? Even if these are not quite the right questions, Marie cannot get to the answers and describes the limits of her sources, the six volumes of archival materials in front of her. She states: "Je sais d'avance que je n'y trouverai aucune réponse à ces questions-là."[33] (I know in advance that I won't find any answer to those questions there.) Marie continues to question the tools and paradigms that she is using: "De quelle manière aurais-je mesuré, si je l'avais rencontrée, combien elle avait vécu heureuse? Jusqu'où le bâtiment, par son état, ses espaces, ses sons et ses circulations, conditionne la forme d'une existence?"[34] (In what way could I have measured, if I had met her, how happy her life was? Up until what point does the building, through its state, its spaces, its sounds and its pathways, determine the form of an existence?) The question of pathways towards understanding and apprehension is posed by the novel, but one might argue that both Marie and Richeux struggle with imagining other non-French paradigms with which to "measure" or understand the conditions of many forms of existence. Ultimately this struggle renders the plural perspectives signified by the title *Climats* less amply plural than they might have been.

In thinking of missing indigenous Algerian or non-French perspectives, perspectives of people who were already repeatedly denied the rights and political voice of citizenship by the French colonial state, we might again ask: What about Malek, Marie's primary interlocutor?[35] What is represented as his perspective? Apart from an affective tenderness, what is owed to him in terms of knowledge and understanding? The novel presents Malek as a kind, understanding old man, subjected to history beyond his control. There is little moral ambiguity in his story—he has never had to participate in political violence. The fact that he marries a white French woman is explained as a reality of his circumstances: he claims he didn't know any Muslim women in Paris. Marie describes Malek speaking about his wife: "Le fait que je rencontre la dame à ce moment-là m'a tenu éloigné, ça m'a sauvé peut-être."[36] (The fact that I met this lady at that precise moment kept me away from things, it saved me perhaps.) In short, the character Malek represents no threat to Marie; he doesn't embody accepted racist histories or moral and sexual orders, and rather than challenge her positionality and assumptions, he produces a safe space of reflection that maintains Marie's moral innocence. But Malek doesn't just maintain her innocence; their relationship gives her permission to enter into different spaces and stories that aren't hers. Indeed, how might Marie see herself reflected in his wife, as a welcome white female savior? When she struggles to describe her writing project, he answers: "'Je te comprends ma fille' Phrase que j'attrape au passage comme un sésame."[37] (I understand you, my daughter. A sentence that I catch hold of like an open *sesame*.) Marie accepts the familial moniker, *ma fille*, as a key to opening new spaces. But the familial relation is not reciprocal. Malek's story becomes less a story leading to familiarity than a set of questions that reveal to Marie the continued gaps in her knowledge of both his experience and the history of the war: "Et où est Malek exactement? Comment savoir?"[38] (And where is Malek exactly? How to know?)

Like Marie's arrival in Algiers, Richeux describes Malek's arrival in France through an affective encounter beyond his immediate understanding:

> La peur ou la lucidité de son entourage, voilà ce qu'il serre contre son cœur, l'avion décollant. Vers quoi l'on vole exactement, quelques mois après avoir terminé son service militaire, quelque temps après le 1er novembre 1954? Vers quoi l'on vole exactement, fils unique, jamais éloigné d'Oran? Puisqu'il sera tenu de choisir l'un ou l'autre camp, puisque son service ne lui a donné à vivre que les débuts des "évènements," puisqu'il est jeune homme et sait manier les armes, puisque, puisque, puisque . . . il ne faut pas rester dans le coin, voilà ce qu'on lui a dit. Les hélices font un sombre bruit.[39]

(The fear or the lucidity of those around him, that is what causes his heart to constrict at takeoff. What is he flying towards, several months after having finished his military service? What is he flying towards exactly, an only child, never away from Oran? Because he would have been forced to choose one side or the other, because his military service showed him only the beginning of the "events," because he is a young man who knows how to handle a weapon, because, because, because... he can't stay in the neighborhood, that's what they told him. The propellers make a dreadful sound.)

His initial political ambivalence, created and then solidified into a position in a French space, echoes Chevallier's. Malek tells Marie: "Si j'étais resté, j'aurais penché pour un côté ou pour l'autre. En partant, je ne penchais ni pour l'un, ni pour l'autre."[40] (If I had stayed, I would have leaned towards one side or the other. By leaving, I wasn't leaning towards one nor the other.) In the end, Malek backs Algerian independence: he pays his monetary dues to the FLN, but he avoids the violence of the war. He doesn't participate in the October 17, 1961, demonstration; instead, he has left Paris on vacation with his French wife.

Malek's pain in this novel is not presented as political: it comes from the death of his son from a drug overdose. The novel claims pain is entirely personal, as though the personal and the political can be separated. Malek keeps asking Marie if she remembers his son, a question that she avoids answering in order not to hurt his feelings. His questioning punctuates their conversations and often lingers at the ends of chapters bearing his name, like here where Malek's question forms the last paragraph: "Tu te souviens de Kader? Tu te souviens un peu de son visage? Les fleurs sur la commode, je vais te dire la vérité, je vais lui apporter demain, au cimetière, ce sera très bien, ces fleurs pour lui."[41] (Do you remember Kader? Do you remember his face a little? The flowers on the chest of drawers, I will tell you the truth, I will bring them to him tomorrow, to the cemetery, it will be very good, these flowers for him.) Toward the end of the novel, Richeux finally devotes text to the son's life. In deference to Malek's request, Marie calls his character by his real name, Abdelkader. But we never actually hear Abdelkader's voice or perspective as a young man, addicted to drugs, living in a housing complex that facilitates their use. Instead, we just hear the opening prayers in the hallway, prayers of mourning for his death.

The novel's starting points are based in affective recognition: a recognition of felt bonds and intimacy, a recognition of attraction to something unknown, a recognition of deep desire and fear that precedes knowing. But the pathways of apprehension and knowing don't lead Marie to a deep transformation of herself in her positionality, nor do they affect a mutual transformation between parties. By the end of the book, Marie has researched, traveled, and listened to people, and the conclusion appears to be that everyone's loss is complex, and their positions at times self-contradictory and difficult to apprehend and fully name in their nuance. If the book, as Richeux describes, is about the power of the "pallier" (hallway or landing) to connect disparate people and histories, the web of connective chapters struggles to realize this power and undo the atomistic architectures of individual housing units. Through the kaleidoscopic structure of the novel, Richeux starts a poetics of relation à la Glissant that is spiral-like in its nomadism, but unlike the poetics articulated by Glissant, which are "latent, open, multilingual in intention, directly in contact with everything possible," this structure remains monolingual.[42] To put it most bluntly, what is missing are diverse Algerian perspectives. Malek's story is very important, but he is one character and, as noted above, functions more like a foil for Marie rather than a fully realized character. Other Algerian characters make appearances but remain in the margins of the book. What is thus present is a limited opening of dialogue from a variety of silences.

Richeux depicts silence and tries to repair it in her novel, but the silence she names is really only silence when viewed from one perspective. Silent to some, these spaces and histories have always been and continue to be loud and vociferous to others, calling for transformation. Richeux doesn't depict the conversations of the men working in the chantier or the speech acts of the buildings' inhabitants, especially the voices calling out for independence. To return to the novel's preface, do Marie and Richeux succeed in actually listening to and understanding what is being said or are they still just overhearing a sound whose meaning they do not recognize?

In her important article "Housing as Battleground," Sheila Crane describes how during the December 1960 protests in Algiers, "increasingly, city streets and apartment interiors became provocative stages for and even vehicles of protest."[43] Pushing back on dominant representations of the street as sole site of protest, Crane writes that:

> Apartment interiors were also activated through coordinated displays of light and sound, transforming dispersed spaces into networked structures of resistance. The architectural logic and relative density of new apartment complexes in Algiers provided ready scaffolding for conjoining multiple voices. The atomized structure of individual apartments could, at least temporarily, be overcome as dispersed voices were united in collective chorus.[44]

Crane's evocative description of voices coming together to overcome the atomized structure of individual apartments provides an important contrast to Richeux's *pallier* (hallway) of silence. Likewise, the buildings' materiality that provokes such a deep feeling in Marie, the limestone, is seen differently in light of the revolution. Crane writes, "The imposing limestone walls of Diar el-Mahçoul and Climat de France in particular offered an additional sense of protection for residents ensconced in their apartments or poised at their windows and balconies. Coordinated chants and ululations were markedly difficult to police as participants could be dispersed throughout a building or neighborhood."[45] "Pouillon's stone" protects but also amplifies the voices of the residents as they speak for freedom.

The Relational Poetics of "A Peculiar Family Album"

Like building residents, poets and writers also turned to mass housing architectures to amplify a poetics of revolution. Writer Mouloud Feraoun describes the fundamental connections between new housing blocks and bidonvilles as mass housing sites of protest. On December 11, 1960, he described this shared geography:

> So today Arabs are in the streets. These are the people "from my neck of the woods"; I mean from the Clos. They have taken over Mahçoul and Saâda, as well as those from Belcourt and the Ruisseau. There were people from the shantytowns of Nador, Scala, El Amal, Bodez, Abulker, and all the others. Kouba was represented also. The Casbah and Bab-el-Oued wanted to join them in the streets.[46]

Two days later, in a less celebratory tone, he describes how Pouillon's apartment interiors activated by Algerians as sites of resistance were also used by European civilians to kill Algerian Muslims:

> Dec 13, 1960
> Both [Aoudia and Rezki] witnessed up close what took place at the Clos and Diar-es-Saâda. They described entire scenes, parts of scenes. There, at least, the Muslims were killed not by the military but by civilians. Rezki says that, in the morning, the Europeans went to the top floor of his apartment complex. They found refuge in a well-situated apartment. From there, they started shooting.[47]

Indeed, mass housing found itself everywhere in the poetry on the war for independence and its different moments of victory and defeat. In June of 1962, a month before the official date of independence, July 2, that ended the war, Jean Sénac wrote a poem entitled "Istiqlal El Djezair" (Algerian independence). In one key section of that long poem, he references mass housing:

> Peuple architecte
> Sur chaque cicatrice une pierre est posée

La mémoire s'ouvre—grenade d'abondance
Bonne faim pour ce peuple jeune
De pain et de savoir
Jubilation et Paix
Il y a pour cette Cité
Un chant à mettre en place.[48]

(Architect people
A stone is placed on every scar
Memory opens up—a grenade of abundance
A deep hunger for this young people
For bread and for knowledge
Jubilation and Peace
For this Cité (Mass Housing)
There is a song to put in place.)

The opening line of this section "peuple architecte" is not only a nationalist call to build an independent nation out of the wounds of war and 132 years of French rule and oppression. It is also a strong repositioning of the dynamics of urban planning in Algiers, a symbolic and healing move away from the hands of individual French architects and planners into the hands of a collective Algerian people. As Sénac would later write in 1963 in his famous poem praising nationalization and autogestion, the people are strong and beautiful in their formation of power-sharing committees and cooperatives: "Tu es belle comme un comité de gestion. Comme une coopérative agricole. Comme une mine nationalisée."[49] (You are beautiful like a management committee, like an agricultural cooperative, like a nationalized mine.). In "Istiqlal El Djezair," it is important to note where Sénac places the architect people and what *they* will actually build in stone and in song: a *cité*. Capitalizing the word *cité* in the poem, Sénac refers to an idealized city in line with the capitalized jubilation and peace, but the word *cité* would have had strong connotations of its lower-case declinations: both the bidonville and the housing project, and the use of the term for both once again shows their inseparability. In this instance, the poem repairs the broken links between the two.

Fifty years later and poetry is still at work, shifting relations between the city and its housing. Indeed, Amina Menia describes the city of Algiers as "a poem" two times in her 2012 film *A Peculiar Family Album / Un album de famille bien particulier*. Archival footage from the 1950s of a bulldozer razing a bidonville is accompanied by the narration: "Algiers has a mysterious poetry, a sort of mystical beauty that transcends all of my daily frustrations" (5:21).

A minute later and the footage has shifted to blocks of stone being moved and a building going up while the narrator exclaims: "It is as though a stroke of magic has turned it into a poem city" (6:18). Where architect Le Corbusier famously positioned himself as the master poet of urban planning in his 1950 text *Poésie sur Alger*, for Menia, the city in its magic and mystery is already its own poetry. Moroever, magic and mystery here evade colonial logics of knowing, creation, and control. By pairing colonial-era film footage of the construction of three housing projects with a contemporary decolonial reading of space and agency, Menia shifts and redefines the relations of architectural authorship.

Menia created the fifteen-minute film from fragments of archival film footage from Jacques Chevallier's personal archives.[50] Filmed by a colleague of Chevallier, this footage (some in black and white, but most in color) documents Fernand Pouillon construction sites in 1950s Algiers, showing building construction in progress, site inaugurations and visits by various political delegations, people and their daily activities in adjacent bidonvilles, and the razing of bidonvilles. As the visual moves these archival clips around, a text written and narrated by Menia in an autofiction genre tells stories of the city, its architecture, Pouillon's buildings, and the artist's relationship to it all.[51] The film ends with a slowed-down image from a film clip of schoolgirls leaving one of Pouillon's buildings. As the camera pans closer to a young girl's face, Menia asks: "Who is she? What is she doing? What does she feel amongst those buildings? Has she heard of Pouillon? Does she live in one of his apartments?" (13:50–14:00). The voice-over pauses for a moment, and then Menia says: "This girl could be me. Probably is me. This girl is Algiers" (14:03–14:08).

Amina Menia was born in 1976 in Algiers where she lives and works to this day. Her 2020 artist biography positions her work in relation to the colonial and postcolonial architectural history of the city: "Without hesitating to confront the history and consequences of the colonial past of her country, her work most often takes the form of in situ installations that pay attention to urban spaces as conflictual and revealing sites when it comes to power structures."[52] Menia's approach to deconstructing official architectural history passes first and foremost through an affective lens. In an interview on the occasion of the 2020 *Notre monde brûle* exhibit, Menia described her general approach as such: "J'espère que ça passe d'abord par l'émotion, ensuite il y aura l'information."[53] (I hope that it is received first of all through emotion. After that, information will follow.) The centering of the affective as the primary means of connection, followed by the transmission of details, narratives, information, and history, places Menia's work in a similar logic of affect and apprehension to

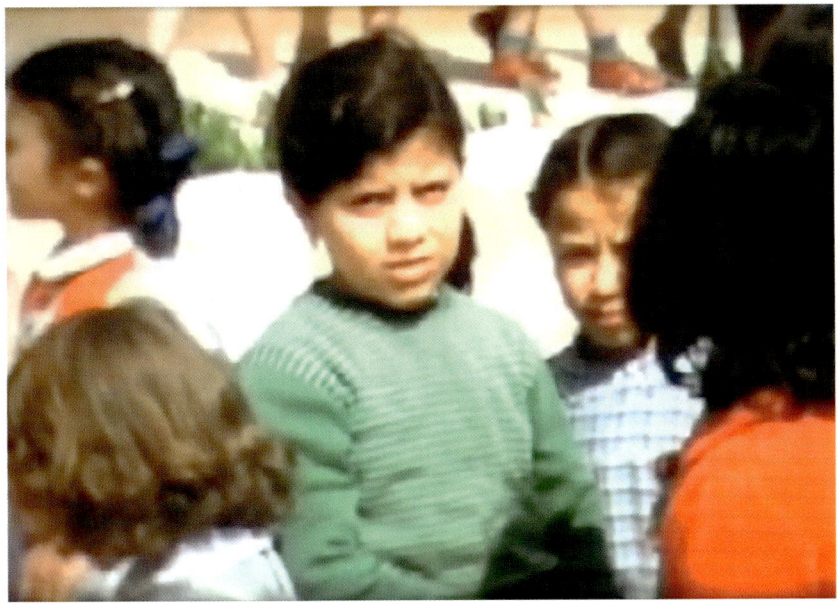

FIGURE 2.1. Still from Amina Menia, *A Peculiar Family Album / Un album de famille bien particulier*, 2012. Video. Courtesy of the artist.

Richeux's approach in *Climats de France*. However, Menia's work differs deeply in both its positionality and the networks of relation that it privileges.

The film *A Peculiar Family Album* begins with a black screen and low hum, and then presents the first clip of footage: a 1953 black-and-white film clip of a view of Algiers from a shaded hill across the city to the sea. With the appearance of this footage, the oral narrative begins, situating Menia's voice in and apart from this geography. The place is 1953 Algiers, but the voice speaks from 2012, in a summer of intense heat that is causing Algiers residents to "suffocate" (0:35) in another climate, another *climat*. In autofiction mode, Menia the narrator describes how she has recently moved neighborhoods and then gives a geographical sketch of her life in the city: from suburbs to a chic neighborhood to Bab El Oued: "Every man's land. The beating heart of the capital and its social barometer. This is where righteous anger rattles and urban revolutions foment" (1:40). In this first minute and a half of narration, the visual has changed eight times: from the black-and-white opening footage, to footage in color of the Climat de France construction billboard going up, to black-and-white footage of Jacques Chevallier, to dignitary visits, and to billboards from Diar el-Mahçoul and Diar es-Saada that advertise the number of days remaining for the completion of construction. Menia's chosen clips are short and at times create an urgent visual pace that mirrors Chevallier and Pouillon's construction goals, but the speed of the visual varies and contrasts with Menia's calm, steady, and low narrative voice. The voice is closely miked and as such draws the viewer into a certain type of intimacy with the narrator and her narrative. Unlike a traditional documentary voice-over that confers a normative authority, we are brought into official historical footage with the sound of breath on the microphone and the feeling of a physical and emotional closeness.

As we see throughout the film, the visual and the narrative do not line up in terms of pace and temporality, and they also often resist superficial conceptual pairing. For example, in this opening sequence, a clip of the Diar el-Mahçoul billboard lines up with Menia's description of needing to live near the water: "I need to smell the sea spray to have a true sense of this town, to feel I am part of this town" (1:10). Menia's practice of creating conceptual gaps has been termed "stepping into the breach" by Clelia Coussonnet who writes:

> [Menia] delves into the most emblematic areas of the Algerian capital to unearth unwelcome histories about her country's past, interrogating public space and her compatriots' relations to it. Over the years, she has become an expert at stepping into the breach so as to physically touch the spaces confiscated from locals. The urban, but also peri-urban, landscape in Algeria is marked by French colonisation, the war of liberation, and the following years of turmoil. After decades of mistrust, how can citizens peacefully interact with these spaces again? How can they apprehend the history their city conveys, and what can they learn from it? Menia dissects the built environment to question the invisible architecture that structures Algeria; she tickles the complex systems and mechanisms organizing her community to reinvent a collective memory. Her ephemeral and minimal actions highlight the precariousness of public space.[54]

I would push Coussonnet's metaphor further to say that stepping into the breach is not only about questioning, dissecting, and highlighting access to historical information and space. In addition, stepping into the breach is an act of reparation: a repair of "collective memory" but also of relation itself, a reconnecting of parts and parties, a reconnecting of multiple languages (verbal, embodied, visual, and aural), and a reconfiguration of gendered positions. As Menia explained to me in July 2023, the film was a way to put her voice and body into the center of all these male geographies, as an "Algérienne."[55] By creating a new relationality between archival footage, personal reflection, and embodied experience, Menia shifts the positionality of all three and introduces another understanding of Climat de France.

In order to pay attention to both the visual and the narrative text in their differing temporalities, speeds, and subjects, I viewed the film many times and sketched out a map connecting the visual timeline and the narrative timeline. But even without such slow attention to detail, a single viewing of the film suffices to impart a sense of complex love (anticolonial, intimate, critical, and affectionate) toward the city's architectural history, present and future. Menia has described the film in the following terms:

> When I found the archive of Chevallier, who was mayor of Algiers during a very sensitive period of Algerian history, I was fascinated and moved. This was the making of an entire part of Algiers, as it still looks today, and these images are totally exclusive. Algerians never saw this period because there is a serious lack of imagery documenting it. In my narration, I'm going back and forth between past and present, relying on the auto-fiction mode. *It's like leafing through a very particular family album: the "Algiers" album, in which small stories become descriptions of the social and historical context.* The countdown for the war had already started, so I underline the parallel movements between the two battles: the housing battle (as it was called at that moment) and the battle for liberation, the battle of Algiers. By articulating related concerns, exploring the legacy of the last century's Utopian projects in Algiers, and situated in the failure of current-day urbanism, this film looks for the aftermath of the push for modernity in my country.[56] (emphasis mine)

I highlight Menia's description of the film as a family album here because indeed the visual component of the film leafs through the archival footage in the nonlinear way that one might leaf through an album, lingering on some images and returning to others as memory does its work to unearth other deeper stories. Sociologists Oksana Sarkisova and Olga Shevchenko write that the family photo album is a site of performance, of curating the visible and invisible histories into a space that is simultaneously private and shared, a space for intimate domestic reflection and a record for posterity.[57] As Sarkisova and Shevchenko question: "What do domestic photo collections make visible, and by contrast, what do they obfuscate? And how do people use performative opportunities that arise from photographs to put forth and pass on their visions of themselves and their pasts?"[58] Drawing on the work of Gillian Rose, Sarkisova and Shevchenko write that the family photo album "articulates and re-creates the bounds of what is to be considered family, reaffirming and modifying existing configurations of kinship. In this sense, the practices of joint looking and shared ownership of family photographs are the currencies that bind the family together."[59]

The term "family" in Menia's Algiers album is capacious. In the narration Menia names the many groups who governed the city (politically and economically) across its history: Berber, Phoenician, Roman, Arab, Andalusian, Ottoman, French, and in terms of recent construction, Chinese. The effect of listing these groups while showing only footage from the French colonial period puts the French part of the family in its place in a history of *longue durée*, even if the French architectural "legacy still dominates" (1:59–4:00). Menia's representation of multivocality beyond the colonial functions in striking contrast to Richeux's limited voice and perspectives. Menia also doesn't reduce the family history to a "national one" but rather narrates the city's history in its irreducible relationality in a move evocative of Glissant when he writes, "Relation informs not simply what is related but also the relative and the related. Its always approximate truth is given in a narrative."[60] The narrative of the city and its history are always approximate in that they are both always proximate to something and someone else.

The performance of the family album and its "modifying configurations of kinship" and relation manifests in Menia's read of Pouillon and his three housing projects: Diar el-Mahçoul, Diar es-Saada, and Climat de France. Similar to photographer Yto Barrada's work (discussed in the previous chapter), the explicit colonial violence that encircles and dominates the buildings' construction at first appears missing from the visual record. Menia writes of this lacuna in the archival visual footage:

> At the same time as the launch of this "housing battle," another battle breaks out, a far more fierce one: the Algerian War. The images in this film, realised by Chevallier's collaborator, don't show this context. They focus on the buildings rising from the ground, on the inspection site visits and the countless inauguration ceremonies. Nevertheless they really depict the making of what would transform the face of the capital city.[61]

And yet, while images of police and army violence are missing, if we look at the scenes of shantytowns being razed or the tired bodies of the construction workers, colonial violence is very present.[62]

Menia's verbal narration amplifies the colonial and anticolonial history that is entwined in the buildings' construction yet relegated beyond the frame. In one striking example, footage of the inauguration of a construction site triggers

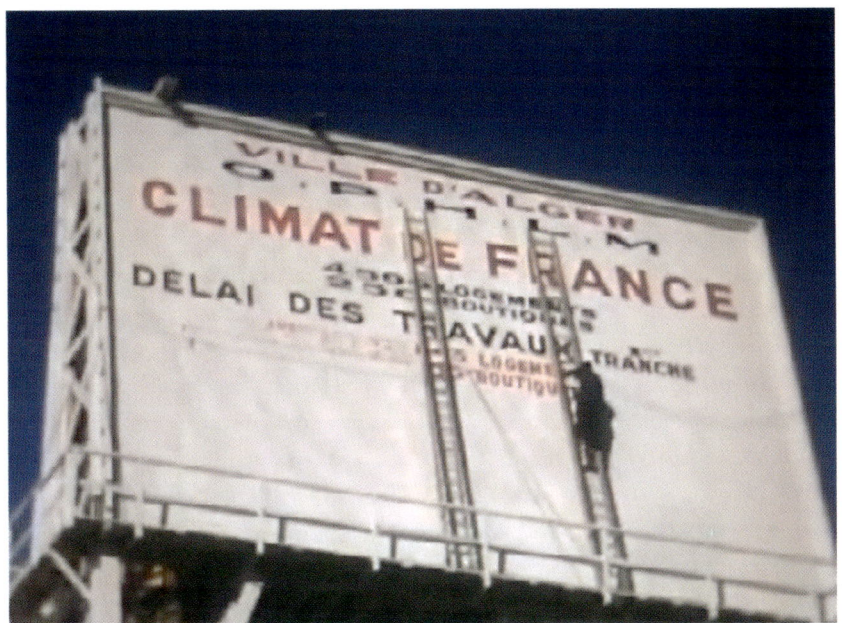

FIGURE 2.2. Still from Amina Menia, *A Peculiar Family Album / Un album de famille bien particulier*, 2012. Video. Courtesy of the artist.

a commentary on Pouillon's obsession with registering the number of days to building completion. While the visual documents the ceremonial beginnings and various stages of construction work, Menia narrates: "The film begins with a date: 1953. This was only a few months before the creation of the FLN and the outbreak of the armed struggle" (8:21), and then continues, "I like to feel in the same countdowns, the rising of the Algerian people against the edifice of French Algeria" (9:04). In this example, we see a moment of appropriation of Pouillon's logic for another end. Menia takes an idea/obsession of Pouillon's and shows how it might describe another battle that he does not articulate. She reconfigures the relation of kinship.

This appropriative or reparative reconfiguration of relation is repeated several times throughout the film as Menia pays attention to Pouillon as a family member with a vision and a legacy, and asks what he might do in the city today.[63] What might the city take from Pouillon today to make life better, to combat "new forms of exclusion" (13:05)? How might Pouillon's aesthetics, in particular his commitment to stone and ceramics, restore "color and gaiety to our drab living quarters" (13:32)? What would Pouillon think of the

AFFECTING RELATION IN CLIMAT DE FRANCE   93

palm tree planting frenzy of 2012 (11:00)? And when Menia sees poverty in the city today, she recalls a Pouillon description of a bidonville (4:50). Menia's attention to Pouillon is neither celebratory nor dismissive. He continues to be a family member, a relative in relation with the city. Two-thirds into the film, the narration asks: "What remains of Pouillon in today's Algiers? His [housing] estates are more alive than ever" (11:51). The openness with which Menia continues to keep Pouillon close and alive in the Algiers family album contrasts with Richeux's complicated postcolonial French/Algerian kinship, where the family across the hall (or the sea) might be recognized but remains still separate. Perhaps this is because Menia centers the plurality of history and its production of kinships. The city and its Algerian residents have a history and future beyond French colonialism and have the power to encounter and assimilate outsiders into their city, even when those outsiders held power over them. Perhaps because, to turn again to Glissant, "we 'know' that the Other is within us and affects how we evolve as well as the bulk of our conceptions and the development of our sensibility."[64]

In the introduction, I wrote that this book is interested in artwork that engages in the afterlives of mass housing, and there is one moment in the film when Menia focuses on the afterlife of Climat de France in particular. The narration exclaims: "Paradoxically, while they used to promote a little dignity for Algerians of the slums, some of them have now become the arenas of new social disparities.... Climat de France is better known for its drug dealers than for its surreal architecture" (12:00). The building's contemporary afterlife is not visualized, however. Instead, this narration lines up with film footage of the Diar el-Mahçoul billboard advertising 180 days to completion and then clips of visiting delegations walking up steps and through construction sites. The afterlife is figured in the tension, "in the breach," between visual and verbal where the archival yet forward-looking footage of building completion lines up with a narrative description of contemporary social disparity and exclusion. It is striking that throughout this artwork Menia constrains her visual record to archival footage while her narration wanders across time and into the future. The effect of looking at newly constructed "surreal architecture" in the 1950s while hearing about its contemporary twenty-first-century afterlife requires the viewer to interrupt the sociological impulse to see the visual in an illustrative function. As such, the film insists that the visual archive is irreducible at the same time as its epistemology is undone. Always in relation to the time of viewing, the visual archive is simultaneously independent from the time of viewing and its range of analytical interpretations, from decolonial critique to various forms of nostalgia.

In describing her relationship to archives of the past, Menia notes: "The impossibility of accessing information—freely and without authorisation—forces me to rummage through books and history. I do not revisit a mythical or glorified Algiers. I reflect what is going on there."[65] It is worth repeating that the footage Menia resplices into her film comes from a personal archive and not a state one. While it could easily be folded into French or Algerian state narratives, and while in fact similar footage exists in French state archives, in this film, the footage from the "family album" is first in Menia's hands and then in the hands of its viewers. This is particularly poignant considering the current debates about the repatriation of colonial-era archives from France to Algeria.[66] The French state continues to deny requests for the return of colonial-era archives, so the fact that Menia finds alternate routes to placing these images in her Algerian viewer's hands is another moment of repair.

The idea of reflecting and relating rather than conscribing or representing is a form of poetics central to Menia's work. In her essay, "The Economy of Hope," Yasmina Reggad writes that

> neither Amina Menia or Mohamed Bourouissa are pretending to resolve any social issues or engaging a collective action. Instead, within the field of relational art practice, they invite us to *critically rethink how the individual and the collective are articulated in our relations to the world*. The artists deconstruct the power relations which impede the quest for alternatives and a better future and remind us that, "only hope [...] has within its powers to oppose the given state of things, the human distress, suffering and privation, and to lead the hoping man into a different, better future."[67] (emphasis mine)

This methodology, described by Reggad as "an economy of hope," resonates with Gabriel Winant's reading of affect in a time of neoliberalism that I cited in the introduction. In his essay "We Found Love in a Hopeless Place," Winant writes: "Affect theory does not discover an authentic self buried by oppression; it constructs one anew from the wreckage of defeat. In doing so, it assembles collective knowledge."[68] Likewise, Menia does not seek to unearth an authentic Algiers buried by histories of oppression and layers of construction. Instead, she builds new structures to understand that history and imagine new collective futures in open relation.

Building new structures in order to understand and collectively interpret the city literally takes the form of scaffolding in some of Menia's other artwork such as *Extra Muros*, *Africaines*, and *Iconoclastes*. In those works, Menia

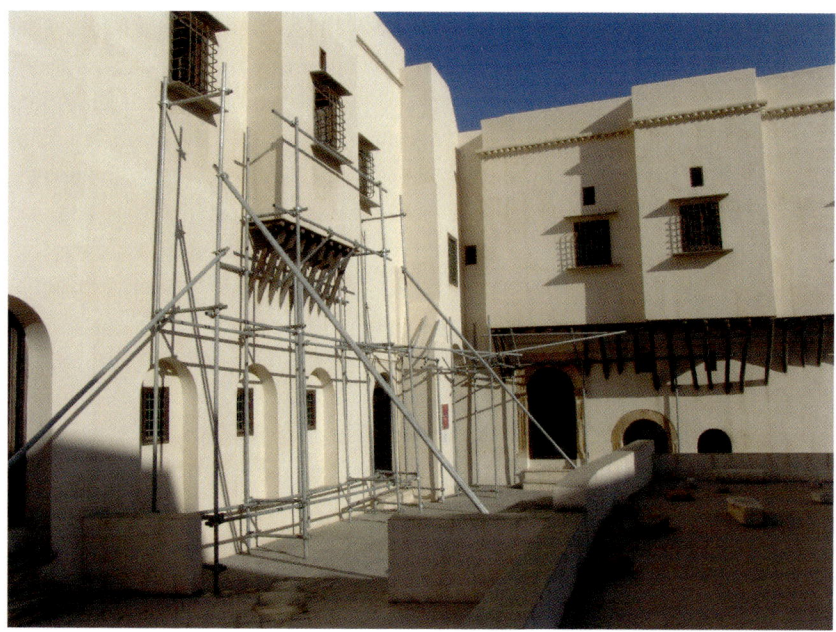

FIGURE 2.3. Amina Menia, *Extra Muros Chapter 1*, Bastion 23 Art Center, 2005. Galvanized steel tubes and brackets, 100 m². Photograph courtesy of the artist.

constructs scaffolding in relation to existing buildings as a path to seeing the built environment differently. She writes:

> It is a kind of alphabet for me, I have written a lot with it. The scaffolding is a bit ironic. The Casbah, like many parts of Algiers, is constantly under renovation. The scaffolds sometimes end up ruined or badly rusted because of the marine air. They portray the passage of time ... embody the eternal renovation and unfinished projects.... With interlocking metaphors, I explore architecture and elements being built, becoming, and under construction. My scaffolds are always pristine. They are not there to be looked at, but to enable us to see something.[69]

The archival footage in the film *A Peculiar Family Album / Un album de famille bien particulier* is in a sense a type of "pristine scaffolding." While irreducible in its materiality, it is also a type of poetics that enables us to see relation at work in the city: from Pouillon and Chevallier, from the buildings they constructed and the bidonvilles they razed, to today's Algiers and the rush to construct new housing as the city ages and transforms.

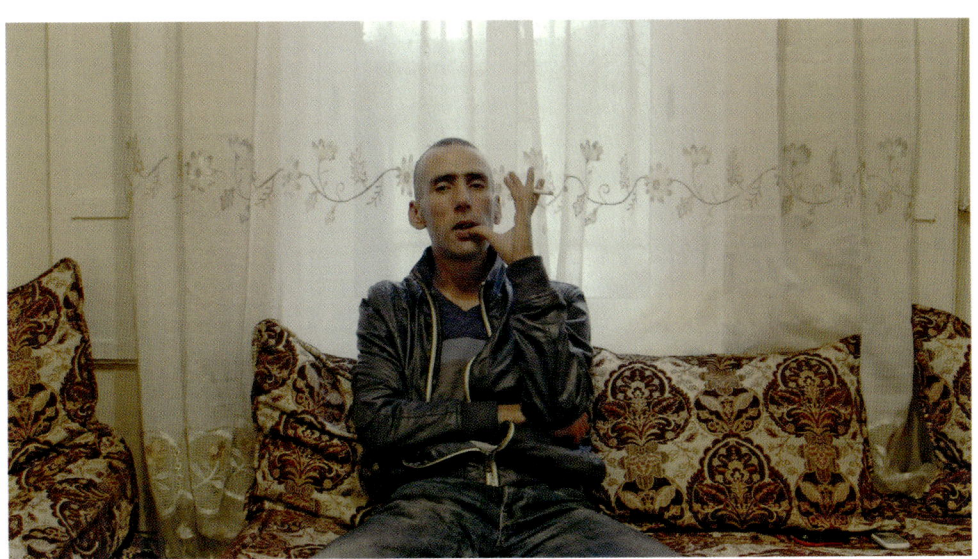

FIGURE 2.4. Still of Hamid Rahiche from the opening sequence of Stéphane Couturier, *Alger—Cité "Climat de France,"* 2015. Video. Courtesy of the artist.

From Facade to Interiority: Stéphane Couturier and Abdelhamid Rahiche's Relational Aesthetics

Where Amina Menia's film ends with the powerful archival image of a young girl and a statement of recognition—"This girl could be me. Probably is me. This girl is Algiers" (14:03–14:08)—Stéphane Couturier's 2015 short film *Alger—Climat de France* concludes with another powerful scene of appropriation and repair. Abdelhamid Rahiche sits in his family's apartment in Climat de France and explains to the camera with the deep and gentle seriousness of an act of self-constitution that is devoid of rancor or resentment: "I am what I am. I'm worth what I am worth, and the people who share this life with me know my worth. This is my land [*pays*], here" (35:24–35:32). This articulation of self-worth and shared recognition is but one instance of the critical love and recognition that Rahiche expresses throughout the film and that is emphasized by Couturier in his sensitive framing of Climat de France and its residents.

It is a surprising film. Surprisingly caring and careful in the face of deeply negative depictions of postindependence Climat de France in the French and Algerian press, but also aesthetically surprising because Couturier's photographic and film work to date has tended to focus primarily on building exteriors, industrial structures, and nonhuman forms. In this film and larger project, Couturier centers the buildings' residents through video portraits and through extensive "airtime" to Rahiche, who frames the narrative, and to another resident who calls himself *le mendiant de Dieu* (the beggar of God) and interrupts colonial and other dominant logics that work to capture the neighborhood. In doing so, Couturier develops a deep relational dynamic between the visual and the embodied experience of Climat de France and moves beyond his previous focus on surface and form into a narrative engagement with architecture and built environment.

In many ways, the film is a collaborative work with a significant artistic afterlife. After Rahiche's initial encounter with Couturier in 2011, the two men formed a professional relationship through photography, and since that time they have produced, together and independently, complex and nuanced artwork that engages the building and its residents.

Stéphane Couturier (born 1957, Paris, France) is known for his photography and video work on urban sites and buildings across the world. His large-format, highly detailed photographs are often compositions of overlapping or time-lapse images, and his video work takes the form of loops that obfuscate any sense of beginning or end. As his official gallery biography describes, "The photographs of Stéphane Couturier, whether of construction sites in Berlin, demolished buildings in Havana, or an automobile assembly plant in Valenciennes, are all about transformation."[70] In his *Melting Point* and *Melting Point (continued)* series, for example, he explores the dynamic potential of industrial sites and structures through large-format photography that he cuts and meticulously recomposes. Couturier's compositional practice, which is committed to repetition in form, produces new structures and surfaces that speak to the space between reality and image. As Damien Sausset writes:

> His desire to deliver fragments of the city (via the tight frame) imposed visual distortions with their forceful effect of abstraction, whilst maintaining the most neutral frontality possible. To achieve this, he also needed to accentuate to the point of paroxysm the physicality of the surface, with this play between macro and micro structure, perpendicular lines and abundance of detail. This gives the photographic artefact a dual value: the value of what it summons as a fragment of reality (its relationship to the world, its theme), while at the same time proposing a surface.[71]

The proposition of a new surface ultimately invites the viewer into an engagement with a familiar architectural world made new, a collaborative type of "world making" in which the viewer re-pieces the images to answer the puzzle of what might be real.

This compositional practice also invites the inclusion and incorporation of different perspectives and modes of perspective. Sausset argues that "through this form of cutting, Stéphane Couturier reinvents a relationship with the world" and that "in Couturier's images, destroying/building/restoring/innovating mingle into one, as if to witness more eloquently to the inclusion of local modes in the face of the power of international architectural codes."[72] These artworks not only invent alternative architectural surfaces but also produce alternative archives that have the potential to chart different relationships between architectural forms (as discussed in chapter 1 in relation to Yto Barrada's photographic engagements with the *cité verticale* and *cité horizontale* in Hay Mohammadi). Shirley Jordan describes Couturier's work through the prism of urban archeology and the creation of these new forms. She writes that "Couturier's distinctiveness in his *Melting Point* work resides in the challenge he sets for his medium since his focus is on between-ness, becoming, dynamism and instability."[73]

In 2011, Couturier arrived in Algiers on a grant tied to Marseille's designation as the "cultural capital" of Europe for 2013.[74] He was eager to understand the links between the two cities, and in line with his portfolio of work on architecture, he turned to their architectural affiliations. Couturier wanted to take an "intuitive" approach to the city, and rather than rely on preconceptions and a network of established artists and diplomats who cautioned him against visiting dangerous neighborhoods, he set out to Climat de France with his camera and a reluctant driver. As he got out of the car in front of the housing complex, which he described as "une force architecturale étonnante" (an astonishing architectural force), he remarked on the attention he was attracting as people looked at him and his camera with distrust. At this point he was approached by Rahiche, who happened to be nearby and asked him what he was doing there. As Rahiche describes the chance encounter, he had just left the building to get a cup of coffee and, becoming aware of the looks people were giving Couturier, decided to help him and invited him for a coffee.[75] The coffee turned into lunch with Rahiche's family and a week of visits and introductions that allowed Couturier and Rahiche to form a relationship and Couturier to become more accepted by the residents of the housing complex. As Couturier describes it, over the course of that visit and the next few years, Rahiche became a "parrain" (benefactor) to Couturier, and Couturier in turn introduced Rahiche to photography, giving him a camera, supporting his artistic training, and hiring him to collaborate on various projects. As Thomas Lallier describes: "[Couturier's] encounter with Hamid Rahiche, an inhabitant of the estate, was decisive. It was then that Stéphane first came up with

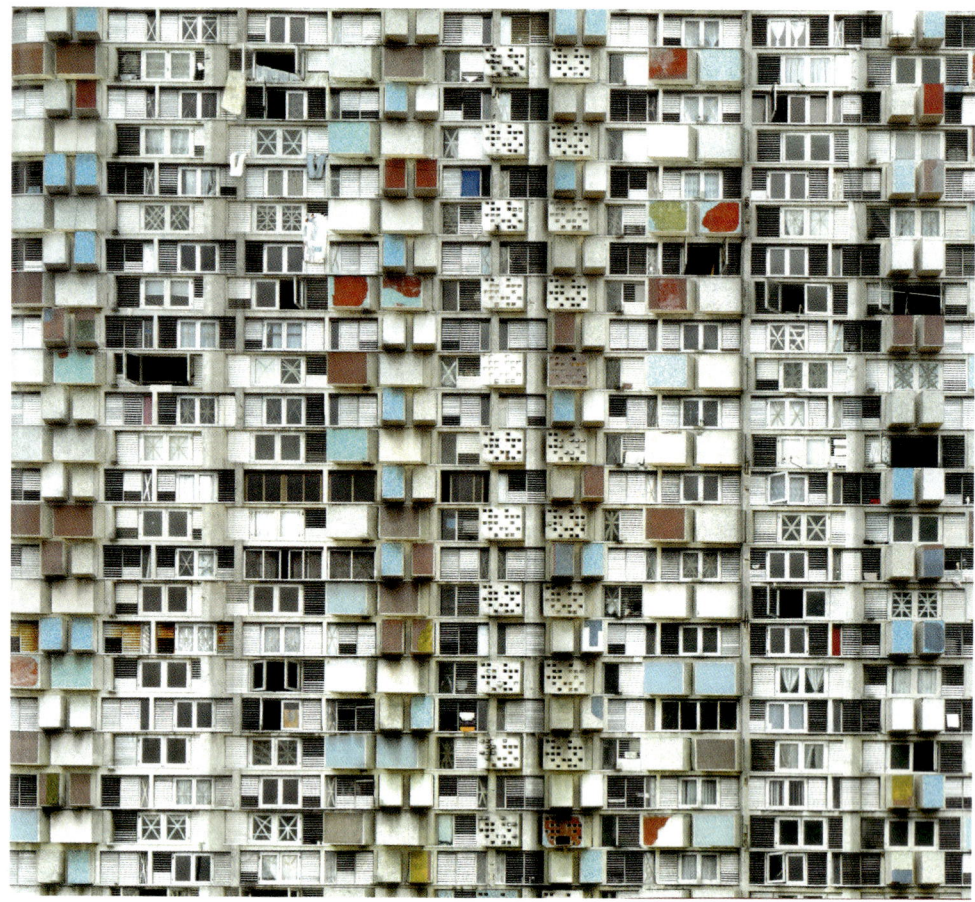

FIGURE 2.5. Stéphane Couturier, *Melting Point La Havane, Giron building*, 2006–7. C-Print, 180 × 189 cm. Courtesy of the artist.

the idea of embarking upon a long-term project, subsequently journeying to Algiers several more times."[76]

From 2011 to 2013, Couturier produced highly detailed large-format photographs of the different facades of Climat de France. The photographs are striking in their attention to geometric form and repetition—in some cases, the exhibited image is a composite of hundreds of individual frames—and their large format amplifies the sheer size of the housing complex. For example, as described by the online art journal *Paris Art*:

> Le polyptyque intitulé *Façade n°1* renvoie l'image d'une façade sous la forme d'une photographie découpée en six bandes verticales espacées

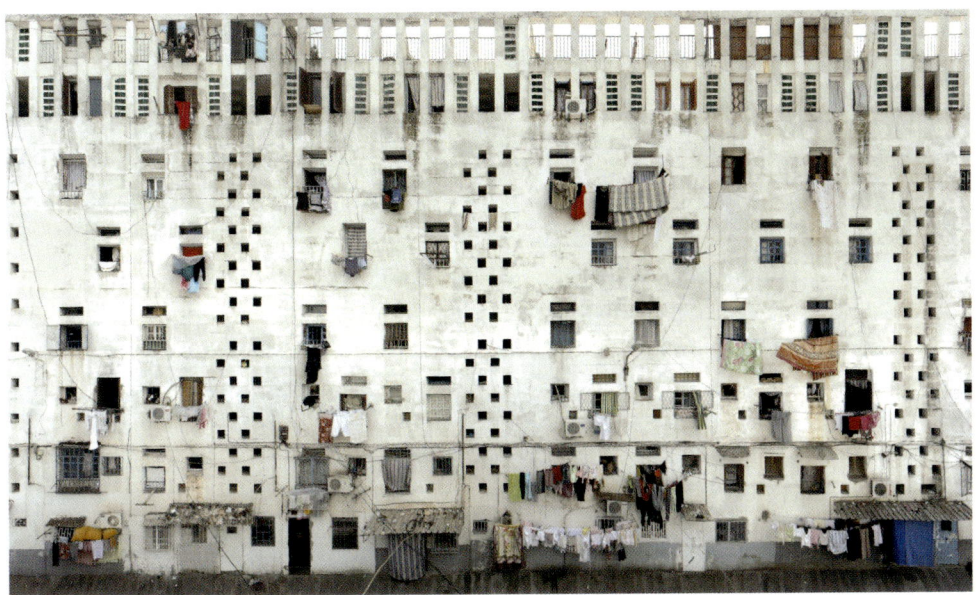

FIGURE 2.6. Stéphane Couturier, *Alger—Cité "Climat de France" Façade #1*, 2011–12. Courtesy of the artist.

et donc séparées par des bandes blanches. Telles les puissantes colonnes qui structurent la cité, les bandes blanches s'opposent à une multitude de détails: le linge coloré séchant aux fenêtres, les systèmes de climatisation, les volets hétéroclites et les traces d'usure du bâtiment.[77]

(The polytyptic entitled *Façade No. 1* refers to the image of a facade in the form of a photograph cut into six vertical strips, spaced and thus separated by white strips. Like the powerful columns that structure the housing project, the white strips are set against a multitude of details: the colorful laundry hanging at the windows, the air conditioning systems, the varied shutters, and the traces of the building's wear and tear.) (See figure 2.6)

While some images tie into his methodology of melting points, composing new abstract images from decomposed and recomposed architectural details, many photographs are less abstract, allowing the building itself to testify to its monumentality without extensive manipulation. The exhibition of his photographs of Climat de France at the annual La Gallicy Photography Festival in 2018 underscores the monumentality of the building and Couturier's work.[78] As festival organizers wrote, the exhibit choice to present one large-scale print that enveloped the exhibit space "surligne à la fois le gigantisme de la Cité Climat de France, mais aussi le talent et la technique dont a usé Stéphane Couturier pour créer une telle image, sur plusieurs années" (underlines at once the enormity of the Climat de France housing project, but also the talent and technique that Stéphane Couturier used to create such an image over multiple years).[79] The large-format print that encircled the courtyard walls creates almost a trompe l'oeil effect, inserting the viewer into the space, as a visitor documented in one YouTube video.[80]

At the same time as he photographed the buildings and their residents, Couturier also started creating videos of Climat de France and video portraits of residents. This methodology of simultaneously working in both still photography and film and often blurring the space between the two is a continuation of a practice he established in Seoul with his loop piece *Seoul—Tanji* (2003–9), in which he created video from spliced, tightly framed photographs of a highrise building in different stages of construction. As his website describes:

> For each video, the process sets out to maintain a certain frontality in relation to the subject portrayed in order to strip it of effect. The intensified image becomes a living scene in which the flows of the city come and go with the current of urban life. Moreover, the videos are in loop, so they are not conceived in the form of a dramatic progression, instead revealing itself as a globality which is somehow outside time, somewhere which stretches, kneads and condenses time.[81]

This intermedial work between photography and film creates new entry points into how we perceive architectural transformation and time.

For Climat de France, Couturier focused on the Deux Cents Colonnes building courtyard, a multiuse common space that serves as a market place in the mornings, a soccer pitch in the afternoons, and a parking lot in the evenings. The resulting eight-minute 2012 piece, *Alger—Cité "Climat de France"—Travelling latéral—Place des deux cents colonnes*, is remarkable for its simultaneous reproduction of flatness and depth. The camera travels from right to left as young men play soccer in its view and move from left to right. Behind them, arcades, closed shop entrances, and passersby can be seen, and behind the columns, the massive building dominates the space. Occasionally a car travels in front of the camera. And yet there is a certain flatness to the perspective with all layers condensing into one as the eye attempts to re-create depth against the red building. When the camera arrives at building passages that link the court-

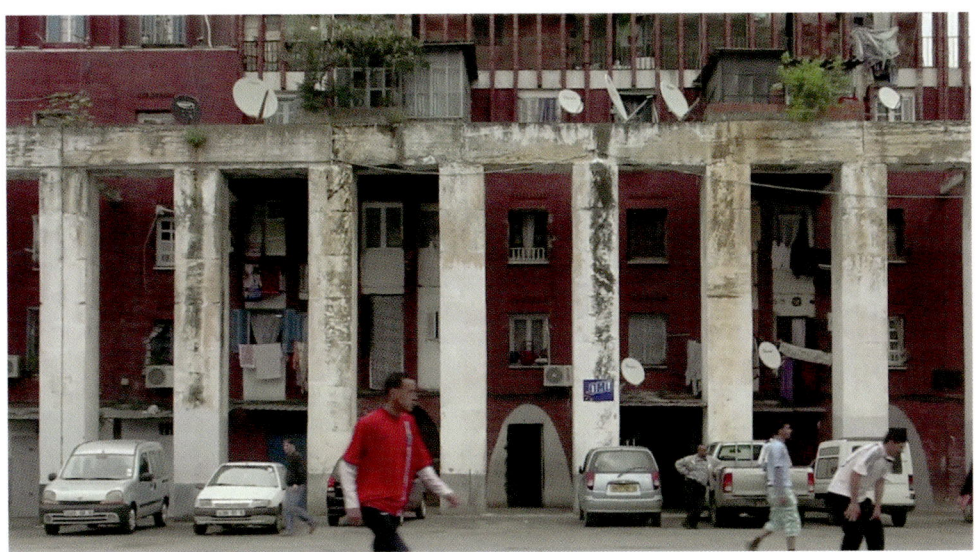

FIGURE 2.7. Still from Stéphane Couturier, *Alger—Cité "Climat de France"—Travelling latéral—Place des deux cents colonnes*, 2012. Video. Courtesy of the artist.

yard to the exterior, such as at 1:09 or 5:48 or 7:40, the red building momentarily breaks with a dash of exterior perspective from the greenery of the el-Kettar cemetery or a glimpse of blue sea, only to close again when the camera moves past the passage again. In a 2014 lecture, Couturier spoke of this video as a continuation of his lateral traveling videos in which he creates loops that go beyond narrative and produce a vocabulary of "frontalité" and fragmentation, prompting the viewer to ask what they are actually looking at.[82] Shot from a slow-moving car, the film loops footage from the north facade of the courtyard to the south facade (*avec paraboles*), creating what Couturier calls an "infinite colonnade" that while revealing difference in repetition also posits that "il n'y a rien de spécifique à voir"(there is nothing specific to see).[83] Such a dynamic of looping, splicing, erasure, and interruption proposes an epistemic repair to the buildings' representation. Visible and invisible scars in the creation of the infinite column invites the viewer to rethink the monumental nature of the Deux Cents Colonnes as defined by Pouillon into an even more monumental, indeed spatially and temporarily endless, built environment that is defined in relation to itself.

In 2014, however, Couturier broke with this nonnarrative film process to produce another type of film based on "everything that Hamid recounted."[84]

AFFECTING RELATION IN CLIMAT DE FRANCE   103

Over the span of two hours, Couturier filmed Rahiche talking spontaneously with him about the building, about his experiences, about Algeria, about life. Couturier edited out his questions and prompts and spliced the interview with other scenes and video portraits he filmed with Thomas Lallier. The result is the remarkable thirty-six-minute 2015 film *Alger—Cité "Climat de France"* that invites a different poetics of relation based in mutual recognition and deeper reciprocal looking.

The film starts with Rahiche sitting on a sofa in his family's apartment. He takes a drag of his cigarette and looks directly at the camera, holding its gaze for twenty seconds while cigarette smoke floats across the screen. Behind him is a curtained window. The film then cuts to a long lateral traveling shot of the building exterior. Unlike the Deux Cents Colonnes film that focused on the red brick exterior of the courtyard, here Couturier chose a white building facade, the rectangular forms of its windows and breezeways interrupted by circular satellite dishes and the whiteness of the wall dotted with colorful laundry hung from windows (see figure 2.6). The soundscape is calm with birds chirping and the muted sound of radios, domestic noise from inside, and market activity from the courtyard. After almost a minute of this soundscape, Rahiche's voice comes in as a voice-over while the camera continues its slow pan. He describes the perception of Climat de France by other Algerians and how the inhabitants of the housing complex are both ashamed of its reputation and proud to live there: proud of its problems and the strength of character that it builds. He concludes with the powerful statement, "A force d'être marginalisés, ils se sont construits" (Due to their marginalization, they constructed themselves) (2:29). The voice-over cuts for a few seconds, and then in the next scene, we are back in Rahiche's apartment, as he smokes and talks.

The film oscillates between interior scenes in Rahiche's apartment and exterior scenes of the buildings and their inhabitants. The interior scenes consist of the same closely framed footage of Rahiche sitting on a sofa in the apartment in Climat de France. This staging might recall the opening scenes in Merzak Allouche's 1976 film *Omar Gatlato* in which Omar speaks to the camera while sitting on the bed in his family's apartment in the same housing complex. But where Omar's descriptions of life in Climat de France ultimately focus on him and his "containment," Rahiche focuses on the larger community, reaching out beyond the apartment walls. Rahiche talks about the history of the building, the war for liberation, and the civil war of the 1990s; he talks about what it means to be a neighbor and the moral codes of the housing complex; he talks about appropriation, pride, and the power of mutual recognition. In the exterior scenes, Couturier emphasizes architectural forms but also interjects video portraits. As in the opening scene with Rahiche, in making the portrait, the camera fixes on the faces of different men and boys who hold its gaze. Shot at close range and tightly framed, these portraits are remarkably intimate. In one portrait, a young man holds himself perfectly still, staring at the camera and barely blinking. Yet in most, we see men struggling to remain still, their faces twitching at times, their deep creases shifting, their eyes sometimes turning away and returning to the camera. The intensity of looking straight at the camera translates into an intense engagement with the viewer. The men hold the camera's gaze as well as ours.[85]

In contrast to Richeux's representation of silent coexistence in the hallways of Meudon-la-Fôret, Rahiche presents Climat de France as an extended family of people that know each other and share a moral code that assures mutual aid and respect among neighbors. Rahiche dives deeply into the dynamics of care between neighbors, discussing a network of people that not only know each other but organize to take care of each other, whether that be late-night hospital trips or cleaning someone's apartment for them. As Rahiche speaks of solidarity and mutual aid, Couturier shows a scene of the courtyard shot from the roof of the building. In the perfectly rectangular courtyard, people and cars slowly weave across the space in gentle curves, and in the lower left of the frame we see a few people slowly pushing a car that won't start. The camera remains still and the perspective doesn't change, and over the course of the scene, the car makes it across the yard to the upper right of the frame. This scene and Rahiche's narrative emphasize what it means to "know" and be known by those you live with.

In another section of the film, Rahiche enlarges the concept of family to talk about the relationship between residents and the buildings as a type of family heritage or inheritance. In an interior scene from his living room, Rahiche explains: "Il y a toujours quelqu'un qui dit, 'Moi, mon père il était manœuvre, il était maçon, il a participé à la construction de Climat de France, et il a vécu, et on est né ici, et il est mort ici mon père.' Donc, c'est comme un héritage que les anciens nous ont laissé, cette cité" (12:31). (There is always someone who says, "My father was a worker, he was a mason, he participated in the construction of Climat de France, and he lived and was born here, and my father died here." So this housing project is like an inheritance, a heritage that our elders left us.) Compare this framing to the earlier passage I cited from Richeux where anonymous Algerian laborers are present on the construction site—but it is Pouillon who offers future residents their experiences. Or compare this footage to Chevallier's archive in which male dignitaries dominate the screen with occasional images of construction workers at the margins. What we see in

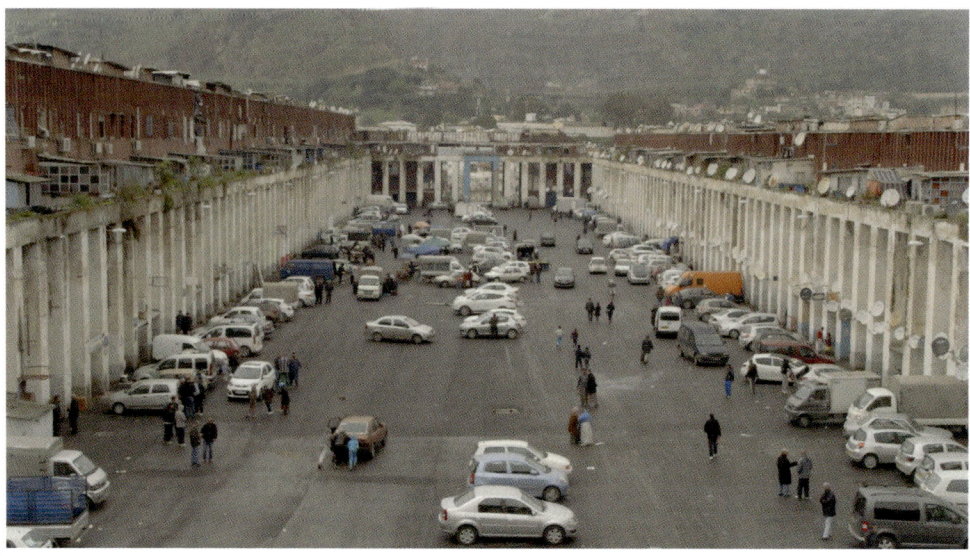

FIGURE 2.8. Still from Stéphane Couturier, *Alger—Cité "Climat de France,"* 2015. Video. Courtesy of the artist.

Couturier's film is a reparative appropriation of the construction process and the ownership of inheritance. The inheritance comes from the laborers and not solely from the architect or the architecture. Rather than an anonymous group following the vision of one man, the laborers are full participants in the construction of their homes.

While this repair is powerful, it is also important to note how it is limited to a primarily male lineage of inheritance. In the scene that follows, Couturier positions his camera at the back of a small neighborhood snack bar full of men talking. The camera then produces three visual portraits of men in the café while Rahiche's voice-over explains how the housing project was intended to move Algerians from shantytowns into housing with dignity and that while some people today would say that France did something positive and are proud of the building for being good solid construction, others see it as "dormitory" housing that isn't fit for large families. This appropriation of the building's origins and origin narratives also takes place visually. As Rahiche describes, many people are proud of the building and even have archival-footage clips of the building on their phones. The next scene, still in the café, consists of a tightly framed close-up of a cell phone playing a 1950s filmed advertisement for Climat de France. For approximately a minute and a half, we see the hand of someone holding the phone while ina.fr footage plays (see figure 2.9) and we

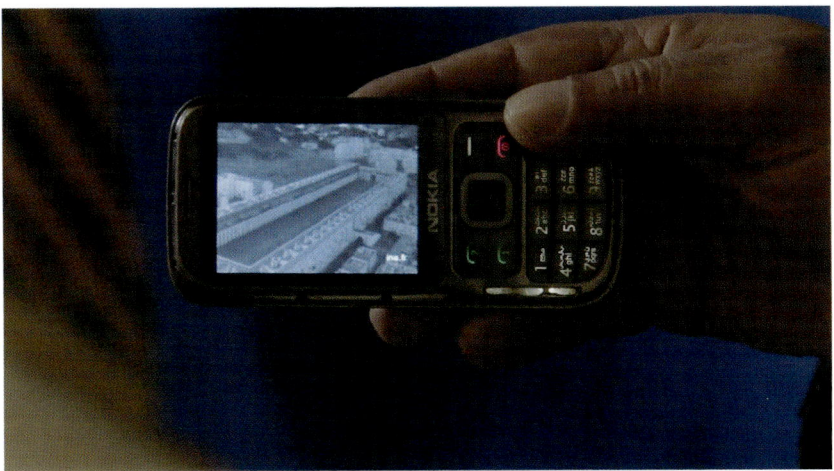

FIGURE 2.9. Still from Stéphane Couturier, *Alger—Cité "Climat de France,"* 2015. Video. Courtesy of the artist.

hear a French script that announces the majesty and enormity of the building and the dignity it will provide. What does it mean that the hand that holds the archival footage is that of a second-generation building resident? Again, like the buildings, French state archival footage becomes part of his inheritance. It also belongs to him.

It is important to note the gendered nature of this representation of appropriation and inheritance in Couturier's film. Unlike in Menia's film in which an Algerian woman's voice is central to the framing of colonial history and architecture, here women are notably absent: their presence only noted in the silent margins of images. In some respects, this is due to Couturier's mediated access to residents by Rahiche, but it is important to underline how the film's repair work replicates a certain male colonial and postcolonial history.

Halfway through the film (at 16:54), there is a long exterior scene in which an elderly man speaks at length with the camera. Calling himself God's Beggar (*Mendiant de Dieu*), the old man introduces himself as a former patient of the Joinville psychiatric hospital in Blida (Fanon's hospital!) and shows the camera his state-issued identity card. He looks at the camera and says: "Toi, tu es un artiste, tu as le sens de l'écoute, et ça c'est rarissimo ici" (17:43). (You, you are an artist, you possess an ability to listen, and that is very rare here.) The old man enters into an extended poetic riff that starts by recounting who he is and meanders through anecdotes and stories that include "the perfume of knowledge of the Sorbonne," Iranian blues, and a story of a dog that says "bismillah."

The old man's poetry in the courtyard is a performance, and a group of curious young boys stay at his side, listening to him with an attitude that sits on the line between incredulous amusement and wide-eyed belief. At this point, the film is deep in the reparative poetics of recognition, showing how the old man is seen and treated with respect while alternately connected and disconnected from the reality around him. God's Beggar tells the camera that a long time ago the ORTF (Office de Radiodiffusion-Télévision Française) came to film the neighborhood, but they didn't really "see" it. Rather, an artist is needed to truly see the building and its residents in their full selves. Couturier does not assume or assert that he is the sole artist for this task or that in his positionality he, and perhaps other outsiders, can fully see and represent the neighborhood.[86] He acknowledges that Rahiche's act of hospitality toward a stranger enables such a task. Couturier ends the film with Rahiche, in his apartment, saying, "On s'en fout de comment toi tu nous regardes" (We don't give a fuck how you see us) (35:04), and asserting his worth based on the community's recognition of who he is.

Hamid Rahiche's reappropriation of representational power is not limited to this comment but is a dominant concept in his own photographic practice. The genesis of Rahiche's photographic practice is linked to Stéphane Couturier and their encounter, and like Couturier, Rahiche (born 1979 in Algiers) has been primarily interested in urban space and architecture, especially in Climat de France and the Algiers Casbah. But while their interests are related, Rahiche's photographic language is distinctly different, using his camera and positionality to create intimate portraits of people amid their housing. Rarely are Rahiche's portraits still and fully frontal in their composition; rather we see a girl running into the frame, a young boy jumping in profile (figure 2.10), a man laughing while turning away (figure 2.11), two men turned to each other in greeting. The photographs are dynamic with people most often in movement or occasionally photographed in relation to means of movement such as a car or a truck.

This approach emerges in part from Rahiche's studies with Bruno Boudjelal, a photographer known for producing an aesthetic of intimate, fleeting, and fluid images that speak to his own personal ties to the people and histories he photographs. Boudjelal's photography often features people walking, and he often takes photographs while in motion as well, producing a dynamic relationship between photographer and subject.[87] Journalist Yasmine Chouaki characterized his style of work as "photo volée" (stolen photography), a label that has persisted, but in a 2010 interview Boudjelal described his methodol-

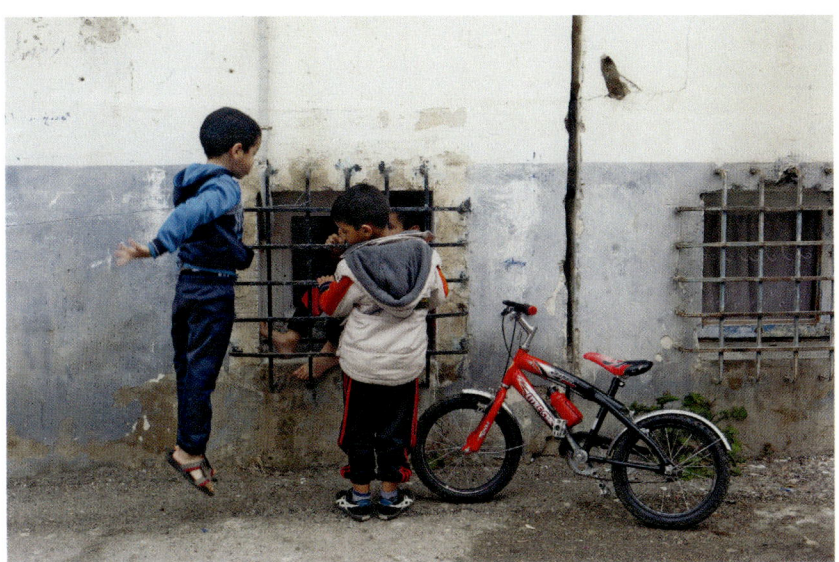

FIGURE 2.10. Hamid Rahiche, *Utopia*, Algiers, Climat de France, March 19, 2015. Courtesy of the artist.

ogy as not about theft but linked to the practical realities of adapting to the environments in which he photographs. He explains how in Algeria taking photographs in public spaces outside familial spaces is a complex and challenging task.[88] One doesn't have any sense that Rahiche's images are stolen from his subjects. The connection between the camera and its subjects seems clearly reciprocal, and the softness in the way people look toward the camera communicates trust and established relationships. Rahiche is not coming to his subjects from the outside. In fact, he sees himself in their position. To that end, he always includes a self-portrait in any exhibited series: "Je ne me dissocie pas de mon sujet. Je suis sujet et photographe en même temps."[89] (I don't disassociate myself from my subject. I am a subject and photographer at the same time.)

One journalist has characterized Rahiche's practice as based on "des images de son enfance passée dans cette cité qu'il dépeint avec un soupçon d'ironie dans laquelle il compare l'architecture des bâtiments avec la physionomie des habitants" (images of his childhood spent in this housing project that he depicts with a hint of irony in which he compares the architecture of the buildings to the physiognomy of their residents).[90] And indeed, the vast majority of Rahiche's photographs are of people amid and in relation to the built

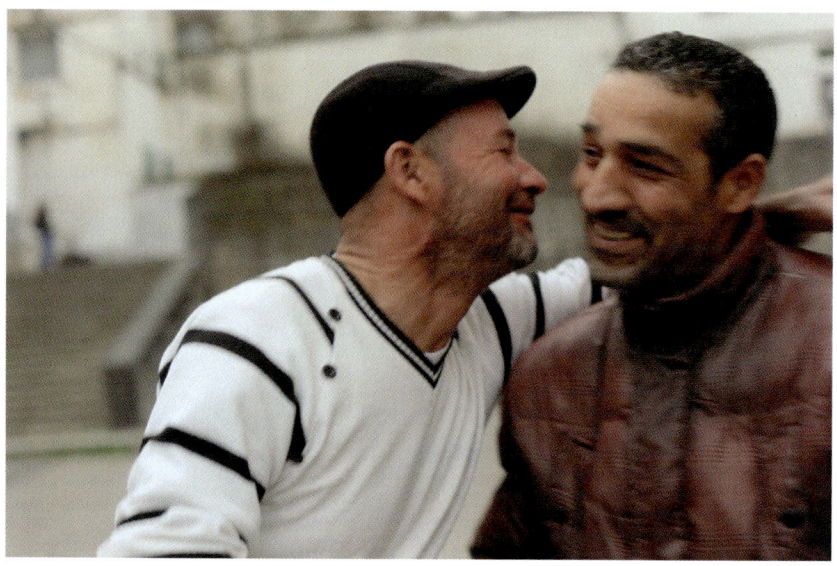

FIGURE 2.11. Hamid Rahiche, *L'Autre Climat de France*, Algiers, Climat de France, March 14, 2015. Courtesy of the artist.

environment of Climat de France. At times, the buildings appear as exterior walls that are crisp and in focus, and at other times architectural elements are present as unfocused fragments (part of a ceiling, part of a door). Rahiche has described his work as telling the story of the built environment and its people against a system of media representation in which the perception of the space remains static and negative.[91] He asks, "Comment changer la perception des lieux? Les lieux évoluent mais la perception n'évolue pas." (How do we change the perception of these places? The place evolves but its perception doesn't.) One photograph in particular speaks to the tension and play between representation and transformation. The photograph, taken from inside an open window looking out at the courtyard and the building across from it, has multiple frames: the window itself, crossed wires, scaffolding outside the window, then columns and finally the courtyard which gives view to the opposing columns and building facade. The multiple frames and scaffolding speak to transformations of both the building and the perspectives in which it is framed and become a way and means to approach and present Climat de France as a world of "multiple truths" ("plusieurs vérités").[92] According to Rahiche, he wants to engage this world of multiplicity, plurality, and severality as a world that is "in-

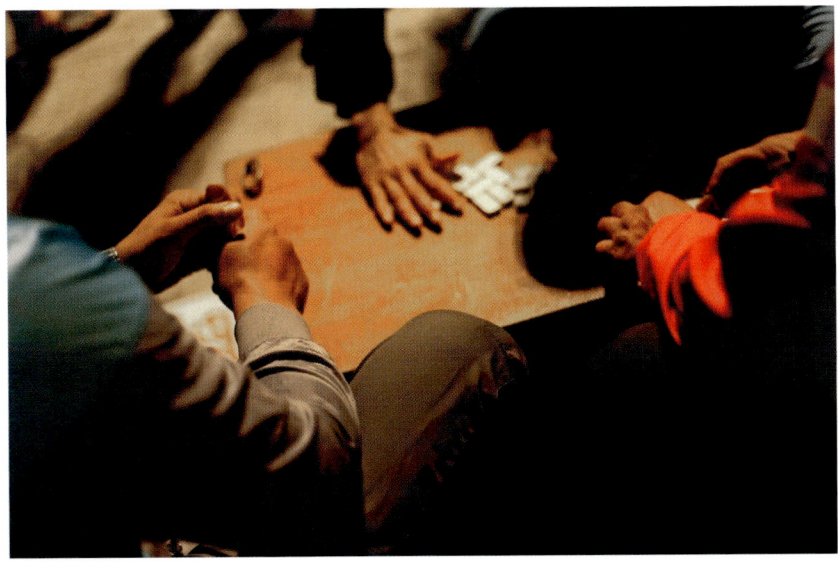

FIGURE 2.12. Hamid Rahiche, *Climat de vie*, Algiers, Climat de France, March 12, 2015. Courtesy of the artist.

saisissable": beyond the grasp and/or not easy for the taking.[93] It is also a world of possibility and potential. Bérengère Chamboissier writes, "Hamid Rahiche a grandi à Climat de France. Il connait la violence, les codes, les passe-droits et les règles de cette cité. Mais l'artiste sait aussi tous les possibles de ce lieu, de l'optimisme dont on ne parle pas."[94] (Hamid Rahiche grew up in Climat de France. He knows the violence, the codes, the special favors and the rules of this housing project. But the artist also knows all the possibilities of this place, of the optimism that isn't spoken about.)

Since his initial encounter with Stéphane Couturier, Rahiche has exhibited his work in both Algeria and France, has led a year-long photography workshop with children in the Casbah, and has held multiple artist residencies, including a project that explores Marseille's northern housing projects. Delayed by the COVID-19 pandemic, in 2022, he finally conducted a residency that took him to Meudon-la-Fôret to photograph and film the relations of everyday life that exist between this Pouillon site and Climat de France. Much like Kamel Daoud's riposte to Camus's *Stranger* in his 2013 novel *Meursault, contre-enquête*, Rahiche's journey and filmic work sets the stage for reparative return to Richeux's novel.

Conclusion

In the previous chapter, I analyzed Marion von Osten's video mapping art project *This Was Tomorrow!* as a way to create new grids of self-representation and constitution onto modernist mass housing in Casablanca. I argued that artwork, including amateur videos, stage the very act of building forms of home—whether that means new grids of understanding, new ledgers, or new catalogues of life. To conclude this chapter, I would like to emphasize the poetics of relation that Marion von Osten's methodology invites. There are many amateur videos on YouTube on Climat de France, from driving tours to views of the building from the cemetery across the hill. One video in particular struck me for its relevance to the discussion of family and reparative relationality that I have explored here.

Entitled "Climat DeFrance, Cassbah, Bab El Oued [*sic*]," the video begins with the following text superimposed on a sunny view of the water of the Bay of Algiers: "Farid presente ouled familia de Climat de France" (Farid presents the sons of the family of Climat de France).[95] With over eighty-seven-thousand views at the time of writing, the seven-minute video presents photographs of smiling men and children interspersed with images of Climat de France: a visual family album. There is no text or narrative, but Abdelmadjid Meskoud's famous song *El Assima* plays throughout. The 1987 song, which propelled Meskoud to prominence, presents a melancholic love song to Algiers that was inspired by the singer witnessing his old neighborhood being razed. Accompanied only by his oud, Meskoud describes the brilliance of the city, its people, its arts, and its culture, and mourns the changes that it is undergoing. He sings that the Hamma neighborhood (where he grew up) is in a state of ruin and that in the heart of his much-loved neighborhood of Belcourt, the perfume of his parents has blown away. In Bab El Oued and the Casbah (the geographic neighbors of Climat de France), he sings that good taste has grown wings and flown away.

Some people critique this song for xenophobia in response to mass migration from rural areas; others see it as a critique of the rise of extremism in the late 1980s. In any case, it is a rousing song that exalts the city while bemoaning what is being lost. However, unlike the song, the video does not evoke melancholy or nostalgia. Instead, the viewer sees image after image of different family members and friends: posing together in front of cars, in front of buildings, sitting on terraces. People are smiling and close to each other.

In 2022, Franco-Algerian musician DJ Snake staged his return to Algeria in an exuberant video for his song "Disco Maghreb."[96] Set in the nearby Diar el-Kef housing project, DJ Snake sings on a stage in the central courtyard, surrounded by residents both on the ground and on balconies. Together, they are celebrating home and projecting it ecstatically outward across the internet. In the amateur YouTube video, we see a similar embodied exuberance but on a smaller, more intimate scale. Between the affecting song and the images on the screen, there arises yet a moment of incipience and a fleeting documentation of what might be: a housing project that harbors hope and celebrates life in kinship.

3

Remembering and Repairing Women's Homes
Nanterre, Bidonville de la Folie

In many of Monique Hervo's 1960s photographs from the Nanterre Bidonville de la Folie, women and young girls stand and sit in front of their homes. Small shacks of metal, brick, paper, and wood frame their bodies while large-scale concrete housing blocks loom in the distance, for many families presciently out of reach. In her series of photographs of the neighborhood celebrating Algerian independence, men and Algerian flags join the women and children in the frame. Everyone is dressed up. The sun shines through the black-and-white images. Women are in the center, and they are smiling for the camera.

In explaining what a bidonville was to her little brothers in 1957, then seven-year-old Akila Hadjdaj also centered women in the frame: "Bidon, c'est comme le Bidoune en fer de Maman, le seau où elle met l'eau pour la lessive."[1] (Bidon, it's like Mama's metal barrel, the bucket where she puts water for the washing up.) For the little girl, the definition of mass housing begins with a mother's bucket.

What room can art make for women in male-dominated histories of architectural modernism, anticolonial liberation, and migration? And what strategies do artists employ to engage women's past and possible future homes?

In the book so far, we have already seen art that engages the male legacies and history of urban planning and modernist architecture from different engendered poetics. Yto Barrada and Marion von Osten rework modernist grids to amplify traces of female domesticity and creative appropriation of space in Casablanca. Marie Richeux and Amina Menia position their own (fictionalized) bodies as a means or "scaffolding" through which to read colonial architecture and its anticolonial histories in Algiers. These female artists have worked to differently gender the histories, lines of inheritance, and formal structures of modernist mass housing. In this chapter on art's engagement with mass housing in Nanterre, I turn to artistic attention to women's spaces and lives within the provisional, and inherently unstable, form of bidonville mass housing in the La Folie neighborhood. In reconstructing women's domestic and political lives in and against this now razed and erased housing, how does contemporary artwork contribute to a process of remembering silenced and complex histories? And how might these art interventions figure into future-facing dynamics of repair?

Bidonville de la Folie was a shantytown mass housing site formed on the land abutting Rue de la Garenne in Nanterre and was named after the larger neighborhood in which it was located. Though some are quick to associate the name La Folie with "madness," the name comes from the old French term *la foillie, feuillie* (leafy) in modern French, and refers to the various wooded areas (La Grande Folie, La Petite Folie, Les Grands Buissons, and so on) that encircled the medieval village of Nanterre. While La Folie has existed as a recognized geographical area since the seventeenth century, first appearing on a map in 1688, there was only one recognized mailing address for the Bidonville de la Folie: 127 Rue de la Garenne.

Bidonville de la Folie was the largest of nine bidonvilles in Nanterre. In 1966, it housed 3,233 people (1,758 individuals and 272 families). The majority of residents were Algerian. Moroccans were the second-largest residential population. Primarily designed and built by Algerian and Moroccan workers, units were built using concrete blocks, bricks, and wood panels for walls, and wood and corrugated metal for roofing. Walls were often insulated with paper. Most units had small interior courtyards used for cooking in the summer and for doing laundry and other household activities. A separate wooden structure housing a toilet would be built off the courtyard. Units had anywhere from one to three rooms: a kitchen with a wood stove that served as a common area and one to two bedrooms. While there was no electricity, most homes had battery-powered radios and a few had battery-powered televisions as well. There was one water pump for the entire housing project. Residents would collect water from the pump using a variety of containers and carry water back to their units by hand or in carts.

There has been a recent flourishing of academic attention given to the former bidonvilles of Nanterre—so much so that some scholars affectionately refer to this work as Nanterrology.[2] Historians have been at the forefront of this movement, and much of their work on the bidonvilles has been driven by the need to establish a new housing history of Nanterre that centers immigration, colonialism, and the Algerian War of Independence in the writing of this space. The historiography of Bidonville de la Folie in particular emerges from two interlinked but not always equally treated analytical frameworks: the housing history of Algerian immigration and the political history of 1961, specifically the protest march and brutal murder of Algerians on October 17, 1961. In housing history, La Folie is most often written as a site for the administration of discriminatory housing policy. For example, in Marie-Claude Blanc-Chaléard's deeply documented *En finir avec les bidonvilles: Immigration et politique du logement dans la France des Trente Glorieuses* (2016), Bidonville de la Folie is approached primarily through a social policy lens that exposes the links between immigration and discriminatory housing policy, but the text barely mentions any of the anticolonial political action of its inhabitants. Yet in political histories, the neighborhood is cited as one of the starting points of the October 17, 1961, march, as well as a space of political repression and organization. Jim House and Neil MacMaster's *Paris 1961: Algerians, State Terror and Memory* presents Bidonville de la Folie simultaneously as a site of police-administered terror and repression driven by discriminatory policing during the Algerian War and a site of Front de Libération Nationale (FLN) political organization. While La Folie is present in both political and social strands of Nanterre historiography, its political and social lives still remain separate despite being so deeply intertwined.

Within this matrix of representation, there is yet another historiographical marginalization present: that of women and their lives and political actions. House and MacMaster's use of oral histories in combination with state archival documents engaged four decades of "memory activist" work, an engagement that led them to conclude that "more work needs to be done on how gender dynamics affect memory transmission, and produce different symbolic investments in memory" and that male-dominated language "has often removed women's visibility from memorial activism."[3] Muriel Cohen's 2020 *Des familles invisibles: Les Algériens de France entre intégrations et discriminations* seeks to correct this male-dominated record, if not in terms of women's political activism, at least in terms of family housing and immigration history. By combining oral histories with social-service archives, Cohen is able to start undoing a history in which women and children are rendered doubly invisible.

As Cohen notes, much of her work owes an intellectual debt to another woman: Monique Hervo. Hervo spent many years talking to and working with people in Bidonville de la Folie, and her notes, photographs, and interview recordings have produced a rare glimpse into the lives of women in particular. Born in Paris in 1929, Monique Hervo joined the International Civil Service in 1956 inspired by her post–World War II work with refugees and as a way to mark her opposition to French colonialism in Algeria. In 1959, she moved to Bidonville de La Folie in order to live with the North African community that she sought to support, and there she created a number of cooperative structures for ameliorating living conditions, including shared hardware tools, administrative services, and children's outings. She aided the French section of the FLN during the Algerian war for liberation all the while maintaining her commitment to nonviolence. Hervo lived in La Folie until the bidonville was razed in 1971. During her time living and working there, she conducted many interviews with people about their living conditions, which she collected as sound recordings. Many of these interviews were transcribed in the book *Bidonvilles: L'enlisement*, cowritten with Marie-Ange Charras and published by François Maspero's press La Découverte in 1971. In the past ten years, there has been renewed interest in her work with exhibitions, essays, interviews, and new editions of her work being published. In a sense, like her photography, her archive is a rare instance in which women are truly at the center of everything—and as we see in this chapter, writers, artists, and scholars return to it again and again.

Literary critic Mildred Mortimer also raises the question of women's marginalization in the historical record, but rather than focus on archival absence, she explores it through the prism of women's own silence in relation to their migration histories, political involvement, and daily lives in 1960s Nanterre.[4] In the introduction to her translation of Leïla Sebbar's 1999 novel *La Seine était rouge*, Mortimer asks, "Why are the women silent?"[5] In response, she quotes Sebbar from a 2002 lecture at the University of Iowa:

> First, "One doesn't speak of painful things." Simply stated, the women do not want to return to traumatic events that caused them pain and suffering and transmit this legacy to the next generation. Second, "Algerian culture had taught them to distinguish between public and private events, male and female space. They consider the events of October 17 as belonging to the realm of men and their politics." Demonstrating alongside the men, these women were clearly supporting the political demonstration but they considered their role to be auxiliary, not central, their own realm being the intimate world of domestic space.[6]

Sebbar's response names the dynamics at play: memory and the intergenerational transmission of trauma and pain, and Algerian culture and its gendered spaces, its private and public divides.[7]

Sebbar's literary work as a whole emerges from this matrix of memory and space and can be characterized as a spatialized work of memory retrieval: a repair of broken transmission that takes place through mediated and alternate pathways that seek to contain traumatic pasts. For example, her early novel *Shérazade, 17 ans, brune, frisée, les yeux verts* (1982) explores the legacies of Orientalist art and the ways in which young Arab/Beur female bodies enter into and against this visual record and its associated grammars. In *La Seine était rouge*, Sebbar chooses the medium of documentary art as the means by which memories of women's political engagement and the massacre of October 17, 1961, can be retrieved and contained. As Mortimer writes, "Speaking to the eye of the camera, Noria is able to recreate scenes of trauma and evoke her personal, painful sense of loss. Although she cannot yet speak to her daughter, she can bear witness via a different medium."[8] In this novel, there is a double mediation at work. Artwork is twice removed: the novel, a fictional form, accesses the history and experience of women through the creation of a fictional documentary that collects their testimony.

While most scholars have focused on the novel's important memory work around October 17, I will argue that the novel's retrieval project is a simultaneous retrieval of women's social, cultural, and political histories in the Bidonville de la Folie. For the process of memory retrieval in *La Seine était rouge* is not limited to political events and their associated traumas. When Noria speaks to the camera, she also recounts ordinary life in the shantytown and bears witness to aspects of her life that have not yet been spoken and named for future generations. Indeed, this narration through a different medium (film) is a protected space in which she can begin to indirectly answer the questions that her daughter Amel asks her and her mother about the past. Importantly, Amel's questions also don't start with the October 17 massacre or the anticolonial war for Algerian liberation. They start with questions about everyday life in the shantytown, about the women in her family's migration story and their social and economic lives.

The artwork discussed in this chapter performs a repair of multiple marginalizations and silences. Rather than tease out and separate women's lives and work into separate political or social histories, artwork *re-pairs* these histories by building a more capacious space to hold everything together, showing how deeply enmeshed and inseparable all these histories truly are. Artwork both identifies and works to repair broken memory chains of transmission. It also names traumas and future threats. Lia Brozgal argues for the power of cultural texts to do this type of work in her 2020 work *Absent the Archive: Cultural Traces of a Massacre in Paris 17 October 1961*. In questioning who is excluded from history, she turns to a "rogue collection of cultural texts" to build a different type of archive, a performative "anarchive," arguing that "literature and culture may do history differently by complicating it; by functioning as first responders and persistent witnesses, by reverberating against reality but also speculating on what might have been; by activating networks of signs and meanings; and sometimes, by showing us things that otherwise cannot be seen."[9]

Cultural texts are not uncomplicated or objective witnesses. Hannah Feldman also asks us to think carefully about image, its production, and the activation of meaning in her analysis of the photojournalism that documented the October 17 massacre. Feldman argues that when read carefully, the circulation of images from the demonstration and its repression reveals how "those who are codified as unequal by the colonial state make claims to the ideal of egalitarian belonging" and how they make claims "for the space of appearance that is the spectacular image."[10] Images and cultural texts thus participate in larger dynamics of aesthetic and political belonging—from the visual to the embodied. Emine Fişek makes a similar argument in her book *Aesthetic Citizenship: Immigration and Theater in Twenty-First-Century Paris*. Performance-based artwork, such as theater, powerfully reveals the links between belonging and national identity because "signification, embodiment, and their corresponding models of theatrical action mobilize specific visions of the body, as well of the self to which the body is attached, and the collective to which that self belongs" and "national participation, belonging, and citizenship are spheres of experiences that require rehearsal."[11] Like image making, theater making thus quite literally stages the space of appearance and rehearses the formation and possible emancipation of a political subject. As Fişek describes: "'Being onstage,' as one theatre workshop leader told me, 'is speaking in a space of liberty, where one is listened to.'"[12] This workshop leader's comment echoes the request for recognition made by Arrif's interlocutor in the preface: What does it mean to be in a space where one both listens and is listened to?

The tension between silence and listening is central in this chapter, and the artwork's use of multiple media shows how the reparative movement between silence and listening is not linear or direct. Leïla Sebbar's *La Seine était rouge* (*The Seine Was Red*), Laurent Maffre's graphic novel *Demain, demain* (Tomorrow, tomorrow), and Mehdi Lallaoui's play *Monique H., Nanterre 1961* all do their repair work through double or multiple media mediations. Like nesting dolls or onion layers, in making a world, these primarily literary arts create yet other art forms, making worlds within made worlds. Sebbar's novel centers around the creation of a film; drawing in part from Monique Hervo's photography, Maffre's graphic novel turns its attention to interior decoration and dance to recount women's restructuring of domestic space; in his play, Lallaoui stages Hervo's photography as well as Frantz Fanon's writing and René Char's poetry. It is as though the single-authored written word alone is not capacious enough to convey the complexity of lived experience, nor is it the primary medium to carry the multiplicity of Algerian women's mass housing stories.[13] The work of memory repair in relation to women's lives in La Folie relies on these multiple aesthetic containers that have the potential to unlock new affective accounts of stories and spaces that have otherwise disappeared from sight. Artwork exaggerates, extends, de-forms, and re-forms intensities, experiences, memories, and futures. It is through this medial manipulation and the formation of aesthetic adjacencies that other paths to knowing and thinking through women's complex lives in bidonville mass housing are formed.

Silence and the Poetics of Containment as Repair

In the opening chapter of *La Seine était rouge*, Amel asks her grandmother yet again to tell her about her past life in the La Folie shantytown. She has asked both her mother and grandmother multiple times and has been met with silence or vague generalities. Amel exclaims: "Le bidonville, tu m'as seulement dit qu'il se trouvait à l'endroit du grand parc ou vers l'université, je ne sais plus, de l'autre côté de la cité. Dis-moi, le bidonville, Nanterre, maman, et la vie."[14] ("As for the shantytown, you only told me it was located at the site of the big park or near the university. I don't know, somewhere on the other side of town. Tell me about the shantytown, Nanterre, Mom and your life.") In this conversation the terms *bidonville, Nanterre, mom*, and *life* are all presented in intimate proximity: each fundamentally tied to the other. The conversation is taking place in 1996, and the Bidonville de La Folie, razed in 1971, has left no physical or geographical traces for Amel to grasp onto. In contrast to the vast number of monuments and historical markers across Paris, there is no symbolic marker to represent the histories of thousands of lives that were lived there. Despite and because of this topographical erasure, Amel's search for the physical site of the bidonville is even more important: "Amel cherche l'emplacement du bidonville dit La Folie où sa mère a vécu. A elle, sa mère n'a rien dit."[15] ("Amel is looking for the site of the shantytown called La Folie where her mother had lived. Her

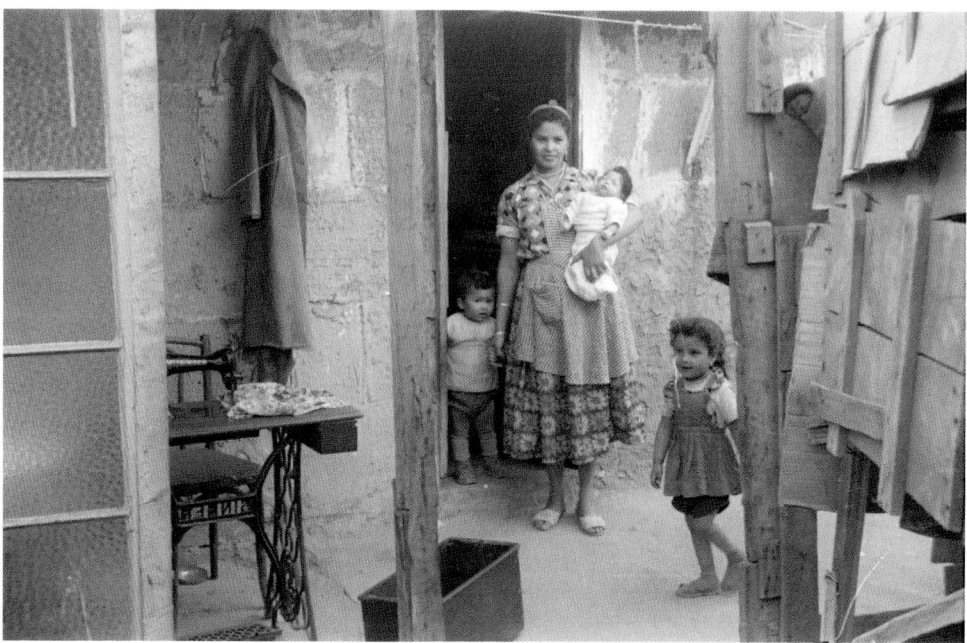

FIGURE 3.1. Monique Hervo, *La Folie*, no. 40, 1963–64. Bibliothèque La Contemporaine, Hervo Archives, Fonds D: HER 03 N / D00—HER 03 N / D35A.

mother never said anything about this to her.") Amel's search for the place, the "emplacement" of the bidonville, is a step toward understanding not just the "site" of the bidonville, as the English translation (mis)terms it, but the social, cultural, political "place" of life there. Her companion Omer, an Algerian journalist seeking refuge in France from the violence of the Algerian Civil War, is frustrated at Amel's approach and chides her:

> "On cherche ton bidonville sans indice, sans repère, comme ça, à l'aveugle. Va à la mairie, regarde le cadastre, le plan de la ville dans les années soixante, aujourd'hui, relève ce qui peut te servir. Tu perds ton temps. Tu sais pas travailler.... Pourquoi tu viens pas ici avec ta mère, elle doit savoir, ou ta grand-mère?" "Elles veulent pas. Chaque fois que je demande, elles disent: 'Un jour tu sauras.'"[16]

("We're looking for your shantytown without a clue, without a signpost, just like that, blindly. Go to city hall, check the land register, the map of the city in the 1960s. Go today: get information that will be useful to you. You're wasting your time. You don't know how to operate....

Why don't you come here with your mother? She must know where it is, or your grandmother?" "They don't want to. Every time I ask, they say: 'You'll find out when the time is right.'")

What Omer cannot understand in this moment is that no archive or city plan can unearth or show her the place. Only the women's words can render the space in its fullness, and they refuse, claiming that one day she will "know." Sebbar highlights the women's reluctance to talk and stresses how the broken communication and chain of transmission between the women of the family block or challenge Amel's ability to find the place, or her place in their story. For Amel, the path to knowledge without her mother's and grandmother's guidance becomes a circuitous one. She roams the city of Paris with Omer. As Lia Brozgal perceptively traces in her chapter "Non-Lieux de mémoire: Maps and Graffiti in the Scriptable City," by tagging various monuments and buildings, Omer and Amel literally highlight the city's history of violence toward North Africans. Omer spray-paints corrective texts on memorial plaques in order to include and make legible the Algerian experience in the memorial record of the city, his graffiti becoming a new map to read and follow.[17]

And so it is surprising and shocking to Amel that, while her mother and grandmother do not speak openly to her about the past, Amel's mother, Noria, speaks voluminously to Amel's friend, a young documentary filmmaker named Louis, the son of Noria's friend Flora.[18] As Mildred Mortimer notes, the mother is able to speak to Louis's camera in a way she can't to her daughter. The camera distances and protects both her and, in her mind, her daughter from the immediacy of both danger and trauma. Noria's first description of the events leading to the October 17 massacre starts with a recollection of her childhood in the bidonville. While her account of the space starts with environmental images of disorder and mud, it ends with a certain almost nostalgic articulation of affection for the neighborhood:

> J'étais petite. Sept ans peut-être. Je me rappelle. On habitait au numéro 7. Le chiffre 7 était écrit sur la porte en bois, avec de la peinture blanche. Le facteur, je sais pas comment il s'y retrouvait, pour le courrier. Des rues sans nom, des noms fantaisistes, souvent illisibles, des rues . . . Si on peut appeler ça des rues . . . Nous, c'était rue de la Fontaine, parce que le point d'eau n'était pas loin. On devait pas faire des centaines de mètres pour l'eau, comme d'autres qui la rapportaient dans des bidons de lait géants sur des chariots. Tu imagines l'hiver, le gel, la pluie, la boue . . . Pour nous, c'était pas si affreux . . . enfin, pour moi. La cité de transit, j'ai pas aimé. Mais notre baraque dans le bidonville, elle me déplaisait pas. Le bidonville

> il s'appelait: La Folie, je sais pas pourquoi, c'était le nom du quartier de Nanterre, un terrain vague, sûrement, avant les baraquements. C'est mon village natal. Je peux pas dire que je le regrette, non, je sais que ma mère a souffert, elle te le dira. Moi, non. Mes frères, je sais pas. On n'en parle pas.[19]

> (I was little, maybe seven years old. I remember that we lived at number 7. The number 7 was written on the wooden door in white paint. I don't know how the mailman was able to deliver the mail. Streets without names, other streets with weird names, street signs that were often illegible... Those streets... if you could even call them streets. Ours was called Rue de La Fontaine, because the fountain wasn't far. We didn't have to go several hundred yards for water, like the others who carried the water back in giant milk cans on dollies. You can imagine in the winter, the frost, the rain, the mud. It wasn't too horrible for us, I mean for me. I didn't like the transit housing project. But our shack in the shantytown didn't bother me too much. The shantytown was called La Folie. I don't know why. It was the name of the section of Nanterre, surely a vacant lot before the shacks were built. It's the town where I was born. I can't say I miss it, but I know my mother suffered; she'll tell you she did. I didn't. I don't know about my brothers. We never speak about it.)

We see a central tension here between the physical environment of life in the bidonville mass housing (cold, mud, rain, unequal access to water, ill-defined streets) and the psychological sense of security the child felt in what she calls her "village natal." Noria's feeling about the bidonville contrasts with how she feels she should feel about it, and she edits her description accordingly. See, for example, the above sentence: "It wasn't too horrible for us, I mean for me." Noria knows that she cannot speak for others, not even for her mother: "she'll tell you" how she suffered. Noria can only describe her own feelings. In another later scene, Noria describes the children's sadness about living in housing without trees or greenery. When the father suggests that they go into foster care in the countryside, the children's decision to stay is one of allegiance to people rather than place:

> Au 7 de la rue de la Fontaine, on pleurait, on voulait pas être là, dans les planches et la tôle. Mon père nous disait: "Si vous voulez, vous vivez là-bas, dans une famille de la campagne j'en connais plusieurs, Henri aussi, elles élèvent des enfants de l'Assistance publique. On peut demander pour vous." On disait non et moi je me cachais dans les plis à fleurs de ma mère.[20]

(At 7 Rue de la Fontaine, everyone was crying. We didn't want to be there, among the planks and the tin roofs. My father told us: "If you wish, you can go live with a family in the country I know several and so does Henri. They take in foster children. They can ask for you." We said no, and I hid in the flowered pleats of my mother's skirt.)

Noria chooses her mother's flowered skirt over meadows of flowers. The psychological security of being near her mother is more important than leaving the harsh physical environment of planks and tin.

In another scene from Louis's documentary, a different person, the owner of the Atlas Café, describes life in La Folie. Here again, Sebbar untangles the physical environment from other structures that produce the experience of living there. The café owner explains: "On allait à l'école pieds nus, dans la neige, l'hiver... Alors la boue du bidonville, ça me fait pas peur. Mon père est mort dans la boue des rizières, en Indochine, sa pension a disparu avec lui et sa compagnie."[21] (We went to school barefoot, in the snow, in winter... So, the mud in the shantytown doesn't scare me. My father died in the mud of the rice paddies in Indochina; his pension disappeared with him and his unit.) Mud does not produce fear, but colonialism is inherently life-threatening, killing both the owner's father and his family's chances for economic security. It is not the physical place that causes harm but rather colonial structures and policies that have decimated families.

As the book progresses, and the reader "sees" new scenes from Noria's documentary interview, Noria describes the actions of other women and how their social and economic lives overlapped with the political on a daily basis. She describes how her mother became a seamstress when she immigrated from Algeria. She sewed dresses to make a living and in so doing participated in a network of women who supported each other and also worked together to further the political cause of Algerian liberation:

> Ma mère est venue à Nanterre, mon père lui a acheté une Singer d'occasion et elle a fait de la couture à domicile. Pas seulement de la couture. Avec des femmes du bidonville, elle a caché des tracts dans les tissus, les robes pour les mariages... Elles les ont distribués. Les musiciennes répandaient la nouvelle de mariage en mariage, d'une fête à l'autre. Je voyais faire ma mère et ses amies, elles disaient que c'était des recettes de cuisine, des lettres pour la famille là-bas... J'ai su plus tard que les tracts étaient signés par le FLN. Ils appelaient à la manifestation du 17 octobre 1961.[22]

(My mother came to Nanterre. My father bought her a secondhand Singer sewing machine and she did dressmaking at home. Not only dressmaking. Working with women of the shantytown, she hid political tracts in fabric, in wedding dresses; the women distributed them. Women musicians would spread the news from wedding to wedding, from one celebration to another. I watched my mother and her friends prepare them; they said they were kitchen recipes and letters for the families back home . . . I later learned that the tracts were signed by the FLN. They were calling for the protest march on October 17, 1961.)

It is important to note that Noria's mother doesn't tell her what she is doing. Noria observes and learns about the FLN pamphlets later. As we have already seen, "learning later" is a dynamic that both grandmother and mother adopt toward Amel. The impulse to protect children from too much knowledge of necessarily clandestine political actions during an anticolonial war is not the same as the impulse not to share too much about that past. However, the continuation of that dynamic points to a felt experience of continued danger. The dangers in 1996 are different from those in 1961, but the older women continue to use silence as a protective structure when they see Amel emerging as a political activist herself.

I want to pause here to talk about the relationship between the three women. Most discussions of the novel focus on Amel as a "memory activist" who is fighting for social justice.[23] Indeed, many of Sebbar's novels present young second-generation women fighting to know their histories in a French society that limits access to this knowledge and an Algerian community that seems to exclude its French-born children from collective memory and shared language. I would like to propose, however, that Noria and her mother are not oppositional figures in this fight for social justice. Rather, when listened to differently, their silence is a loud warning that the dangers their generation lived through are still present even if their forms have shifted. Contemporary France is still not a space of liberty; it is still not a social and political stage where they can speak freely and be listened to.

Apart from a description of how her mother dressed and bathed her and her siblings before setting out for the October 17 demonstration, Noria doesn't describe life in the bidonville any further. The book, and Amel, move on to other geographies in Paris, ultimately retracing the path of the October 17, 1961, march and the subsequent 1996 commemorative march by antiracism activists. While Sebbar's novel retrieves but a few traces of women's lives in La Folie, most importantly it articulates a method for doing so. Rather than relying on maps, city plans, and written archives, the process to repair memory is one of talking and listening or bringing people and stories back into "pairings" even if such acts need to be indirect and mediated. Distanced and contained within another embedded aesthetic form (here the documentary film within a novel), the fragments of women's lives in the bidonville pose important questions for the future and reveal how women seek to limit harm when physical structures are dismantled but racially discriminatory structures remain.

Building in and against the Mud

The café owner in *La Seine était rouge* distinguished between two forms of mud. The mud of the rice fields in Indochina where her Algerian father was sent to fight for colonial France is deadly and produces intergenerational harm and trauma. But the mud of the bidonville is a relatively harmless mud or at the very least produces limited bodily harm. Indeed, as Akila Hadjadj describes in her 2014 memoir, *Vol au-dessus des bidonvilles*, for children, the mud of Bidonville de la Folie could even be a material that is positive, joy-producing: "Mais moi, dans cette boue, j'étais toujours d'humeur joyeuse."[24] (But me, I was always in a joyful mood in that mud.) But there is also another type of mud, mud used discursively to stigmatize Algerian and Moroccans in France and block their pathways to inclusion in French society. This stigmatizing mud and its mitigation by women in the bidonville appears as a central element in Laurent Maffre's 2012 graphic novel *Demain, demain*.

The cover of *Demain, demain: Nanterre, bidonville de la Folie, 1962–1966* is a curious collage of unreasonable juxtapositions literally positioned in mud (see figure 3.2). Images of characters from the book are taken from the inside pages, from different interior and exterior scenes, and placed together in an open outdoor space loosely framed by the shantytown. People going about their daily lives appear next to policemen violently conducting a raid; the policemen in turn are placed right next to two dancing women. In the center of the cover, we find the main characters of the novel, the Saïfi family, united visually here, but each figure taken from different panels and points of time in the novel. Behind them, Maffre places images of protesters heading out from the bidonville on October 17, 1961. And behind those protesters, the horizon reveals housing projects in various stages of construction. With the bidonville and high-rise buildings in the background, the open muddy space in the foreground serves as a visual palimpsest that links ordinary lives with violence, that links destruction with the recuperation of materials, and that links the rebuilding of lives with political action.

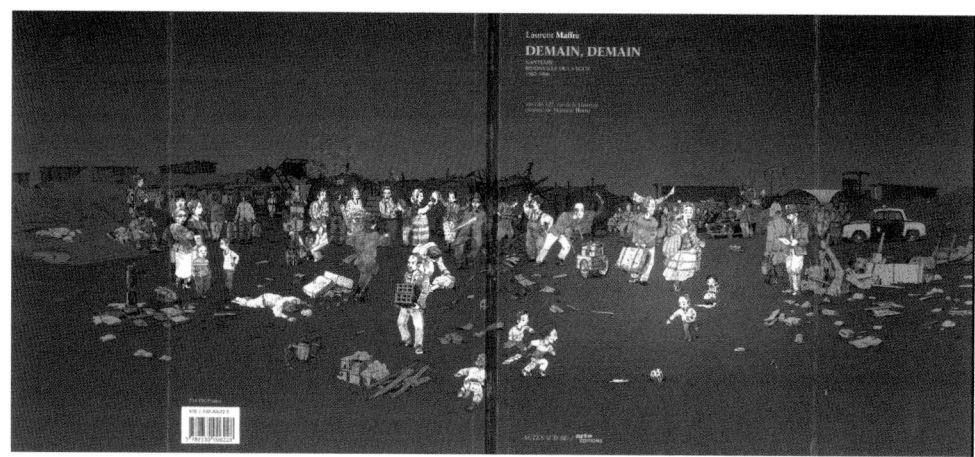

FIGURE 3.2. Cover of Laurent Maffre, *Demain, demain: Nanterre, bidonville de la Folie*, 2012.

By foregrounding all the events and people of his novel into one space, into one image bounded in mud, Maffre makes the statement that not only is it possible to aesthetically represent the Nanterre bidonville of 1962–66 but that it is also necessary to render visible the populations and stories that define its history. In some ways, Maffre's is an argument about "aesthetic belonging"—a term I borrow from Hannah Feldman's work on the visual making of the October 17, 1961, massacre.[25] Belonging does not simply mean inclusion or, in the French case, assimilation into the visual record. Rather, through his unreasonable visual juxtapositions of who belongs with whom Maffre raises the question of ownership of both spatial representation and self-representation. Who/what gets remembered? And by whom? Maffre's attention to self-constitution and self-fashioning are at the heart of a project that seeks to counter a long-standing racist discourse linking Arab immigration to unformed mud and dirt.

While *Demain, demain* has a large cast of characters, in many ways the graphic novel is about the life of women in the bidonville. Drawing on Monique Hervo's photographs and ethnographic accounts, Maffre creates a black-and-white visual language of geometrically contained panels that transmit the stark material conditions of their built environment and its existential language of confinement and containment. In comparing Maffre's creative process of memory retrieval with that of Sebbar's characters, one could argue that Maffre is a type of Louis—a progressive white man from outside the community whose political solidarity with the community and pursuit of social justice lead him to represent their story. Maffre is careful to rely on Monique Hervo's archival records: photographs but also interviews that she was able to conduct with families during her ten years of living in the bidonville (1961–71). And like Louis, Maffre conducts his own interviews with former residents, relying extensively on the story of one family in his representation of the Saïfi family. What we read when we read the graphic novel then is a deeply intermedial and mediated account of women's lives. Like Louis's film, it transmits a testimony that has been silenced or subsumed by other migration stories. In Sebbar's work, the white men who lead efforts to document Algerian life are presented as walking a fine line between neo-Orientalizing their female subjects and offering them a certain love and intimacy that creates space for the women in their paths to self-recognition. In *Shérazade, 17 ans, brune, frisée, les yeux verts*, Sebbar is much more explicit in her presentation of this dynamic, linking the character Julien to Orientalists such as Delacroix. This leads me to Assia Djebar's powerful take on Delacroix: her articulation that despite its deeply problematic positionality, the gaze of the white man may actually reveal something powerful about the lives of Algerian women if women, and particularly Algerian women, read those images for something else. For Djebar, Eugène Delacroix's painting *Women of Algiers in Their Apartment*, when looked at differently, reveals a painful isolation and records a silence that she recognizes in contemporary Algerian women: "Ces femmes, que Delacroix—peut-être malgré lui—a su regarder comme personne ne l'avait fait avant lui, ne cessent de nous dire, depuis, quelque chose d'insoutenable et d'actuellement présent."[26] (Since then, these women, whom Delacroix—perhaps in spite of himself—knew how to observe as no one had done before him, have not stopped telling us something that is unbearably painful and still very much with us today.) To be clear, Maffre is not Delacroix. Neither is he Julien or Louis, but there is something to be said about positionality and what he might inherit or disown of their representational practices.

With all this in mind, let's turn to the graphic novel and its construction of domestic space in and against the stigmatizing politics of mud. The central story of *Demain, demain* revolves around the Saïfi family and the arrival of Soraya and her two children in Nanterre in 1962 to join her husband, Kader, a worker in the French automobile industry. From the outset, Soraya is horrified by the material conditions of the bidonville. Upon entering the space, she exclaims, "Des baraques, ce ne sont que des baraques" (Shacks, nothing but shacks), and repeatedly tells Kader that they cannot live there.[27] Her exhortations are structured through a set of negations: "Pas d'eau, pas de lumière, pas de vue" (No water, no light, no view) and "rien du tout!" (nothing at all!). Maffre repeatedly uses small panels to create a sense of claustrophobia, each panel oscillating from the small details of the housing to the images of Soraya framed by her new environment. After asking Kader, "Mais comment veux-tu que l'on vive ici?" (But how can you want us to live here?), the scene changes to an outside space as Soraya is greeted by two women, Fathia and Yamina, both from her village in Algeria, who welcome her and the children.

After this initial introduction to the space (for both Soraya and the reader), Maffre underscores the monumental shock that Soraya feels by drawing two large consecutive landscapes that each take up two-page spreads. In the first spread (figure 3.4), he presents a landscape of shacks, in the second a rural landscape of an Algerian village. The first drawing is dynamic: short pen strokes create movement and represent people going about their business between the crowded shacks. In contrast, the second landscape is peaceful, if eerily quiet: open natural space dominates the page, and two shepherds are the only human figures present. In his article on memory and place in *Demain, demain*, Mark McKinney writes that in these two panoramas, Maffre "produces a dialogic contrast between a confined scene of urban destitution in France and a much more open, peaceful vision of life in the Algerian countryside. This reverses the typical (neo-)colonial polarity between French modernization and Algerian underdevelopment, Western progress and Third World backwardness."[28] But I would argue that the view of Algeria is not that peaceful—its countryside, a recent site of war, sits emptied of its inhabitants. Soraya is psychologically stuck between the mud of the bidonville and the arid earth of the village, neither offering her a life that is acceptable.

The novel returns to the shack interior and continues to narrate Soraya's adaptation to the space. Maffre focuses on Soraya's attention to hygiene and cleanliness in reaction to the muddiness of the bidonville: he shows her cooking, cleaning the children, feeding them breakfast, and taking out buckets of dirty water. She warns the children to stay inside: "Ne bouge pas d'ici Samia. Ali, fais attention où tu mets les pieds." (Don't move from here Samia. Ali, watch where you step.) This is the first representation of a mud that stigmatizes and has the potential to mark them as physically and metaphorically "dirty" in the eyes of fellow Algeriens and French society. In a later conversation, quoted directly from one of Monique Hervo's interviews,[29] Maffre shows a neighbor telling Soraya:

> Quand j'ai raconté tout ça à ma mère, elle ne m'a pas crue, elle m'a dit: "à Paris, vous n'êtes pas dans un gourbi. En Algérie, tu n'habites pas comme

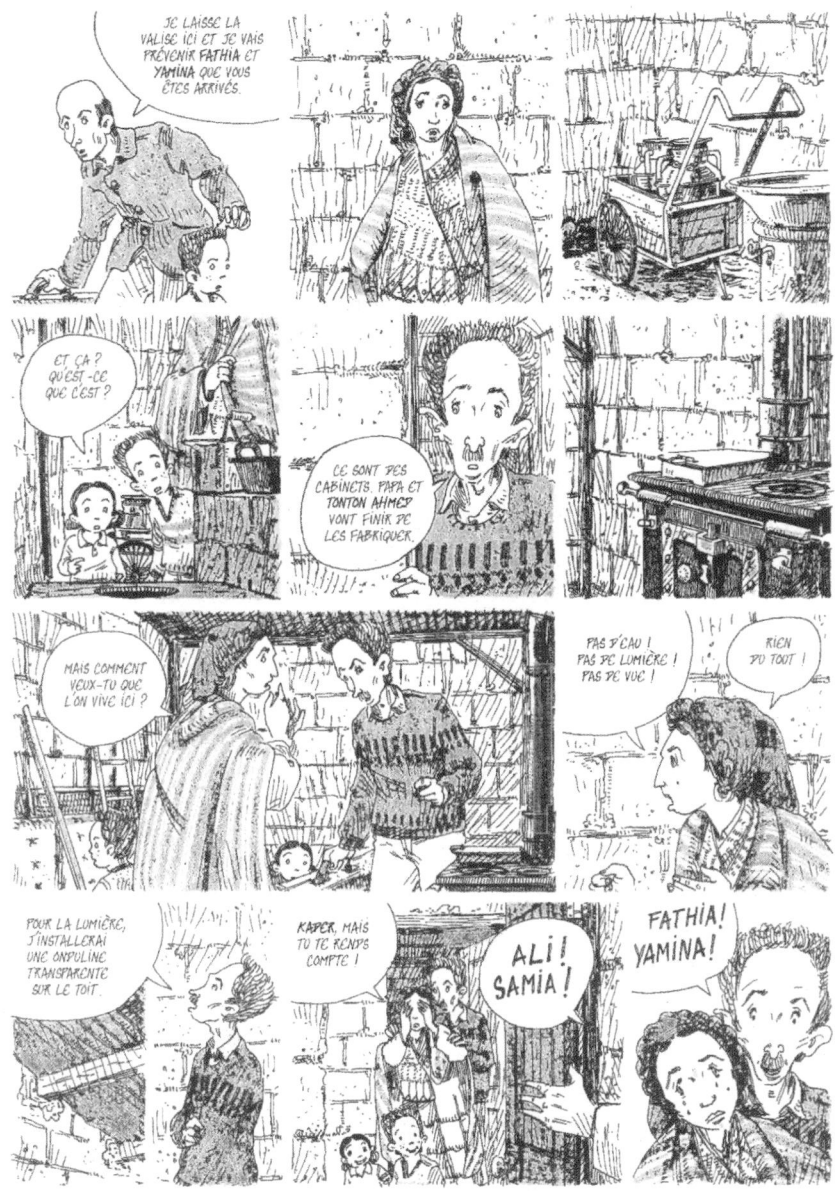

FIGURE 3.3. Laurent Maffre, *Demain, demain: Nanterre bidonville de la Folie*, 2012.

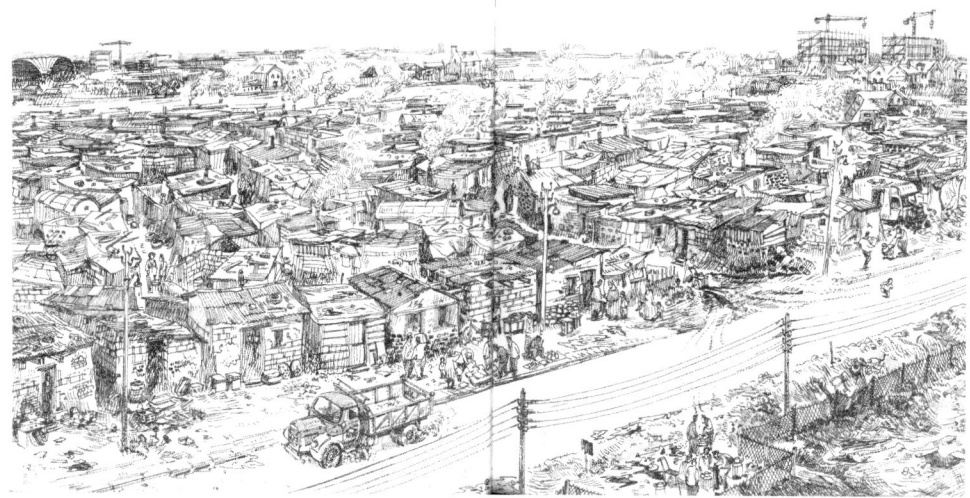

FIGURE 3.4. Laurent Maffre, *Demain, demain: Nanterre, bidonville de la Folie*, 2012.

ça, et à Paris tu serais dans un gourbi? Non! Je ne crois pas que tu es dans un gourbi!" Alors je lui dis: "Mais je te jure ma mère, que je suis dans un gourbi, que c'est sale et sans lumière." Ils ne nous croient pas.

(When I told my mother everything, she didn't believe me. She said: "In Paris, you aren't living in a *gourbi* [shack]. In Algeria you don't live like that, and in Paris you do? No, I don't believe you are living in a gourbi!" So I told her: "But I swear to you, my mother, that I am in a gourbi, that it is dirty and without light." They don't believe us.)

The term *gourbi* means hut or simple dwelling in Algerian Arabic and references rural dwellings made from the natural materials of their environment as well as the shacks that emerge in urban industrial shantytowns.[30] It is a term tied to poverty, and the family in Algeria struggles with the idea that the *gourbi*, a North African stigmatized space of poverty, would exist in France. Indeed it is inconceivable to them that migrating to France, seen as an economic necessity and opportunity, should transport them somewhere lower on the scale of respectability where they risk remaining stuck. As Hervo described it, for many, "Nanterre représente tout l'espoir d'une vie moins abominable" (Nanterre represents all the hope of a less abominable life).[31] It represented a way out of poverty.

However, not all of La Folie's residents came from poor urban or rural communities. One La Folie family that Hervo interviewed lived in a social housing project in Algiers (Habitation à loyer modéré, or HLM in French), reversing the well-worn expression "du bidonville aux HLM" (from bidonville to HLM) to "des HLM au bidonville" (from HLM to bidonville). In fact, as Hervo shows in a chart comparing the type of lodging in Algeria and Morocco with that in La Folie, 110 of 138 interviewed families reported living conditions in their communities of origin as better than La Folie: "Habitat rural correct (eau à proximité, puits, source) habitat urbain à confort minimum (eau courante, électricité)" (Proper rural habitat [water nearby, well, spring], urban habitat with minimum comfort [running water, electricity]).[32] Of that approximate 110, a little less than half reported living conditions in their communities of origin as much better, "conforme aux normes HLM" (conforming to the norms of HLM). One interviewee, Dalila, compares life in her hometown of "Philippeville" (Skikda) with life in La Folie:

> J'habitais dans un bâtiment, au deuxième étage. Je mettais mes enfants sur le balcon avec des petits jouets et moi je restais à coudre, je repassais, enfin j'étais tranquille, tandis que là je suis toute "perdue": pour raccommoder je n'ai pas le temps, pour sortir avec mes enfants, je n'y arrive pas; je perds tout mon temps pour le lavage. Ici on n'arrive jamais à rien, tandis que, quand tu habites bien proprement, aujourd'hui tu laves tout et le lendemain c'est encore propre; au bidonville, tu laves, tu nettoies mais il y a toujours de la poussière et c'est toujours sale, comme si tu n'avais rien fait.[33]

(I lived in a building, on the second floor. I would put the children out on the balcony with their toys and I would stay inside sewing, ironing. In short, I was at peace. Whereas here I am completely "lost": I don't have the time to mend things, to go out with my children, I just can't make it; I lose all my time doing laundry. Here, you never get to anything, whereas when you live cleanly, today you wash everything and tomorrow it is still clean; in the shantytown, you wash, you clean, but there is always dust and it's always dirty as though you had done nothing.)

For Dalila, mud is the sign of incapacitating living conditions in the bidonville. Mud takes over every aspect of life, becoming the central logic in the measurement of time. It erases progress and the possibility of movement through its inescapable presence.

In French racist popular discourse, dirt, mud, and dust aren't solely descriptors of living and working conditions but also markers of Arab identity and worth. Sociologist Abdelmalek Sayad quotes one of the La Folie bidonville residents describing this dynamic of racist stigmatization:

> Le bidonville, c'est le bidonville des Arabes . . . Et s'ils disent "les Arabes sont sales," c'est du racisme, personne ne peut dire le contraire. Et quand ils disent "les gens du bidonville sont sales" tout le monde pense qu'il s'agit au fond des Arabes. Les Arabes, on peut être doublement sales, sales parce que c'est le bidonville, sales parce qu'Arabes. C'est comme ça.[34]

> (The shantytown is the shantytown of Arabs . . . And if they say, "Arabs are dirty," it's racism, no one can deny it. And when they say, "the people of the shantytown are dirty" everyone thinks that it fundamentally means Arabs. Arabs can be doubly dirty, dirty because it's the shantytown, dirty because it's Arab. It's like that.)

In Monique Hervo's ethnographic notes, residents she interviewed also remarked on this form of French discriminatory representational practice. One man states: "Ils disent aussi: 'Les Algériens sont sales,' parce qu'ils nous voient habiter comme ça, mais c'est forcé qu'on devienne sales ici, dans les bidonvilles!"[35] (They also say: "Algerians are dirty" because they see us living like that, but it's unavoidable for us to become dirty here, in the shantytowns.) French discourse labels Algerians as physically dirty (and by extension existentially less-than), but it is French housing policy that forces them into that built environment and discursive mode of representation.

Writer Tassadit Imache famously referred to Nanterre as a "non-terre," a "non-land."[36] Imache's first novel, *Une fille sans histoire* (1989), grapples with the idea of Nanterre as a site of exclusion and fundamental instability. In *Une fille sans histoire* (A girl without history), the central character Lil is constantly displaced: from the run-down attic of a house next to the Bezons bridge to numerous children's homes and two HLM apartments. While she never lives in a bidonville, the bidonville is a central geography that shows the threat of material deprivation that the Algerian side of her mixed identity represents (her mother is French, her father Algerian). When her French mother decides to send the children to church, this tension emerges most dramatically in the children's walk to mass:

> Pour se rendre à l'église, il fallait longer le bidonville. D'abord ils accéléraient le pas puis ils s'arrêtaient net et regardaient les cabanes serrées les unes contre les autres. Des enfants sales et mal vêtus s'agitaient autour d'une marmite. Rougies, les plumes des poules saignés vives voletaient, collaient à leurs semelles. Le vernis clinquant des souliers et le rose résolu des rubans de Lil et d'Isa étincelaient sur fond de misère.[37]

> (In order to get to the church, it was necessary to go by the shantytown. At first they quickened their steps, then they just stopped and looked around at the shacks squeezed one on the other. Dirty and badly-dressed children were busy around a pot. The red feathers of the chickens that had been butchered, fluttered around and stuck to the soles of their shoes. The flashy gloss of their shoes and the bright pink of their hair ribbons sparkled against this background of misery.)

Living in poverty themselves, but cleaned up for church, the children's shoes and hair ribbons sparkle precisely because of the destitution of the Algerian bidonville's surroundings: their French "brightness" is a function of the Algerian "dirt" that surrounds them. The poverty of the bidonville is even greater than theirs, but like the Algerian part of their identity, they cannot escape it. It sticks to them, to the soles of their shoes, as they ultimately pass through.[38] As Jeannine Murray-Román writes: "Imache's protagonists are unable to define home in such a way that they might root themselves in a physical space, or a mental place of respite and emotionally inviolate safety.... The unquestioned comfort implied by 'home' in all its formulations is ultimately inaccessible.... The journeys of Imache's protagonists are always indirect, circular, deviant, and the point of return forever deferred."[39]

For Maffre, the graphic novel is a space in which he hopes to dissolve some of these racist discourses, structures, and images of stigmatization by changing the very representation of the space. To do this, he focuses on self-constitution, showing how residents construct their physical selves and their homes within and against the physical and discursive mud around them. Much of this construction is done by women. Maffre presents Soraya's neighbor telling her that she will feel better once she creates her own space and urging her to decorate:

> Tu vas décorer et tu te sentiras mieux. Le sol est en ciment, pas en terre battue. Ça restera propre. Moi, pour habiller les murs, j'ai collé du papier peint à fleurs et des photos. Et puis dans la cour, ils ont laissé un peu

de terre pour planter des patates douces. Elles vont grimper et avec le vert, ça fera beau.

(You will decorate and you will feel better. The floor is cement, not pounded earth. It will stay clean. Me, to dress the walls, I pasted wallpaper with flowers and photographs. And then there is the courtyard. They left some earth to plant sweet potatoes. They will climb, and with that greenery, it will be beautiful.)

While the text gives advice, the visuals point to the various areas of her shack that have transformative potential. The neighbor's comments underline how women have the capacity to transform a negative mud into a different earth that can bear life, whether that is through flowered wallpaper or flowering sweet-potato vines. Again, Maffre draws on Hervo's archive here, echoing her observation that despite the bare necessity, home repair also becomes something of aesthetic value:

Solutions de fortune. Celles de la misère. Ne pas mourir de froid. Ce sont les femmes qui s'occupent des fourneaux, de les rafistoler avec de la terre réfractaire. Et très souvent elles plâtrent. Sans truelle, avec leurs mains, elles appliquent, donnent une forme, lissent ce matériau comme si elles le sculptaient, comme si elles tournaient la poterie de chez elles.[40]

(Band-Aid solutions. Made out of misery. In order not to die of cold. It is the women who take care of stoves, patching them up with heat-resistant earth. And very often they also plaster. Without trowels, with their hands, they apply, give form, smooth the material as if they were sculpting it, as if they were making pottery from back home.)

Note how repairing the house with plaster is described by Hervo as simultaneously functional and aesthetic; the women are repairing cracks and sculpting at the same time. And indeed, in a later celebratory dinner scene, we see Soraya's shack transformed into both a functional and aesthetic space through textiles and wall decorations (see figure 3.5). Paul Silverstein terms this type of thorough decorative transformation a tactic of spatial appropriation in his work on the creation of Amazigh homes (*axxam*) within French mass housing projects.[41] Maffre insists on the centrality of this spatial appropriation for self-constitution throughout the novel and as an illustrator invests deeply in the details. In one scene representing the aftermath of a fire, the last panel shows us the charred remains of a shack, with everything gone except the hand-painted decorations (see figure 3.6). In this panel, Maffre preserves the care with which

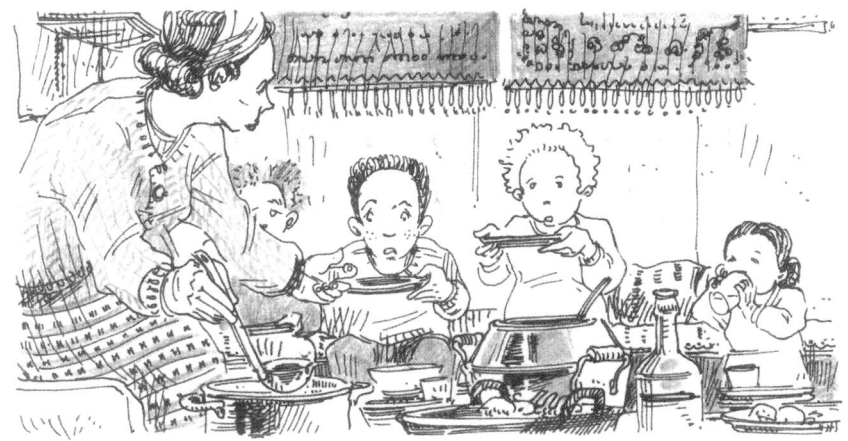

FIGURE 3.5. Laurent Maffre, *Demain, demain: Nanterre, bidonville de la Folie*, 2012.

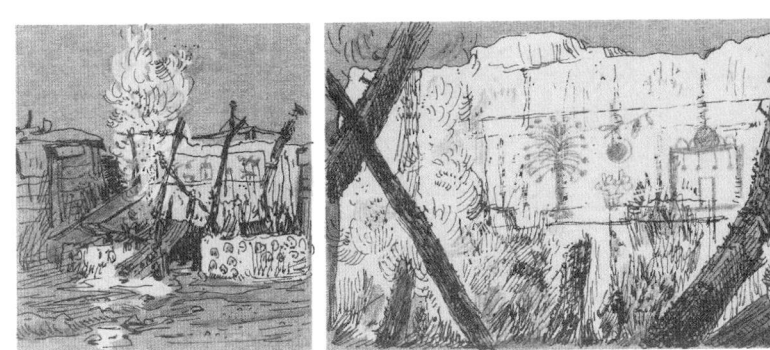

FIGURE 3.6. Laurent Maffre, *Demain, demain: Nanterre, bidonville de la Folie*, 2012.

the residents decorated and transformed the space despite, and perhaps in spite of, the home's destruction.

How do women create space in what Frantz Fanon describes as a "zone of non-being"? For Maffre, it is important to represent survival as coming in part from the ability to create space without limits through various decorative practices, but also through expansive social domestic life. While most of his panels take small rectangular geometric forms, in certain scenes when families meet or interact, Maffre dissolves the panels and allows for images to scatter across the pages or to bleed into one another. In the scene showing the celebratory dinner, the community gathers to eat and dance together, and Maffre dissolves the containers entirely. In scenes of friends dancing together, collective, shared,

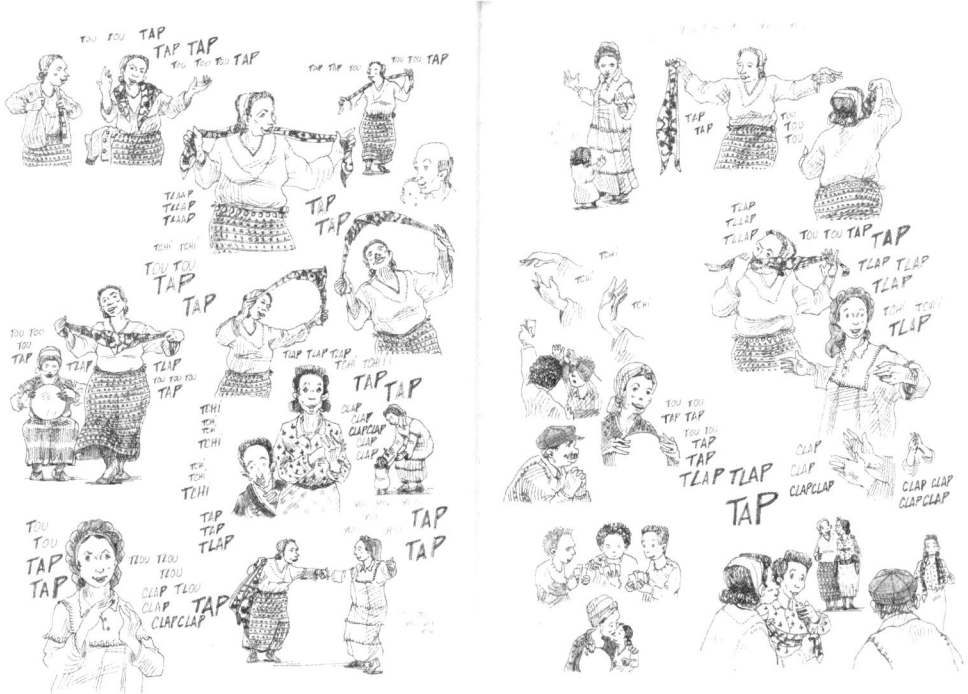

FIGURE 3.7. Laurent Maffre, *Demain, demain: Nanterre, bidonville de la Folie*, 2012.

joyous space emerges from restricted spaces of containment (see figure 3.7). As we saw in Zrika's poem in the preface, dance functions as a powerful reclaiming of space and time through embodiment and occupation of place. There is a powerful decolonial dimension to this: from Langston Hughes's lines "To whirl and to dance / Till the White day is gone" in his poem "Dream Variations" to Fanon's interpretation of dance and possession in *Damnés de la terre* as creating space without limits in colonial orders of containment.[42] Indeed in Maffre's novel, dance in the bidonville is life-affirming, self-fashioning, and community-constituting in the face of state discrimination and harm, and his panels visually enact the contrast of containment with spaces of freedom.

In addition to decoration and dance to counter the discourse of mud, Maffre uses his graphic novel as a platform for amplifying resident voices. It is not enough to represent the community through a single-authored text. Rather, the novel becomes a platform that hosts other texts, sounds, and voices. The graphic novel includes a short "dossier" entitled "127, rue de la Garenne" that is narrated by Monique Hervo and brings together excerpts from her archive:

photographs, documents, and notes chosen and commented by Hervo for the dossier. The graphic novel also points readers to an online *fresque sonore* (unfortunately no longer accessible) that accompanied the graphic novel, created together by Maffre and Hervo: a multimedia piece that "animated" the contained and immobile text and added Hervo's 1960s sound recordings of residents.[43] By including sound recordings of life in the housing project, the *fresque sonore* was another enactment of creating space beyond containment.

According to Muriel Cohen, the attention to voice and testimony in Maffre's novel fits into what she terms the third phase of a literary history of the French bidonville.[44] According to Cohen, the first phase of literary texts and autobiographies of bidonvilles in the France of the late 1970s to early 1980s presented a very "somber" vision of life in the bidonville and "insisted on the violence of social relations, within the heart of the families, and between families and the police."[45] Cohen writes that the bidonville's principal function was a backdrop to explain the trajectory of delinquency of the author. The second phase of literary texts and autobiographies of bidonvilles—during the mid-1980s—focused on the lives of young people who "managed to get out" through education. Here, according to Cohen, the bidonville is configured as both a playful space of childhood and an obstacle to their success. Cohen argues that the third phase of this representational history, starting around 2005, is a less coherent set of narratives that emerge from online testimonies by former residents. These texts are invested in showing social stability and "solidarity" within the bidonville. Cohen situates Maffre in this third generation of literary production and critiques how the focus on solidarity ultimately creates an idealized version of the bidonville that obscures, among other things, the isolated condition of women in the bidonville and the tension between neighbors as different families are resettled. Cohen writes: "Cette représentation 'enchantée' de la vie au bidonville s'explique sans doute en partie par les sources utilisés, mais tient à la volonté de rompre avec les représentations caricaturales de familles sous-prolétaires et 'asociales' qui prévalaient à l'époque."[46] (This enchanted representation of life in the bidonville is explained, in part, by the sources used, but also by its desire to break with caricatures of under-proletariat and asocial families that were prevalent at the time.) Cohen's critique here is important. In his eagerness to combat the racist discourse of mud, what and who does Maffre leave out in his centering of collective domestic repair over other existing dynamics such as social and political isolation? That said, I do not think that Maffre's project is one-sided or even primarily representational—after all, a complex archive already exists, especially Monique Hervo's archive on which the graphic novel is based. Rather, I would

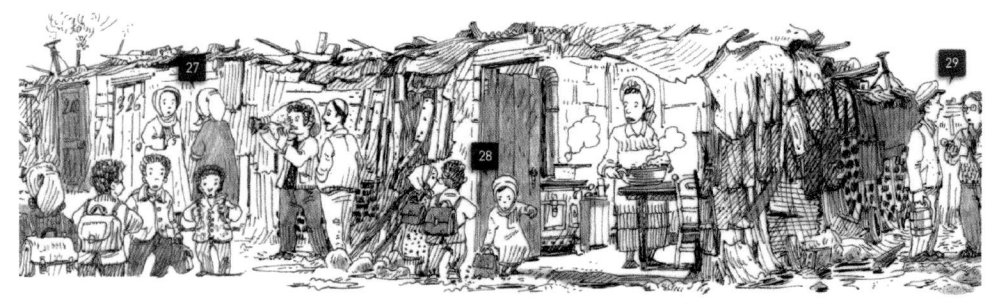

FIGURE 3.8. Screenshot of the *fresque sonore* from Laurent Maffre, *Demain, demain: Nanterre, bidonville de la Folie*, www.bidonville-nanterre.arte.tv.fr (no longer accessible).

argue that elevating solidarity over isolation is an affective strategy to invite the reader into a future solidarity. Where Cohen, as a historian, characterizes enchantment as negative, Maffre's graphic novel attempts a repair work through aesthetic enchantment to undo a colonial politics of representation and imagine a different historical record, however incomplete.

Like Cohen, Mireille Rosello also warns of one-sided representations of bidonvilles: "They were always ambivalent spaces and the difficulty is to find a viewpoint that eschews both a racist amalgamation between the inhabitants and their housing conditions and the temptation to glorify the immigrants' capacity to survive under conditions that we would find unacceptable in the name of a sort of paternalistic admiration for what 'these people' can endure, for their ingenuity, for their courage."[47] Here Rosello names the central difficulty that the graphic novel engages: How does an aesthetic representation of a complex and ambivalent space bear witness to its own limits? Maffre partially answers this question on the cover of the book.

Maffre's novel takes place from 1962 to 1966, after Algerian independence; the war now is against racist discriminatory practices and structures. Nonetheless, the Algerian War and the October 17, 1961, march haunt the novel and its work of constructing home from and in mud. In the center-left of the back cover, a man lies face down in the mud (see figure 3.9). The figure is a drowned protester from the violent suppression of the October 17, 1961, march. Whereas inside the novel his body is shown floating in the Seine, on the cover the body is returned to the bidonville and sinks into its mud. There is something troubling in this movement from water to mud, from central Paris to La Folie—something more unreasonable than the other juxtapositions. One could argue that this partial burial perhaps speaks to an incomplete memorialization of the people killed during the march. One could also argue that placing his body in full sight of schoolchildren is meant to reflect on the historiography (or lack thereof) of the state-sanctioned disappearance of the demonstrators. But there is something troubling here in the disjointed nature of the composition: the children are not looking. In fact, no one is looking. Ultimately, the depiction of the drowned man, reduced to an immobile corpse partially submerged in the material of the domestic space, speaks to the novel's own struggle to reconcile Algerian political agency with the politics of humanization, visibility, and "recognition" in which the novel is invested. It haunts Maffre's narrative of the bidonville's fight for the right to the city and insists that the reparative work for justice and inclusion is still unfinished.

The October 17 march is featured in the novel as a twelve-page flashback triggered by the women looking with Yamina through her old photographs. The flashback transmits the memory of the march and murder of Yamina's husband, Slimane, though the narrative is not from Yamina's point of view—in fact, it is not certain that the women ever talk about it. Rather, Maffre creates a cinematographic set of panels that distance the viewer from the characters we have come to know in their daily lives. While we can still recognize individual faces in the crowd, the panels move quickly through the events: from the organization of the march, to its departure, to police repression, brutality, and state-sanctioned murder, and finally to the family mourning Slimane's death.

Interestingly, at all points in the text, the march for independence is articulated in terms of economic justice, not decolonization. The revolution is termed a socialist one, and the crowd literally emerges from poverty. No talk occurs about the violence of colonial history, but Maffre does directly show us the violence of the "forces of order." While this might be a powerful move, given the history of representation of the massacre, the panels become more about French policing than Algerian political agency. Hannah Feldman critiques such a history of representation of the demonstration, writing:

> It bears repeating that all of the recent and better-known, book-length texts that aim to "recuperate" or restore the 1961 demonstration to its significance feature on their covers images of police coercion and violence. The eclipse of images of the marchers' confirmation of their "right to the city" in favor of their victimization encourages the sense that the most important aspect of the demonstration remains its suppression, thus continuing to place the question of history and its narrative out of the hands of those Algerians who protested.[48]

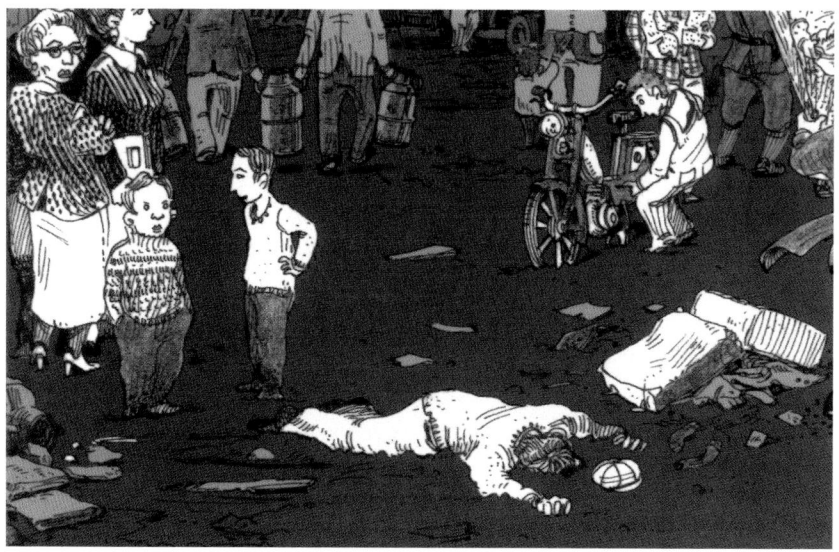

FIGURE 3.9. Detail of back cover, Laurent Maffre, *Demain, demain: Nanterre, bidonville de la Folie*, 2012.

On the final pages of this episode, Maffre presents us with a full-page spread of bodies floating in the Seine and quotes from four contemporaneous French newspapers describing what happened. The texts, which show the censorship of the massacre, jar with the image he presents to the reader. In citing four different contemporaneous journalistic accounts of the event, Maffre never relays what historians and activists have been working to reveal ever since: that over two hundred people were killed that day.

And so we return to the corpse in the mud on the cover that haunts Maffre's narrative of life in the bidonville. The political body lies partly subsumed in mud. The political body remains partially bound in the racial-colonialist aesthetics that Maffre attempts to trouble and dissolve. As Avery Gordon writes:

> Ghosts appear when the trouble they represent and symptomize is no longer being contained or repressed or blocked from view . . . haunting is that moment when things are not in their assigned places, when the cracks and rigging are exposed, when the people who are meant to be invisible show up without any sign of leaving, when disturbed feelings cannot be put away, when something else, something different from before, seems like it must be done.[49]

The figure on the cover can easily be overlooked, but it reappears from the inside of the novel in a new way, demanding that something else must be done. The unreasonable juxtapositions on the cover reveal their power at this moment, and the "ordinariness" of life that Maffre produces within the narrative is disrupted. Ultimately the project is an unfinished one, a project deferred. *Demain, demain* (Tomorrow, tomorrow) refers to a comment in the novel by an urban planner who tells the bidonville residents that they must continue to wait to be rehoused, to enter the city, to enter history. Social history, housing history, must still reckon with the political history that continues to haunt it.

In 2019, Maffre published the sequel to *Demain, demain: Nanterre, bidonville de la folie*. Entitled *Demain, demain: Gennevilliers, cité de transit 51*, the second volume picks up the story of Kader, Soraya, and their family in their temporary housing in the Cité de Transit 51.[50] The address is no longer Nanterre but the neighboring town of Gennevilliers. The date is 1973. But Slimane's ghost is still there.

Demain, demain: Gennevilliers, cité de transit 51 begins with images of rain and a funeral. Neighbors from La Folie come together to mourn the death of Raymond Jobert, the owner of the local garage next to La Folie who had welcomed and helped many of the characters in the first book. Kader, Soraya, and their neighbors now have been relocated to different "cités de transit" after the closing of the bidonville in 1971. When one of the characters asks what La Folie has turned into, another answers: "Ben . . . on reconnaît pas grand-chose. C'est comme si la Folie n'avait jamais existé. Ils ont fait un parc. Puis, autour, c'est que des parkings et des immeubles en construction." (Well . . . there isn't much to recognize. It's as if la Folie never existed. They built a park. And then around it, there are parking lots and apartment buildings under construction.) The neighborhood and its erasure weighs heavily on its former residents, and Maffre pairs this mourning with that of Raymond's death. As the rain continues and former neighbors huddle together, yet another body emerges. A very small panel on the top of the fifth page shows Slimane's body, floating face down in the Seine. The narrative text bubble notes: "Il y a douze ans, c'était Slimane." (Twelve years ago it was Slimane.) In some sense, it is just another unreasonable juxtaposition: Algerian Slimane dies from state-sponsored political violence and Frenchman Raymond dies of old age. The text cannot seem to process this difference analytically. Instead, it draws on affect: the deep mourning of death and loss to transmit the intensity of the injustice. But Slimane's small panel (the smallest size used by Maffre in this book) only makes its appearance in the text this one time. Slimane and October 17th, 1961, are not referred to again. Haunting but contained.

Unlike in the first volume, in this second book there is less emphasis on living conditions in the *cité de transit* (transitory housing), and Maffre focuses more on work conditions at the car factory. But when housing is presented, it is described as even more imprisoning and isolating than La Folie. Kader says: "Parfois je regrette l'époque du bidonville. Au moins, on était ensemble." (Sometimes I miss the time of the bidonville. At least we were together.) One woman says: "Au bidonville, on se sentait plus libres. Les policiers hésitaient à rentrer. Ils surveillaient La Folie de l'extérieur, comme s'il s'agissait d'une seule et même personne. Mais au Port c'est différent, chacun d'entre nous se sent contrôlé." (In the bidonville, we felt more free. The police would hesitate to enter. They would watch La Folie from the outside, as though it was one and the same person. But at the Port [Gennevilliers] it's different; each one of us feels under surveillance.) The structures of containment are not only more visible (the housing is surrounded with fencing and there is only one way out past the guard), their discriminatory essence is also felt more acutely.[51] One woman notes: "Ils ont mis des grillages partout. Ils veulent nous enfermer comme des poules." (They put chain-link fences everywhere. They want to lock us in like chickens.) Maffre illustrates this sense of imprisonment most dramatically in chapter 10, "La passerelle," which starts with a page of nine small squares featuring a small child playing, ending with an adult hand helping the child. A black line cuts across each square in a different diagonal. On the next page the small squares with black diagonals continue, and we see the French guard playing with his small child. The perspective changes halfway down the page, and now we see teenager Ali and his friends framed and cut by the black diagonals that are now revealed to be a chain-link fence separating the French guard's lush garden from the dusty compound.

The discussion about life in this new yet still-temporary housing is primarily carried out by the women characters who comment on the state of the *cité* while doing domestic work together outside, such as hanging laundry. Clean laundry is again a focal point in the fight against the stigmatizing discourse of mud. However, now that mud is not just in the courtyard; with the proximity of the housing to construction, it is everywhere and threatens to bury them. One woman notes: "Ils font des tas de terre pendant des semaines, une vraie montagne, et un jour, ils changent d'avis et ils enlèvent tout. Bientôt il n'y aura plus rien mais on ne pourra toujours pas traverser." (They create mounds of earth for weeks, a real mountain, and then one day, they change their minds and they take everything away. Soon there won't be anything left, but we still won't be able to cross [from the housing projects to the town].) The moving around of mounds of earth can be seen as construction realities and errors. But it can, and also should, be seen as a prolonged campaign of terror and societal exclusion, a state-administered randomness that threatens and prevents the families from feeling safe and "at home." Brian Massumi theorizes the relationship between threat and time in this way: "Threat is from the future. It is what might come next. Its eventual location and ultimate extent are undefined. Its nature is open-ended. It is not just that it is not: it is not in a way that is never over. We can never be done with it."[52] What differs in this volume is that in 1973, over ten years after their arrival in France, the discriminatory discourse of mud that marked Soraya and her family and its production of threat have intensified rather than lessened. What was thought to be temporary is now permanently temporary.[53] And the women realize that they can "never be done with it."

The Embodied Poetics of Possible Shared Futures in *Monique H., Nanterre 1961*

Amina Menia's concept of the family photo album as a pathway to past and future memory appears in Laurent Maffre's *Demain, demain: Nanterre, bidonville de la Folie* when Yamina and her female neighbors look through a tin of photographs of her life in the bidonville. The beginning of Mehdi Lallaoui's 2014 play, *Monique H., Nanterre 1961*, also begins with a box of photographs and the reconstitution of familial memory.

The opening of act 1, scene 1, gives the following stage directions: "Monique est vêtue d'un grand imperméable qu'une ceinture ensure à la taille. A pas lents, elle arpente sa baraque de long en large, une boîte de chaussures sous le bras. Sur le mur de planches, deux photos sont restées punaisées. Elle en décroche la première."[54] (Monique is dressed in a large raincoat that a belt secures at her waist. Taking slow steps, she paces around in her shack, a shoe box under her arm. On the wall made of planks, two photographs are still pinned up. She takes down the first one.) The stage directions continue to instruct Monique to look "sadly" at the photograph. This action triggers the scene: a monologue that reflects on her twelve years of life in the bidonville. She looks at yet another photo and reflects on the disappearance of her friend Fryette. Halfway through the scene she looks through more photographs from the box, making them "défiler une à une entre ses doigts" (pass through her fingers one by one).[55] For Monique, like Yamina, the family album is not organized and bound in a book but stored in a box, the order of photographs easily reshuffled.[56] Structured through loss and disappearance, Monique's family album collects the intimate experiences of people that she identifies as family but who are no longer there with her. We later find out that this scene occurs during the razing of La Folie with the demolition crew waiting outside her door.

This is not the first time that Mehdi Lallaoui has used the trope of the family album in connection with representations of life in the bidonvilles of Nanterre. The preface of Lallaoui's 1993 book *Du bidonville aux HLM* (From the shantytown to low-income housing) is titled "Un album de famille" (A family album), and indeed the book brings together stories and images from shantytowns across France, a disparate and diverse family that shares the experience of living in shantytowns and housing blocks from the end of World War II to the present. In that preface Lallaoui writes:

> Nous avons voulu ce livre comme un album de famille. Des gens, ces gens qui ont fait et qui font la banlieue parlent de leur itinéraire et font revivre une multitude de bribes de vie. C'est leur histoire, où chaque parole est un peu comme la lumière de ces milliers d'ampoules qui, la nuit, dans les grandes barres d'Argenteuil, de Mantes ou de Marseille, éclairent les passants de la cité.[57]

> (We wanted this book to be like a family album. People, these people, that made and make the suburbs speak of their journeys and bring a multitude of memory fragments to life. It's their history. Each word is a bit like the light of those thousand lightbulbs in the housing blocks of Argenteuil, Mantes, or Marseille that light up those who walk through the projects.)

In the play, the family album does more than recollect the brilliance of thousands of lives; it also testifies to their deep loss. In an interview with the French newspaper *Le Midi Libre*, Lallaoui talks about the family loss that occurred in the bidonvilles, not just at the hands of police on October 17, 1961, but in its traumatic aftermaths: "'Même si certains issus de ces bidonvilles ont réussi, nombreux se sont suicidés ou ont fini en prison. Cela a été une hécatombe pour la jeunesse,' a-t-il affirmé, relevant que plus de quinze familles ayant vécu dans ces bidonvilles ont eu des enfants qui sont morts avant l'âge de vingt ans." ("Even if some who came from the shantytown succeeded, many committed suicide or ended up in jail. It was like a disaster for the youth," he affirmed, revealing that more than fifteen families who lived in those shantytowns had children who died before the age of twenty.)[58] Rather than collecting the stories of loss of hundreds of residents, in the play Lallaoui zooms in on two people: Monique Hervo and a female Algerian FLN activist whose identity Lallaoui has kept anonymous per her wishes.[59] Inspired by these two women and their work and lives, Lallaoui fictionalizes them and centers their voices on the stage as Monique H. and Fryette.

As we know, Monique Hervo lived and worked for twelve years in the La Folie bidonville working with immigrant families to claim state benefits and access to health care, education, and social-support services. Her published notes and photographs draw on her extensive experience and interviews with residents. From a historian's perspective, she produced a copious archive of that time and place. In Lallaoui's play, the character Monique H. steps out of that academic archive and becomes a complex, embodied person. The fictional nature of the character Monique allows Lallaoui to hold the shutter open on the archive and to imagine her in different sets of relations, with both her own feelings and experiences and those of the other residents she served.[60]

Lallaoui underscores Monique's personal sense of belonging and shared life in La Folie in her opening monologue. Looking at her photographs of the bidonville, and the many lives they represent, she exclaims:

> Les gens ont vécu là, ils se sont aimés, entraidés, engueulés. Des couples s'y sont mariés. Des enfants sont nés, beaucoup d'enfants. Des hommes y sont morts. Les visages sont inquiets. Ils ont peur de perdre ce grand village qu'ils ont fondé ici. Un village, malgré toute la misère. Ensemble, nous étions un, et tout ce qui touchait un seul d'entre nous affectait tout le monde. Nous étions ensemble! . . . En-sem-ble.[61]

> (People lived there, they loved each other, helped each other, argued with each other. Couples married there. Children were born, many children. Men died there. The faces look worried. They are afraid to lose this big village that they established here. One village, despite all the misery. Together, we were one, and everything that touched one of us, affected everyone. We were together! . . . To-ge-ther.)

In this part of her monologue, "they" becomes "us," and a declaration of solidarity is made through the repetition and insistence on the word "ensemble" (together). These are intimate moments of remembered connection. Monique walks about in her shack, hums the lyrics to a song, repeats gestures made by residents as she recounts fragments of their stories, looks quietly out of the small window. She speaks to herself, to her photographs, and to her missing friend Fryette. When she addresses Fryette, she repeats her statements as if trying to break through the silence of her absence. The scene concludes with the questions: "Qu'es-tu devenue, la Fryette? Qu'es-tu devenue, mon amie?"[62]

(What happened to you, Fryette? What happened to you, my friend?) The scene is powerful in its ability to narrate togetherness while showing absence. Monique is with the community in spirit and memory but alone in her room. She carries their stories and embodies their gestures, but we see only her body in a space that is about to be razed. In this scene, Monique's evocation of Fryette's disappearance and absence sets up the nuanced themes of friendship, love, political solidarity, and proximity that the play will explore. If one accepts Cohen's critique of Maffre's enchanted representations of solidarity, then Lallaoui's take on solidarity, its limits, its fault lines, and its vulnerabilities is more satisfying. However, while Lallaoui presents a more complex dynamic, I would argue that he doesn't shatter the potential presented by enchantment either. Instead he weaves poetry and philosophy into the relationship between the two women as another space of expression and enchanted imagination.

Lallaoui slowly brings Monique and Fryette together and apart through the structure of the play. The play is organized into three acts with a short descriptive prologue and an epilogue in the form of monologue. As described above, act 1, scene 1, takes place in 1971 inside Monique's shack on the eve of its razing. The play returns to this time and place in the epilogue, but otherwise it takes place entirely in 1961 and in two locations: Monique's shack and the communal water fountain. As the back cover text describes: "Deux lieux sont signifiés dans cet univers de boue et de misère: l'intérieur d'une baraque (où vit Monique Hervo) et un extérieur, près de la fontaine à bras où les gens du bidonville font des queues interminables."[63] (Two places are shown in this universe of mud and misery: the interior of a shack [where Monique Hervo lives] and an exterior, near the communal fountain where the people of the shantytown stand in endless lines.) These two spaces are the two key structures of the bidonville—the somewhat protected and intimate private interior and the shared communal water fountain that provides water, the most important resource for life in the bidonville, from cooking and personal hygiene and to the washing away of stigmatizing mud. The first act presents three scenes of monologues by Monique; the second act presents Monique and Fryette in dialogue, two monologues by Fryette, and a monologue by Monique. These scenes span various points of time in 1961 leading up to the October 17 protest march. The final act takes place entirely inside Monique's shack during the evening and night of October 17. The four scenes in act 3 are bookended by dialogues between Monique and Fryette, with two scenes of monologues by Monique sandwiched in the middle. I have gone into such structural detail because it shows how Lallaoui brings the two women, their identities, and their voices

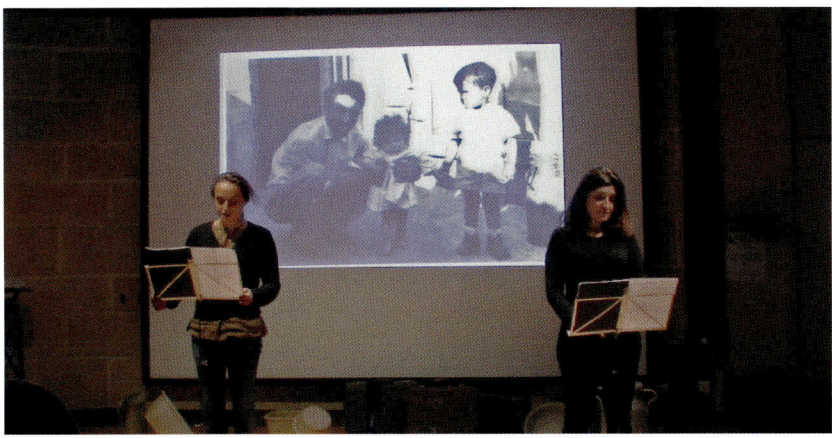

FIGURE 3.10. Screenshot of YouTube video excerpts of 2015 staged reading in Rennes, France, with actresses Leila Guérémy in the role of Fryette and Myriem Allal as Monique.

together and apart. At times they speak directly to each other; at other times they address the absent other in their monologues.

The play is entitled *Monique H.*, but the play is not about Monique alone. Rather, Lallaoui focuses on Monique and the relationships she forms. Reflecting the role Hervo chose for herself in real life, Monique is presented as a collector or a platform for the multiple stories and lives of others. Intimately joined to and in relation with Monique, the character Fryette also has her own voice. As Lallaoui described, the inspiration for Fryette came from an Algerian woman who insisted on remaining anonymous and who lived under multiple identities in order to survive and carry out her anticolonial political work.[64] As a reflection of their capacious identities, Lallaoui resists reducing Monique and Fryette to single national identities and histories, but he also doesn't erase the difference that identity and history produce between their structural positions. Monique has access to services and institutions that Fryette doesn't, and she cannot completely see and understand everything that Fryette does. Fryette also actively questions Monique's positions and actions from her perspective. Resisting a simple and direct representation honors the multiple positions these women held and further underscores how, as in Sebbar's text, the path to Algerian women's memory of the bidonville is not linear and is in fact necessarily indirect.

This particularly plays out in the performance of the play and the different embodiments of Monique and Fryette. Different casting choices made by different productions complicate any single reading of universal female experience, political allegory, or memory transmission. In one 2015 staged reading in Rennes, two French actors of North African descent play the two roles. In a 2019 touring production, Lallaoui described the play as a "pièce pour la lecture à une seule voix" (a one-voice play) and cast Algerian actor, author, and women's rights activist Nadia Kaci in both roles.[65] In a 2018 staged reading in Tulle, one of the actresses, Myriam Amarouchène, described herself as the daughter of an Algerian who marched in the October 17 demonstration, stating: "Mon père était à la manifestation de Paris, raconte Myriam Amarouchène. Il y a perdu des amis. Pour moi, le fait de lire ce texte est d'une importance sacrée."[66] (My father was at the protest in Paris, recounts Myriam Amarouchène. He lost friends there. For me, the act of reading this text is of sacred importance.)

The many different castings of the two female characters show that the line between French and Algerian, between first- and second-generation immigrants, is not always clear but is certainly not broken. Diana Taylor's articulation of the difference and relation between the archive, scenario, and the repertoire is useful here as we think about ways in which Lallaoui's play creates new embodied pathways for memory transmission. As Taylor writes in *The Archive and the Repertoire*:

> The bodies participating in the transmission of knowledge and memory are themselves a product of certain taxonomic, disciplinary, and mnemonic systems. Gender impacts how these bodies participate, as does ethnicity. The techniques of transmission vary from group to group. The mental frameworks—which include images, stories, and behaviors—constitute a specific archive and repertoire.[67]

What if we think of the actresses and casting through the prism of Sebbar's novel and its women's memory work? The actresses, like Amel, present themselves in proximity to an inherited family history they did not experience firsthand but that they understand to carry a "sacred importance." In the play, they literally put themselves into that history and create new embodiments of that memory.

Theater, or the embodiment of the characters, not only is a way to carry memory but also takes a didactic role in staging and rehearsing past and future relationships between the self and the community. In her 2014 memoir, *Vol au-dessus des bidonvilles: Parcours d'un femme des Aurès à Paris (1957–2010)*, Akila Hadjadj, who grew up in the Bidonville de La Folie and became one of the cofounders of the 1970s Nanterre theater troupe La Kahina, writes about her discovery of theater and the collective writing process of the play *Que les larmes de nos mères deviennent une légende* (May the tears of our mothers become a legend):

> Au cours de mes années universitaires, pendant lesquelles je voulais découvrir, entreprendre ou réaliser tant de choses, j'avais rencontré des camarades qui avaient à peu près le même âge que moi et surtout les mêmes objectifs: nous voulions parler de la vie de nos mères algériennes.... Pendant presque une année, nous nous réunissons plusieurs après-midis par semaine pour composer cette pièce. Nous étions entièrement consacrés à notre création. Une fois la pièce écrite, on distribua les rôles.... On répéta longuement, on créa les costumes, on trouva des chants de chez nous pour les intermèdes, ce fut une expérience vivante et exceptionnelle.[68]

> (During my university years, during which I wanted to discover, take on and create so many things, I made friends who were about the same age as me and who, most importantly, had the same objective: we wanted to talk about the lives of our Algerian mothers.... For almost a year, we met several afternoons a week to write this play. We were entirely devoted to our creation. Once it was written, we distributed the roles.... We rehearsed for a long time, we created costumes, we found songs from home for between acts. It was an exceptional experience, full of life.)

Hadjadj's description of the play's creation and performance as an experience that is *vivante*, or "full of life," echoes Taylor's definitions of the repertoire, which unlike the archive consist of "those acts usually thought of as ephemeral, nonreproducible knowledge."[69] As Taylor writes: "The repertoire requires presence: people participate in the production and reproduction of knowledge by 'being there,' being a part of the transmission. As opposed to the supposedly stable objects in the archive, the actions that are the repertoire do not remain the same. The repertoire both keeps and transforms choreographies of meaning."[70] As La Kahina member Youssef Boussaa describes, the La Kahina repertoire was not just a symbolic transformation of meaning, it also led to concrete social work. He describes how after the plays, women who were in abusive households, for example, would see themselves in the play and seek help from the actors and actresses. He writes:

> Every presentation is followed by a debate, sometimes bitter, between spectators and the actors/actresses. These debates provide an opportunity for people to narrate their personal experiences, experiences of constraints that were imposed on them, of being runaways, and the outcome of this for both them and their families. The [debates] also constitute a

time for meetings, prompted by the [exchange] of secrets and requests for help: "I saw your piece, I recognize myself in it, it's my history, I ran away as well, and now please help me for I am alone, sometimes I feel lost but it has done me good to meet you."[71]

As Emine Fişek recounts in her history of La Kahina, theater "had the ability to recall and make witness events, sensibilities, and expectations that may or may not have been shared, but whose unfolding could provide the groundwork for communication."[72] And I would also add reparative social action: in 1983, growing out of its theatrical work and talkbacks, La Kahina founded a shelter for North African immigrant women.[73]

Let us now turn more deeply to the relationship between Monique and Fryette as it develops in the play to see how representation, communication, and memory transmission take shape in Lallaoui's play. In act 1, Monique describes Fryette a couple of times through the multiple ways she is seen and understood by others. Referencing Fanon's articulation of a compartmentalized racial-colonial order, Monique explains:

> J'ai cette sensation bizarre de vivre dans deux mondes. Deux continents qui s'ignorent. Ils se frôlent et ne se voient pas. Ici, au bidonville de Nanterre, nous sommes sur une autre planète, alors que les Champs Elysées ne sont qu'à cinq kilomètres. Les gens de l'extérieur... ceux de l'autre continent, prennent Fryette pour une moitié folle, un peu niaise. En vérité, elle est très futée.[74]
>
> (I have the strange feeling of living in two worlds. Two continents who don't know each other. They rub against each other but don't see each other. Here in the shantytown of Nanterre, we are on another planet, even though the Champs-Elysées is only five kilometers away. The people from the outside... those from the other continent see Fryette as a half-crazy woman, a bit simple. But in truth, she is very clever.)

Those people outside of the bidonville space can only see Fryette as "half-crazy" or "simple" and reduce her to her environment of mud. But Monique insists that Fryette actively manipulates this dynamic to her advantage: "C'est ma meilleure amie. La belle sait lire, écrire et le dissimule très bien à l'extérieur. C'est elle qui rédige les comptes rendus du FLN dans le bidonville."[75] (She is my best friend. The beauty knows how to read and write, and she hides it very well to the outside. She is the one who writes up the FLN summaries in the shantytown.) Fryette conceals her capacities and performs the image assumed by French colonial society in order to move her political work forward. Monique describes a scene she witnessed when Fryette was approached by the police at the water fountain and asked for her papers. Fryette refuses to engage with the police, crying out, "Pas comprendre, pas savoir" (Don't understand, don't know).[76] Monique intervenes by telling the police to leave her alone but is rebuked by the officers. Meanwhile Fryette continues to cry out "pas comprendre, pas savoir" while other women arrive in solidarity and mutual protection: "Les femmes du bidonville, de plus en plus nombreuses, s'approchent des flics en leur criant *Nahdine Babek*."[77] (The women of the shantytown, greater and greater in number, approach the cops, shouting *Nahdine Babek* at them [literally: "May your father's religion be damned," but used as an insult equivalent to "Go fuck yourself"].) The police finally leave her alone, and when Monique and Fryette later meet up at Monique's shack, Monique learns that Fryette had been carrying two revolvers in her water cans. The statement "pas comprendre, pas savoir" that Fryette repeats can be read in two ways: she is communicating to the police that she doesn't understand what they are saying, but at the same time the phrase can be read as Fryette exclaiming that they don't understand or know her. Monique is able to see Fryette as her fuller self, and their friendship is born from that practice/act of recognition and ability to read and engage each other in multiple ways.

When Fryette first describes her relationship with Monique in act 2, scene 2, during her first monologue, she confirms this friendship—"Monique est mon amie" (Monique is my friend)—but also reveals that this was never a given.[78] She recounts the gradual building and deepening of trust between them since their initial meeting. This trust emerges from Monique's social behavior and political actions. At their first meeting at the water fountain, Monique stands in line with the others, and Fryette remembers her father telling her: "L'égalité entre eux et nous, nous les indigènes . . . ce serait lorsque plus personne ne profiterait de son statut ou de son origine pour double dans la file."[79] (Equality between them and us, us the natives . . . that will exist when no one takes advantage of their status or origins to skip ahead in the line.) When Monique and a priest help to transport an FLN militant to the Belgian border, Fryette's trust in her is cemented. It's important to note that Lallaoui doesn't construct their friendship through an assumably shared gender experience of the bidonville. Rather, it is the ethical and political that binds the two women together even if, or perhaps because, at times they disagree on strategies for action. Monique insists on nonviolence, based on Ghandi's teaching, while Fryette asks: "Comment peut-on être non-violent au milieu de tout cet enfer? Comment peut-on être non-violent lorsque chaque jour on nous humilie, lorsque chaque heure on nous désintègre, lorsque chaque minute on nous refuse notre humanité?"⁸⁰ (How can one be nonviolent in the midst of this hell? How can one be nonviolent when each day they humiliate us, when each hour they break us apart, when every minute they refuse us our humanity?) Lallaoui maintains the tension in the differing positionalities of their identities, never collapsing their differences and perspectives.

At the same time, Lallaoui retains and underlines their deep sorority. The play shows how this ability to dialogue through difference builds a bond that leads to an affirmation of life and love over death and terror. Fryette states: "Monique est mon amie, elle m'a ramenée à la vie. Lorsque je suis arrivée ici, j'étais déjà morte. Il ne suffit pas d'avoir un cœur qui palpite pour être vivante."⁸¹ (Monique is my friend, she brought me back to life. When I arrived here, I was already dead. It's not enough to have a heart that beats to be alive.) A survivor of a French massacre in her Algerian village, Fryette lives with the trauma of that event, and Monique helps her to process colonial violence by sharing with her the writings of Frantz Fanon. By reading Fanon and learning about his work with children orphaned by French violence, Fryette is able to think and speak of the future again: "Plus tard, moi aussi je serai comme Fanon. Je m'occuperai des enfants le jour et de la Révolution la nuit. Pfff... je divague encore... L'autre nuit, j'ai fait un rêve étrange... j'ai rêvé qu'à l'indépendance, au fronton de l'hôpital de Blida, le nom de Frantz Fanon s'étalait en grosses lettres."⁸² (Later, I too will be like Fanon. I will take care of children during the day, and take care of the Revolution at night. Pfff... I'm digressing again. The other night, I had a strange dream. I dreamt that after Independence, the name Frantz Fanon would be displayed in large letters on the front of the hospital in Blida.) She not only can see a future for herself but also is able to see a collective future, a postindependence Algeria where, as is the case today, Fanon's name is given to the hospital where he worked.

Fryette's slow healing enables her to see love as a framework for liberation and possible postwar repair. This is something that Monique also deeply believes in:

> Ne parle pas d'elle [la mort], Fryette. Parle de l'amour à venir et de la liberté. Parle de l'espoir de la fin de cette maudite guerre. Parlons des cœurs qui tambourinent, des jours heureux, parlons de la fête que nous organiserons ici, à Nanterre, le jour de l'indépendance, et de cette bouteille de Bourbon que nous nous sommes promises et que nous sifflerons ensemble.⁸³

(Don't speak of death, Fryette. Speak of love to come and of freedom. Speak of hope for the end of this cursed war. Let's speak of hearts that beat, happy days, let's speak of the party we will throw here, in Nanterre, the day of independence, and of that bottle of Bourbon that we promised each other and that we will drink together.)

Fryette acknowledges the connection between *love* and *liberation*, two words that carry potential healing and sustain her. In one of her monologues, Fryette recounts: "Monique m'a promis de me faire une robe pour le jour de l'indépendance. Elle me taquine aussi. Elle dit que cela pourrait servir pour mon mariage si par hasard, un jour, l'amour me tombait dessus... Avant de rencontrer ce bébé de Moussa, je n'y croyais pas du tout... Est-on capable d'aimer lorsque tout son être subit la guerre?"[84] (Monique promised to sew me a dress for independence day. She teases me as well. She says that it could also be used for my wedding, if by chance, one day, love fell upon me... Before meeting Moussa, I didn't believe in it at all... Is one able to love when one's whole being is subjected to war?) While Lallaoui introduces a romantic-love plot line between Fryette and Moussa, it is in the two women's relationship that the question is most deeply explored. How do Fryette and Monique care for each other, look out for each other, and make space for new dreams together? One form of care takes place when Moussa is arrested and Monique takes advantage of her identity as a French woman to make inquiries with the police. Another mutual form of care occurs when Monique and Fryette pray together for Moussa's return:

FRYETTE: Tu... tu crois en Dieu maintenant?
MONIQUE: Ben... pas trop, mais je vais quand même prier avec toi. Pour se faire entendre, deux voix valent mieux qu'une...
FRYETTE: Tu es ma grande sœur, Monique. "Deux voix valent mieux qu'une."[85]

(FRYETTE: You... you believe in God now?
MONIQUE: Well, not so much, but I will pray with you anyway. To be heard, two voices are worth more than one...
FRYETTE: You are my older sister Monique. "Two voices are worth more than one.")

Monique makes space for prayer and Fryette makes space for Monique's voice to join with hers.

Yet another form of mutual care is the creation of space against the confines of a racialized colonial order. Rather than through interior decoration or dance, as we see in Maffre, in Lallaoui's play this creation of space comes through shared reading. Together Monique and Fryette read and discuss political writing, anticolonial theory, and poetry. Lallaoui shows how in these literary conversations the women take refuge in writing that can contain their experiences, reflect their hopes, and ultimately create new epistemologies that are grounded in liberation. For example, in one conversation in which Fryette discusses her love of René Char's poetry, Lallaoui shows the women negotiating the entry point for a discourse on dignity:

> FRYETTE: J'ai dit à Moussa que... malgré la noirceur des textes qui le composent, et la mort de ses camarades de résistance... on sentait sous la plume de René Char l'espoir, une fois le nazisme vaincu, l'espoir d'un monde meilleur. L'intuition d'un jour où tous les possibles seraient convoqués, où l'homme ferait "triompher la dignité de l'esprit."... "Chaque fois qu'un homme a fait triompher la dignité de l'esprit, chaque fois qu'un homme a dit non à une tentative d'asservissement de son semblable, je me suis senti solidaire de son acte."
> MONIQUE: Voltaire!
> FRYETTE: Non, Frantz Fanon![86]
>
> (FRYETTE: I told Moussa that... despite the darkness of the texts he wrote, and the death of his comrades in the resistance... one feels hope in René Char's pen, the hope of a better world once Nazism is vanquished. An intuition of the day when all that is possible will be summoned forth together, when man will make "the dignity of the human spirit triumph."... "Every time a man makes the dignity of human spirit triumph, every time a man says no to an attempt to subject another, I feel myself in solidarity with his act."
> MONIQUE: Voltaire!
> FRYETTE: No, Frantz Fanon!)

Monique misreads the Fanon quotes in Fryette's articulation for Voltaire, and Fryette corrects her, shifting the prism of understanding from a French universalist perspective to one emerging from a specifically racialized colonial paradigm. But what is even more powerful in this exchange is not the negotiation of attribution or origin but the way in which Fryette shapes the very discourse itself. The sentence that most stands out to me in the above quote is when Fryette states, "L'intuition d'un jour où tous les possibles seraient convoqués" (An intuition of the day when all that is possible will be summoned forth together). Fryette's epistemology, her poetics, emerge from this statement of radical irreducibility, an affective premonition ("intuition") of a larger world of possibilities brought together.

Monique challenges Fryette's turn to poetry from a Marxist perspective, saying, "La poésie n'est qu'un pansement... le caviar des pauvres" (Poetry is but a Band-Aid... the caviar of the poor), but Fryette replies, "Non, Monique, la poésie est bien plus que ça... C'est un baume, un état, un éclat de cristal, une arme, la plus intime et la plus efficace des armes" (No, Monique, poetry is much more than that. It's a solace, a state, a burst of radiance, a weapon, the most intimate and effective weapon).[87] In this statement Fryette links poetry to healing and repair (*baume*), to a burst of radiance (*un éclat*), to an intimate and efficacious tool in the war for life. This list of words arranged without causality echoes the vocabulary of affect in which shimmers and unnamed intensities provide another entry point to knowledge and possible world making.

Let us take a closer look at the poetry that Fryette characterizes as an affective and affecting "hymne à la vie" (hymn to life).[88] Toward the end of the play, Lallaoui reveals the text of the René Char poem that Fryette shares with Moussa and Monique, the first verse of Char's "À***":

> Tu es mon amour depuis tant d'années,
> Mon vertige devant tant d'attente
> Que rien ne peut vieillir, froidir,
> Même ce qui attendait notre mort
> Ou lentement su nous combattre
> Même ce qui nous est étranger,
> Et mes éclipses et mes retours.[89]

> (You have been my love for so many years,
> It makes me dizzy to think of so much hope,
> And my dizziness won't be aged, or cooled;
> Even by what waited for our death,
> Or slowly learned how to fight us,
> Even by what is foreign to us,
> Or by my eclipses and my returns.)

In this verse, we see the connection between love, irreducibility, and liberation that Fryette and Monique discuss together. In later verses Char develops the sense of irreducibility of the other in a relationship of love even further, writing:

> Chacun de nous peut recevoir
> La part de mystère de l'autre
> Sans en répandre le secret.[90]

(Each of us can receive
The mystery of the other
Without divulging it.)

While Char wrote the poem in the aftermath of World War II, we can read the poem in the context of the Algerian war, repositioning the subject "nous" from French to Algerian resistance fighter, or more specifically "nous" to Fryette/Moussa and Fryette/Monique. Indeed, the title of the poem "À***" (To . . .) holds space for and invites these different inhabitations.

Whereas acts 1 and 2 build up relationships that sustain the two women, act 3 stages Fryette's disappearance and the breaking of that bond amid and in the immediate aftermath of the October 17 march. In the first scene, Fryette and Monique are shown in Monique's shack discussing the demonstration. Monique points out the danger of police violence, but Fryette encourages her to attend, and the two leave together. In the stage directions for the scene, Lallaoui suggests the possibility of playing a video clip of Jacques Panijel's film *Octobre à Paris* showing Algerians leaving the bidonville to attend the rally. The story of two women is decentered as the story of a people is shown. In the following scene Monique returns alone and in a short monologue recounts the events of the march: Fryette's joy and the police officers' violent suppression and murder of the protesters. Scene 3 is an even shorter monologue by Monique in which we learn of Fryette's disappearance. Scene 4 stages Fryette's reappearance and finds her deeply traumatized by what she witnessed at the march. As Fryette recounts the horrifying deaths that she witnessed, Monique tries to slow down her narrative, interrupting it with phrases such as "Regarde-moi, Fryette, regarde-moi, c'est moi, Monique, ton amie, sors de ce cauchemar, reviens avec nous . . . Reviens avec nous" (Look at me Fryette, look at me, it's me Monique, your friend, come out of this nightmare, come back to us . . . Come back to us); "Calme-toi" (Calm yourself); "Tais-toi" (Be quiet), and "Repose-toi" (Rest yourself).[91] Monique's exhortations do not succeed, and Fryette continues to speak the images in her head. She finally asks Monique for the dress she has been sewing. When Monique questions her and asks her again to slow down and rest, Fryette takes the dress and leaves, delivering her final words to Monique: "Je n'ai plus le temps, Monique, je n'ai plus le temps. Il faut que j'aille réveiller nos sœurs, nous repartons manifester, nous repartons réclamer notre liberté."[92] (I no longer have the time, Monique, I no longer have the time. I must go to wake up our sisters, we are going back to protest, we are going back to demand our freedom.) The enchanted circle of love that bound the two women in the "nous" of solidarity is broken in this scene.

Fryette seizes her liberty, the dress and the possible love it represents, from Monique and the space of the bidonville. She does not return.

What does Fryette's disappearance mean? How does it relate to the disappearance of the place itself? Lallaoui resists a romanticized vision of anticolonial female activism. Unlike in films such as *Vivre au paradis* or *Bataille d'Algers* where the final images of female fighters are celebratory, Lallaoui takes the path of feminists who have written about women's silencing after the revolution.[93] Women that are making history are also in a painful relationship to that history, often silenced, often disappeared. His female political agent exits the stage in determination but also carrying pain and trauma. Likewise, he resists conveying a sense of permanence to the space of the bidonville. Like in the first scene, the epilogue takes place in 1971, ten years after Fryette's disappearance, on the eve of the razing of the bidonville. Monique is alone in the shack but speaks to Fryette as though she were still there. She asks Fryette if she read the famous poem Kateb Yacine wrote about the October 17 massacre. She narrates the return of the other women to the bidonville after the marches, the death of Fanon, the celebration of Algerian liberation, the liberation of Algerian prisoners, and the subsequent ten years of living and fighting for better conditions in the mud of the bidonville. Monique mourns Fryette's absence and with it the absence of shared emotions. When speaking of Algerian independence, Monique exclaims: "Et comme j'aurais aimé que tu partages avec nous cette joie intense, profonde, débordante!"[94] (Oh how I would have loved for you to share this intense, deep, and overflowing joy with us!) In speaking of the bidonville's resistance to policing, again she says: "Qu'est-ce que j'aurais aimé que tu voies ça, Fryette!"[95] (How I would have loved for you to see that, Fryette!)

In this monologue, Monique addresses her testimony to a missing witness, an absent interlocutor, a silence. In this play, Lallaoui addresses his testimony to a now missing place and its people, and a historiographical silence that is too slowly being broken. The La Folie bidonville was an unstable form of mass housing and an ambivalent and impermanent space of political and social engagement. By starting and ending his play with the razing of the housing, he underlines its precarious existence and the difficulty and importance of retrieving its memory, especially of the lives of the women who lived in and created the place. The play attempts to repair the distance between social and political love, between social and political intimacy, and build what Laurent Berlant might name "other kinds of infrastructure for proximity ... that will bind us to the world in which we find each other; or bind us to each other and, in such binding, make a world."[96] In so doing, the play rehearses a repair and stages a possibility for a fuller understanding of women's lives in La Folie.

A Tale of Two Parks

In Sebbar's novel, Amel's grandmother tells Amel that the former bidonville was located near the "grand parc" (large park).[97] Likewise, in volume 2 of Laurent Maffre's *Demain, demain*, the former bidonville residents learn that a park has been built where their homes once stood. The park they refer to is undoubtedly the park now known as the Parc André Malraux.[98] Approved by André Malraux in 1964 when he was minister of cultural affairs, designed by Jacques Sgard, and built between 1972 and 1981, the park was proposed to be a space of art and culture with a museum and four art schools.[99] What does it mean that already in 1964 a whole branch of state government was looking at a bidonville but only seeing a future site of high culture? Put differently, what does it mean that a whole branch of government was imagining a construction zone for cultural buildings and spaces of leisure while thousands of underserved people lived in remarkably difficult conditions? I suppose these questions aren't surprising. One need only look at histories of race and city zoning across the world to recognize this as a widespread dynamic in which whole neighborhoods are never seen and certainly never seen as having futures. Faced with the monumentality of a twenty-five-hectare park that was conceived as a cultural green space for the La Défense *grand projet*, it is not surprising that Amel struggles to see her family history in the space. Ultimately, the museum and art schools were never built, and needless to say, the Parc André Malraux does not bear any historical markers remembering La Folie either.

La Folie had only one mailing address for the entire neighborhood: 127 Rue de la Garenne. There is another small park near this address today: 290 Rue de la Garenne is the site of a small park run by the association Vive les Groues, founded in 2019. Like the Parc André Malraux, it is a future-facing project of its (now neoliberal) time. According to the association, the park is a site to unite neighbors in collective projects revolving around a fruit-and-vegetable garden, gathering space, and campground. Initiated by the NGO Yes We Camp, Vive les Groues seeks to build a collective future-looking space that inserts nature and urban agricultural practices into development-heavy city areas. As the mission statement elaborates:

> Dans des contextes de friche, de vacance ou d'urbanisme transitoire, Yes We Camp peut engager un protocole partenarial qui permet que ces espaces disponibles deviennent, pendant un temps donné, une zone de tentative possible et d'invention facilitée, à la rencontre de plusieurs ambitions: production locale, accueil des plus fragiles, relation au vivant,

développement des apprentissages, création artistique, réalisations collectives.[100]

(In the contexts of industrial wasteland, of vacancy or transitory urbanism, Yes We Camp can engage in partnership protocols that allow for these available spaces to become, during a certain time, zones of possibility and facilitated invention that meet several goals: local production, the welcome of the most fragile, the relationship to living organisms, the development of apprenticeships, artistic creation, collective productions.)

As we can see from photographs of Vive les Groues, a lush green garden has been created at 290 Rue de la Garenne (see figure 3.11), an otherwise postindustrial site next to the highway. Metal shipping containers have been used to create an indoor gathering space and café. The association hopes to bring people together through "micro-projets inclusifs et expérimentaux" (inclusive and experimental micro projects).

Would Amel see herself and her family history any more in this park than the other? Decorated metal housing containers and a garden rising from the mud of construction echo the work of women in the bidonville past. But the echo rings oddly, refracted through a neoliberal structure in which inclusion works by choice and opting-in, where an interest in camping out and urban farming is often more of a lifestyle choice than a political necessity, and where history seems strangely absent.[101]

The artistic repair work that I have discussed in this chapter expands the limited and bounded geographic space where the park currently sits. That work is important but also fragile considering how the physical space has been transformed and how that time period continues to be both remembered and forgotten. As the Vive les Groues garden shows, the capacious lives, networks, histories, and built environments of women that were once on this land can easily disappear from sight.

Likewise, women can, and too often do, disappear from contemporary artwork's remembrances of October 17, 1961. A recent, powerful piece by Franco-Maghrebi artist Wiame Haddad illustrates this point. In her 2020 piece "A propos d'une chambre occupée (vision d'une soirée d'octobre 1961)," Haddad reconstructs a room from 1961 (perhaps from the Bidonville de la Folie) and then photographs it (see figure 3.12). She fills the housing with signs of life interrupted: drying socks, half-eaten food, an open newspaper, an unmade bed. In the doorway, we see a man leaving this home to join the October 17 march.

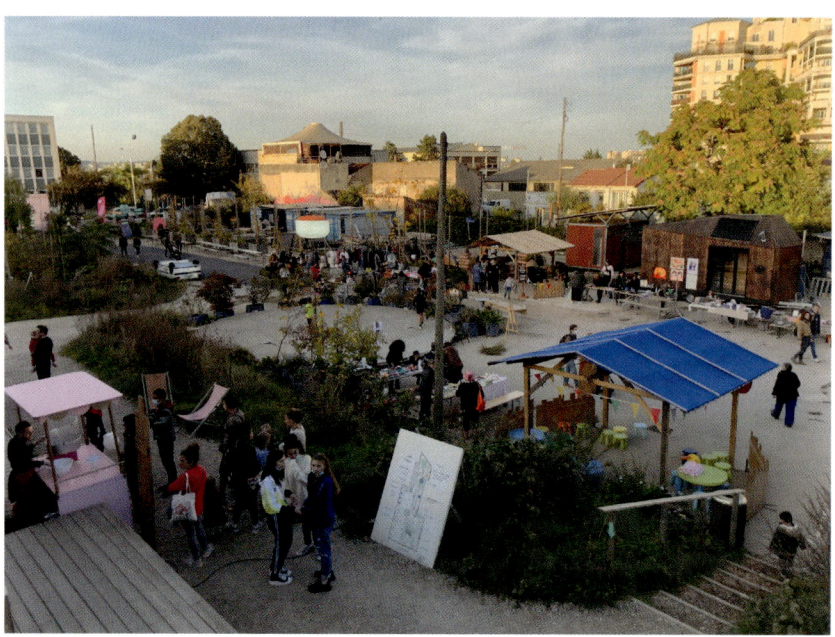

FIGURE 3.11. Image of Vive les Groues, Yes We Camp website (yeswecamp.com).

Haddad explains the genesis of the piece as a response to French denial of colonial history and more specifically the history of the October 17 march, which she had never studied or heard about as a young person. I quote her at length:

> My research was an attempt to understand that era despite the emptiness.
>
> I never wanted to reproduce violent images that I had already seen. I wanted to create an image out of the existing void. I didn't want to create an abundance of images around this event, instead, it was an exercise in constructing a single image that attempted to encapsulate the nuance and depth of this historical event.
>
> ... There is also a piece of construction wood that I include in the top left corner of the frame, right outside the door to this room. This is a conscious revelation that this is a built set and not a photograph documenting a reality. I wanted to point to the constructed nature of the image (even archival photos) and beyond that, to gesture towards images that are missing altogether. It is about creating an image out of the absence of photos of these moments.[102]

Haddad emphasizes that her photograph is a construction, a singular reparative gesture to other missing images. She doesn't articulate what these absent

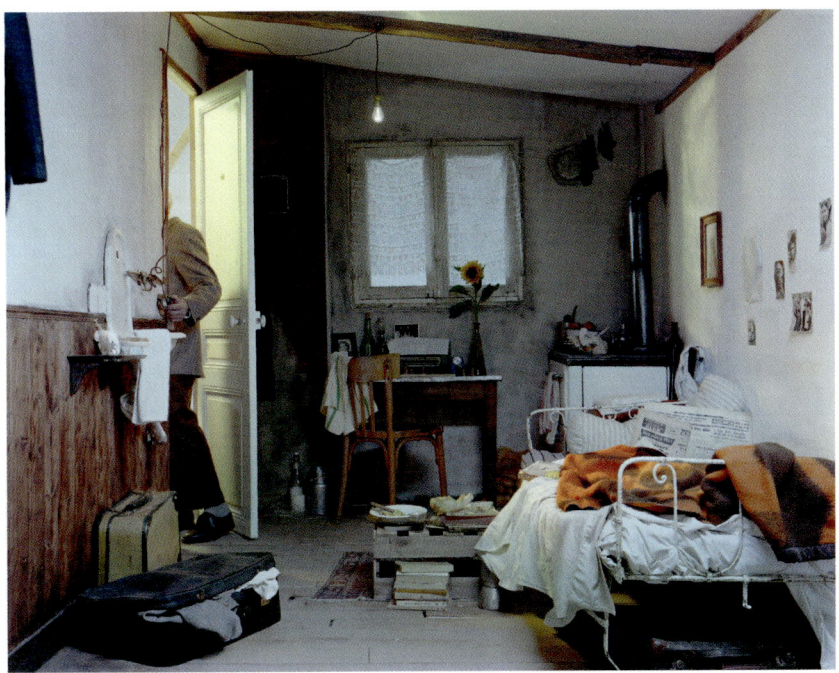

FIGURE 3.12. Wiame Haddad, *À propos d'une chambre occupée (vision d'une soirée d'octobre 1961)*, 2021. Inkjet print based on film photography, 150 × 168 cm. Courtesy of the artist.

images might be or of whom, but as this chapter has argued, the history of women's participation in the march and women's lives in the shantytowns is still slight and underdocumented and calls for attention. That Haddad chooses to represent a male space of housing and male political work is her decision, and I do not question the importance of her perspective. Her artistic choice reveals, however, how repair work related to gender is all the more important to sustain.

Contemporary artwork such as Sebbar's novel, Maffre's graphic novels, and Lallaoui's play slowly and carefully explore women's memories of La Folie through different types of photographic, ethnographic, and embodied archives and through the imagination of different pathways of retrieval and repair. Their work remembering women and their social and political lives are crucial engagements that repair housing history but, even more importantly perhaps, attempt to rebuild once-capacious structures for solidarity, security, and support for the future.

Conclusion

Touching Feet and Moving Hands: Art's Repair from
Affective Gesture to Capacious Home

Meryem Jazouli dances on and next to buildings in Casablanca. Her body takes on the cityscape through gesture: her arms echo the shape of construction cranes, her upright form speaks to the high-rise towers, her hands touch walls, momentarily uniting bodily and architectural skins. Artwork's practice of repair often takes the form of a gesture—a visual sign, a sonic signal or an embodied movement that opens a pathway to meaning. In the context of colonial-era mass housing, how might those gestures point us to more capacious understandings of the possibility of home?

In 2011, Jazouli led a dance workshop with women in the Casablanca SOCICA housing project as part of a two-day music, dance, video, storytelling, and artwork celebration of the neighborhood entitled Nass SOCICA: Veiller par le geste (People of SOCICA: Watching/caring through gesture).[1] Accounts of Jazouli's workshop describe a sense of curiosity, lightness, and laughter as women experimented with different movements and poses in the space around them. Photographs focus on women's legs and lower bodies as they move across the floor. In one particularly powerful image, we see two sets of feet touching each other—an intimate gesture that signals connection and proximity between two women (see figure C.1).[2] This gesture momentarily gives shape to the affects of connection and belonging emerging from that space, affects that

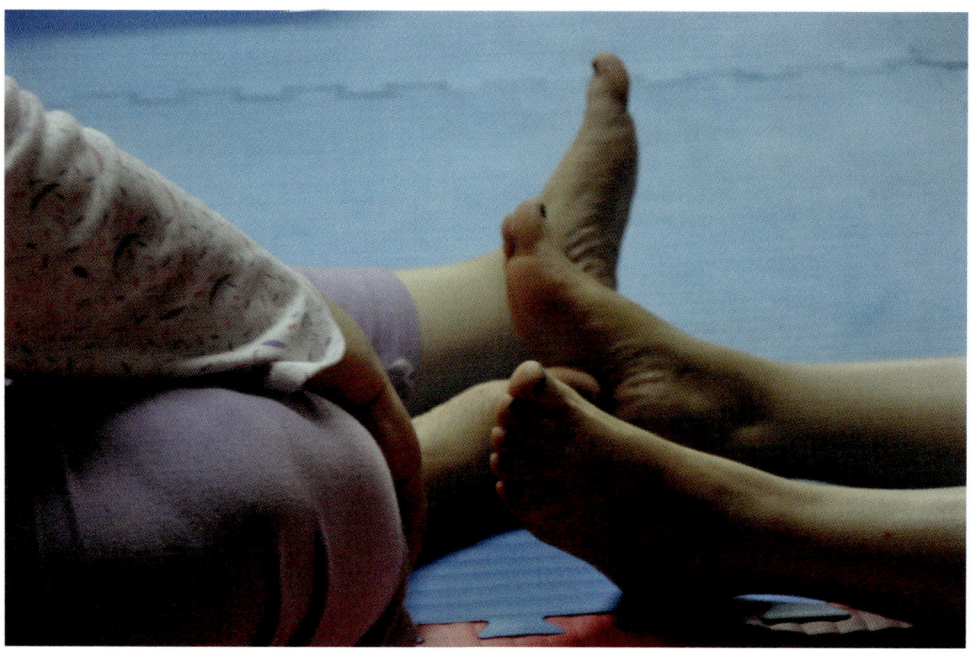

FIGURE C.1. Photograph from Meryem Jazouli, *Cuisine corporelle*, 2011. Dance workshop. Image courtesy of the artist.

bind the two women to each other and to the ground they sit upon. These are touching feet, both literally and figuratively.

Disciplines such as dance theory, art history, linguistic anthropology, literary theory, film, and performance studies have each paid attention to gesture and its staging of the relationships between body and meaning.[3] Despite a wide variation in definitions of what gesture is and does, many disciplines tie gesture to a precedence or incipience of meaning, defining gesture as an embodied action that precedes or points the way toward something else, whether that be verbal meaning, a fully articulated argument, or an executed act of a social, political, or performative code. Furthermore, gesture's capacity to carry incipience relates to its capacity to hold or shape prelinguistic affect. As Carrie Noland writes: "Performed gestures have the capacity to move us—in all senses. As types of 'modeled energy' (Eugenio Barba's term), gestures give shape to affects that might not have precise, codified, or translatable meanings."[4] Gesture holds and shapes affect before translation attempts to turn affect into meaning.

Artwork's reparative gesture, like the affects it carries and shapes, can be imprecise or not easily translatable, but the gesture is not empty. Rather, quite

166 CONCLUSION

the opposite, artwork's reparative gesture is a capacious point of departure. In her work with women in the SOCICA neighborhood, Jazouli names gesture (*le geste*) as the starting point for a communal coming toward each other and a reclaiming of shared forms and bonds. During the two-day event, participants were invited to engage with "un espace vivant où les gestes de ceux qui y habitent les unissent dans un dialogue, ouvert, qui resserre les liens. Des gestes créateurs qui parlent de chacun de nous dans un présent partagé et dans un espace commun" (a living space where the gestures of those who reside there unite them in dialogue, open dialogue, that tightens what binds. Creative gestures that speak to each of us in a shared present and in a common space). Participatory gestures were centered with the understanding that "chacun fera le geste d'être au milieu des autres en ayant le sentiment fort d'être intimement relié sous une quelconque forme aux autres" (everyone will make the gesture of being in the middle of others with the strong feeling of being intimately linked to others through some sort of form).[5] In these quotes taken from the Nass SOCICA flyer, gesture is seen as having the ability to unite and open dialogues in a common space, and the common space here is a colonial-era mass housing project that is also a "living space" in both senses of the word. SOCICA is a space where people live, and it is also a space alive and vibrant.

In writing of encounters in shared space, art historian Serge Gruzinski states that repair "often consists in inventing a way to insert one world into another, not in a gratuitous manner, but to yield meaning and social customs."[6] In chapter 1, we saw dancer Lahcen Zinoun struggle with the limited space and opportunities for art in the SOCICA housing project. In *The Piano*, the insertion of the piano into his family's house inserted one already established world into another without much consideration of the social customs of that world. Jazouli's 2011 SOCICA project attempts repair differently; it brings together professional and amateur dance into a guided practice of exploratory self-expression and co-creation. This is not the insertion of one closed art system into another but the co-creation of new vocabularies of the body, self, and space. Jazouli's attention to the common space of mass housing highlights the existence of another type of commons: "an infrastructure for experimentation" that emerges from "cooperation, sharing, self-empowerment, collaboration, and coordination among peers."[7]

From a different angle, Oussama Tabti's 2019 artwork *Sweethome!* reparatively inserts the hands of the laborer into the world of the architect.[8] For this work, Algerian artist Tabti invited older Maghrebi men to draw sketches while talking about where they lived when they first arrived in France in the 1940s and 1960s to work in construction. As the men describe their living conditions,

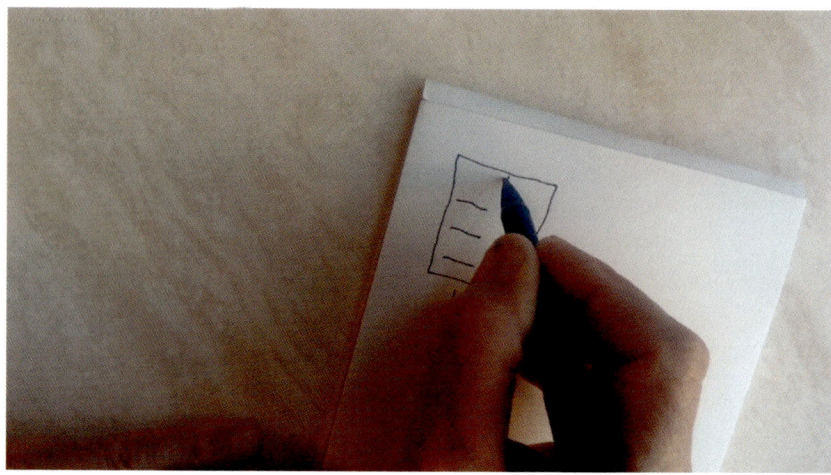

FIGURE C.2. Still from Oussama Tabti, *Sweethome!*, 2019. Video and drawing installation. Courtesy of the artist.

the camera focuses on their hands, hands that draw squares and lines on blank pads of white A5 paper (see figure C.2). The drawings are abstract—gestural lines and shapes that emerge as they talk about their housing in shantytowns and overcrowded apartments in Nanterre, Marseille, and Nice. The hands are worn and calloused but also cared for, clipped nails on fingers tinged reddish-brown from nicotine.

As the viewer watches their hands, we see a dance of connection and disconnection between form and meaning, between presence and absence.[9] Hand gestures punctuate and supplement their drawing and storytelling. And while Tabti presents each man's story separately, the repetitive hand gestures in the film show many lines of connection between the men, their experiences, and the forms they took. Structures of exclusion and isolation thus give way to a deeply shared experience, and in that moment, authorial voice and authority literally change hands. As in the scene in Couturier's film on Climat de France, described in chapter 2, in which a man holds a cell phone that plays a 1950s-era film reel about the housing project, the hands of residents appropriate architectural history and legacy, and pass it between them. In Tabti's work, former construction workers tasked to build French mass housing projects but relegated to self-built shantytowns produce hand-drawn sketches that in their abstract forms echo modernist pen and paper drawings of architects. The hands are moving, both literally and figuratively, in the contradictory affects they reveal about the meaning of home: exclusion, exploitation, and a sense of ownership and pride.

The feet and hands in Jazouli's and Tabti's artworks produce affective gestures that point toward possible repair in the context of colonial-era mass housing. Touching feet point toward a female appropriation of male-dominated built environments in the SOCICA housing project. Women's movement, women's interpretation of space, and women's shared laughter reconfigure the occupation and possession of space, creating a safe and even joyous collective space of well-being. Moving hands invite the repair of an architectural history of racialized erasure. Gestures that emerge from and pass through men's hands signal the possibility of repairing the distance between bidonville and high-rise, between marginalizing representations and centering self-constitution, between the isolation of individual stories and the solidarity of shared experience.

In *Potential History: Unlearning Imperialism*, Ariella Aïsha Azoulay asks, "When can those made near-worldless feel at home?"[10] For Azoulay, home means belonging to the world, defined as a place, time, and practice of common care. It is not a question of restoring a past world; it is a question of remaking that world and that home. In concluding this book, I would like to repeat her question in the context of colonial-era modernist mass housing and the artwork that seeks to repair it. When can marginalized and excluded peoples feel at home in the context of colonial-era modernist mass housing?

In some respects, the women and men who have lived in colonial-era mass housing have always labored to create a home in a world constructed in and from exclusion and alienation, and in which state administration of neglect and threat leads to conditions of "permanently temporary" housing. They have been repairing and reinventing their built environment from the moment of stepping foot into it, transforming it as much as they can into their own shared space: a home that creates refuge, shelter, and care in a world structured to contain or expel them. As AbdouMaliq Simone might put it, they have been living both "within and beyond capture."[11] And they certainly haven't been waiting for artwork to do this for them.

That their lives and their creative relationships within, alongside, and beyond mass housing are still rarely recognized as having value by dominant histories—political, social, or architectural—necessitates epistemological repair. Azoulay writes that undoing and unlearning imperial history and its legacies necessitates a rewinding of history to foundational moments of imperial violence and asking what might have been different. She urges us to rethink those split seconds that came before the creation of defining images and founding documents, when something could have been different, when there was/is a potential other way of being in what Imani Perry terms "right relation with each other."[12] Rewinding history to ask "What *could have happened*, what *could have been prevented*, that which *should not* have been possible, *could not ever* have been possible, *ought not to* have happened"?[13] is a political act of imagination, and these questions, when asked incessantly, constitute a labor of repair.[14] Ultimately the goal is not to right history but to labor for a "shared world of common care."[15]

Through maximizing exposures and reworking relations, the artwork in this book rewinds to the times this mass housing was ontologically defined as a space of nonbeing, a negative space represented as less-than. Through its attention to affect and gesture, artwork registers moments that precede fixed images and words, and points us to the physical and immaterial wounds that have broken both space and sense of home. Affect and incipience in artwork hold potential for political action and social change. At their very core, they unsettle what might be seen as settled history and structures of domination.

Yet, the artwork in this book not only looks back in time. It also imagines and articulates futures for mass housing that are more capacious and that exist beyond narrow existing visions. Both Jazouli's and Tabti's pieces create new gestural vocabularies through feet and hands to show what it might mean to inherit colonial housing and pass it on to the future generations. In this sense, artwork is both poetic and political, constantly creating other angles and frameworks so that these built environments may continue to be seen and known differently.

Whether artwork's reparative gestures produce anything more than affective instances of incipience, or epistemic moments of potential departure toward something that may or may not be transformative, is not the point here. Unlike material or monetary reparations, incipience and potential is harder to measure and evaluate as political or social action. Indeed, how would we evaluate the "effectiveness" of an intense moment of sudden possibility—a possibility of transformation, of shifting, of belonging, of imagining a different way of being in this world? (And why should we use metrics of existing political, economic, and social structures to evaluate a gesture that seeks to bring us beyond the limits of these systems?) Instead, this book has taken art on its own terms and attended to its poetics, its affective gestures, as potent and incipient and full of possibility even when repair seems incomplete or somehow falls short.

In conclusion, let us return again to Jean Sénac's poem "Istiqlal El Djezair" (Algerian independence), discussed in chapter 2. It was published on the eve of Algerian independence, at that moment of incipience and potential. Sénac writes:

> Peuple architecte
> Sur chaque cicatrice une pierre est posée
> La mémoire s'ouvre—grenade d'abondance
> Bonne faim pour ce peuple jeune
> De pain et de savoir
> Jubilation et Paix
> Il y a pour cette Cité
> Un chant à mettre en place.[16]
>
> (Architect people
> A stone is placed on every scar
> Memory opens up—a grenade of abundance
> A deep hunger for this young people
> For bread and for knowledge
> Jubilation and Peace
> For this Mass Housing
> There is a song to put in place.)

The gesture that the poem articulates here, that of people building new environments upon the scars of the past, is a reparative gesture that brings together past and future horizons of abundance. As in Jazouli's and Tabti's work, there is no longer a separation between architecture and the people. The people are an architect people. But it is the gesture in the final two lines that moves me most: "For this Mass Housing / there is a song to put in place." The poetic gesture not only invites the creation of art to celebrate mass housing. This decolonial gesture claims that songs, works of art, can become new foundational documents that unsettle history and put colonial mass housing and its people in a rightful place, in right relation to their futures.

This book has been an exercise in listening carefully to Maghrebi artwork and its articulations of repair for colonial-era mass housing, from low vibrations underneath supposed silence to unsettling tremors and exuberant songs. This book is an accompaniment to the work of art and artists that labor to reclaim home space and communal time from histories of domination and narratives of exclusion. An accompanying register that seeks to amplify their poetics of repair.

ACKNOWLEDGMENTS

I would like to acknowledge the deep generosity of artists, colleagues, and friends who have taken time to enter into conversation with me on this project. I can't overstate how grateful I am to them for sharing their work, discussing ideas, reading drafts, and introducing me to new concepts and artwork.

The beginnings of this book predate the COVID-19 pandemic, and I am thankful for the opportunities I had to meet artists and present the conceptual beginnings of the project in person. In particular I thank my colleagues and friends for those foundational exchanges in Morocco: Hassan Darsi, Florence Renault-Darsi, Maud Houssais, Fatima-Zahra Lakrissa, Marion von Osten, Kader Attia, Salima El Mandjra and everyone at Le Cube art space in Rabat. Likewise, my colleagues and friends in the United States gave me opportunities to present early versions of the project that focused on affect and shantytowns. Thank you to Sheila Crane, Magali Compan, Cynthia Becker, Felicia McCarren, Carrie Noland, and Emma Chubb for your invitations and your indispensable engagements with the project.

The majority of the writing occurred after the pandemic started, and I am so thankful for the long WhatsApp calls, Zooms, and outdoor conversations that sustained the book's development during the height of the pandemic. I'm truly grateful to people for making the time to respond to my questions, to read, to talk, to look at things together, even as their worlds entered different periods of difficulty. I don't take that for granted. First of all, thank you Amina Menia, Stéphane Couturier, and Hamid Rahiche for your remarkable work and your generosity in taking the time to talk about it at length. Thank you, Medhi Lallaoui, Jim House, Lia Brozgal, and Meryem Jazouli for responding to questions in depth and sharing resources with me. Thank you, Brahim El Guabli, Omar

Berrada, and Kristen Scheid for reading early drafts of chapters and providing invaluable feedback and suggestions. Thank you to the Williams College Oakley Center for the Humanities and Social Sciences fellows in the spring of 2022 for their comments on the Climat de France chapter, especially my dear colleague Sophie Saint-Just.

I would also like to thank the Oakley Center for funding a manuscript review that brought together five amazing scholars and readers to engage with a draft of the entire manuscript in the summer of 2022: Sheila Crane, Hannah Feldman, Edwidge Tamalet Talbayev, Jeffrey Israel, and Denise Buell. Their critical engagement and enthusiasm for the project fueled its completion.

Thank you to my students at Williams College. My undergraduate research assistants tracked down texts both in the United States and in Morocco—in particular, thank you, Neftaly Lara and Ryan Buggy. My undergrad and grad students in my spring 2023 course on North African Contemporary Art and Practices of Repair wowed me with their comments and engagements with comparative theories of repair and reparations. Thank you to grad students Meghan Considine and Talia Abrahams for their editorial work on the final manuscript.

At Duke University Press, thank you to Elizabeth Ault for her enthusiastic support of the book project, to Benjamin Kossak for shepherding the book into production, and to Ihsan Taylor for his attentive work on the book's production. Thank you also to the entire production staff at Duke UP, some of whose names I now know and others whose names I look forward to learning. I am extremely grateful to Williams College, particularly the Office of the Dean of Faculty and the Oakley Center for the Humanities and Social Sciences for their financial support enabling me to print the book in color.

Finally, I would like to acknowledge a deeply supportive group of women scholars whose conversations and long-lasting friendships have meant the world to me. Thank you, Theo Davis, Denise Buell, Sheila Crane, Jackie Hidalgo, Magali Compan, and Mérida Rúa.

To my family, parents Ella and Andy, parents-in-law Marc and Merle, and children Stella and Margot, thank you for your unending support and love. Last, but never least, thank you Matthew, for your brilliant insights into all things sound and music and for your remarkable ability to bring laughter and joy into our lives.

NOTES

PREFACE

1. This latest census number reflects the arrondissement of Ben M'Sik, also referred to as Ben M'Sick or Ben Msik in transliterated Moroccan Arabic. The Prefecture d'Arrondissements Ben M'Sik, which includes Ben M'Sik and Sbata, counted 248,138 residents. Haut-Commissariat au Plan, *Recensement général*.

2. "Casablanca, Morocco Metro Area Population 1950–2023," Macrotrends, accessed June 2, 2021, https://www.macrotrends.net/cities/21891/casablanca/population.

3. These moving television reports chronicled the last evictions from the area: Reportage 2M, "Āḫir āyām kāryān bn msīk" (Last Days of Karian Ben M'Sik), September 10, 2015, YouTube video, https://www.youtube.com/watch?v=RzAq34ycSfc; and Hespress, "Kāryān bn msīk—al-ḥqīqa al-mtʾakhira" (Karian Ben M'Sik—A delayed truth), March 11, 2016, YouTube video, https://www.youtube.com/watch?v=P_0II2JvYHI.

4. See Arrif, "Le Passage précaire," and "Fragments d'une enquête."

5. Arrif, "Fragments d'une enquête," 29.

6. See Pieprzak, "Beautiful Grave," and "Participation as Patrimony."

7. For a complete history and visual documentation of the collective, see *La Source du Lion de 1 à Z*.

8. Joris and Tengour, *Poems for the Millenium*, 715.

9. Zrika, "Danse de Ben M'Sik," in *Rires de l'arbre à palabre*, 102–3 (my translation).

10. In particular, see Zrika, "Le Soleil de Ben M'Sik," also in *Rires de l'arbre à palabre*.

11. Zaki, "Transforming the City," 118.

12. Mbembe, *Necropolitics*, 90.

13. Salti, "Shall We Dance?" 170.

14. Jocelyne Dakhlia and Irene Maffi claim that poetry and the written text are the primary carriers of memory and patrimony in North Africa and the Middle East. Pierre Joris and Habib Tengour's 2013 volume on North Africa in the Poems for the Millennium series showcases a long history of poetry that begins with the earliest pictograms and ends with twenty-first-century poets, spans the region from Mauritania to Libya, and includes

translations from at least six languages. Dakhlia, *L'oubli de la cité*; Maffi, *Pratiques du patrimoine*; Joris and Tengour, *Poems for the Millennium*.

15. This statement appears in multiple essays and interviews. Cited in Alessandra, *Abdellatif Laâbi*, 21.

16. For full disclosure, I have lived in Casablanca and Paris on multiple occasions, but I have yet to travel to Algeria.

17. Simone, *Improvised Lives*, 124.

INTRODUCTION

1. Jouder, *Enfilade*. HDB is the abbreviation for Singapore's Housing and Development Board buildings.
2. Jouder, *Tiles*.
3. Jouder, "Poetics of Mass Housing."
4. Jouder, "Poetics of Mass Housing."
5. In his essay on repair and technology, Steven J. Jackson asks: "Can the fixer know and see different things—indeed, different worlds—than the better-known figures of 'designer' or 'user'?" Jackson, "Rethinking Repair," 229.
6. Popescu, "Three Tenses," 319.
7. Popescu, "Three Tenses," 319.
8. Popescu, "Three Tenses," 310.
9. Popescu, "Three Tenses," 315, 319
10. I am grateful to one of the external readers for the press for their call for strategic qualification of reparative potential and for this phrasing.
11. Kılınç and Gharipour, *Social Housing*, 2.
12. Architectural historians such as Jean-Louis Cohen, Monique Eleb, Zeynep Çelik, and Sheila Crane have started to show how typologies of mass housing such as shantytowns and apartment buildings did not evolve in a purely causal relationship but existed simultaneously, responding relationally to each other.
13. See Sheila Crane's forthcoming book, *The City in the Shadow of the Shantytown: A Critical History of the Bidonville*.
14. It is not my intent to erase mass housing sites or exclude artist's work in Tunisia, Libya, or Mauritania from this geography. Rather, this book is an experiment in putting specific sites, artworks, and histories in relation to forge a different, resonant, temporary, and nondefinitive geography. Talbayev, *Transcontinental Maghreb*, 6.
15. Key texts include: Crane, *Mediterranean Crossroads*; Crane, "Housing as Battleground"; Çelik, *Urban Forms*; Avermaete, Karakayali, and von Osten, *Colonial Modern*; Cohen and Eleb, *Casablanca*; Chaouni "Depoliticizing Group Gamma"; Henni, *Architecture of Counterrevolution*; Kılınç and Gharipour, *Social Housing*; and Cupers, *Social Project*.
16. Feldman, *From a Nation Torn*, 69.
17. As Léopold Lambert shows in his book *Etats d'urgence*, charting colonial history through comparison does not erase the specific histories of these spaces but rather puts them into productive spatial and temporal relations with one another. In his forthcoming book *Shantytowns and the City*, Jim House also turns to comparison, arguing that

shantytowns "constitute an unparalleled vantage point from which to analyze colonial internal migrations, urban history, re-housing and repression, everyday lived experience, anti-colonial resistance, and social memory since independence." Centering the Maghreb and producing comparative accounts when we consider the lives, afterlives, and futures of modernist mass housing moves us beyond narrow nationalist perspectives into deeper forms of relationality.

18. Benkirane, *Bidonville et recasement*.
19. Zaki, "Après le bidonville."
20. Zaki, "Après le bidonville."
21. Hamid Rahiche, interview by the author, February 2, 2021.
22. Benkirane, *Bidonville et recasement*.
23. Fanon, *Oeuvres*, 526, and *Wretched of the Earth*, 130.
24. Gordon, *What Fanon Said*, 20.
25. Gordon, "Through the Hellish Zone," 7.
26. Gordon, *What Fanon Said*, 23.
27. Mud and its appearance in artwork that engages the bidonville is discussed most fully in chapter 3.
28. I thank Brahim El Guabli for his comments on this terminology.
29. Sekyi-Otu, "Fanon," 53, 50.
30. For further reading on Moroccan and Algerian shantytowns as sites of political action, see the work of historian Jim House, specifically "Shantytowns in the City."
31. Simone, *Surrounds*, 11.
32. Simone, *Surrounds*, 7.
33. Azoulay, *Potential History*, 580.
34. For scholarship that focuses on architectural history and urban planning from this structural perspective, see Jim House's work. Scholarship that includes perspectives on mass housing from the ground-up includes: Silverstein, *Algeria in France*; Cohen, *Des familles invisibles*; Benkirane, *Bidonville et recasement*; Zaki, "Après le bidonville"; Arrif, *Le Passage précaire*, and "Fragments d'une enquête."
35. For more details on the design and construction of the two monuments, see Caillet, "Le Monument d'Alger."
36. Grabar, "Reclaiming the City," 403–4.
37. For more reading on this project, see Amina Menia, "Enclosed @Mosaic Rooms," accessed April 2, 2024, https://aminamenia.com/works/enclosed-at-mosaic-rooms/.
38. Reeves-Evison and Rainey, "Ethico-Aesthetic Repairs," 2.
39. Menia, ""Enclosed @Mosaic Rooms."
40. Best, "Anger and Repair," 80.
41. Slyomovics, "Repairing Colonial Symmetry," 208.
42. Massumi et al., "Affect and Immediation."
43. O'Sullivan, "Aesthetics of Affect," 128.
44. Avenue Mers Sultan, which cuts across a central district of formerly European colonial Casablanca, is known for its art deco and modernist architecture. It was also one of many sites of anticolonial resistance and demonstration, notably the July 14, 1955, anticolonial bombing of the Café Mers-Sultan that was followed by French

police suppression, anti-Moroccan violence by French residents, and a large Moroccan independence demonstration on the avenue where the Legal Frères building stood.

45. Kraftl and Adey, "Architecture/Affect/Inhabitation," 226.

46. Reed, "Bureaucratic Theory," 568.

47. Toufic, *Withdrawal of Tradition*.

48. Toufic's concepts as described by Finbarr Barry Flood, "Part 2: 'Staging Traces of Histories Not Easily Disavowed,'" *Post: Notes on Modern and Contemporary Art around the Globe*, April 14, 2016, https://post.at.moma.org/content_items/783-part-2-staging-traces-of-histories-not-easily-disavowed.

49. While Attia's work on repair is in some respects central to the conceptualization of this book, it is not the subject of the book and my analysis of his work is limited to this section. For further reading, there has been an abundance of scholarship dedicated to Attia's art and writing, notably by scholars such as Hannah Feldman, Kobena Mercer, Françoise Vergès, Achille Mbembe, Jacinto Lageira, Manthia Diawara, Tarek El-Ariss, Emily Apter, and Ana Teixeira Pinto, to name but a few. In 2021, Attia also started a multipart project entitled *Fragments of Repair* with BAK, basis voor actuele kunst, Utrecht and Attia's decolonial forum La Colonie, which brought together scholars, writers, and critics: Souleymane Bachir Diagne, Maria Hlavajova, La Colonie, Sven Lütticken, Wietske Maas, Catherine Malabou, Olivier Marboeuf, Jamila Mascat, Achille Mbembe, Wayne Modest, Omedi Ochieng, Stefania Pandolfo, Rachael Rakes, Rolando Vázquez, Françoise Vergès, and Ruth Wilson Gilmore. "Fragments of Repair," BAK, basis voor actuele kunst, accessed April 2, 2024, https://www.bakonline.org/program-item/fragments-of-repair/.

50. Attia, "Accident as Repair," 35:52–37:00.

51. Feldman, "As the World Constricts," 65.

52. Feldman, "As the World Constricts," 65.

53. This description relies on images of the exhibit and the detailed description provided in West, "Repair as Redemption."

54. This top-down aestheticizing gaze continues to this day when we think for example of Rem Koolhaas's engagement with shantytowns in Lagos.

55. In her forthcoming book on the bidonville, *In the Shadow of the City*, Sheila Crane challenges the idea that shantytowns in North Africa were informal settlements, showing how they were in fact formal spaces administered by colonial administrations. When we look at televised reports of bidonville razing in Morocco, many inhabitants show official documentation from the colonial period that allowed them to inhabit their space. In particular see Hespress, "Kāryān bn msīk—al-ḥqīqa al-mtʾakhira" (Karian Ben M'Sik—A delayed truth), March 11, 2016, YouTube video, https://www.youtube.com/watch?v=P_oII2JvYHI.

56. Jackson, "Rethinking Repair," 229.

57. Jackson, "Rethinking Repair," 221.

58. Winant, "We Found Love."

59. I follow the definition of affect as it emerges in the work of Brian Massumi. Affect differs from emotion and feelings. Furthermore, as Eric Shouse elucidates: "Affect is not a personal feeling. Feelings are *personal* and *biographical*, emotions are *social* and

affects are *prepersonal.*" Unlike emotion and feeling, affect "cannot be fully realized in language" and is "always prior to and/or outside of consciousness." Shouse, "Feeling, Emotion, Affect."

60. The participants were Laure Augereau, Yasmina Bouzid, Zineb Benjelloun, Aicha El Beloui, Nisrine Chiba, Armelle Dakouo, Soraya El Kahlaoui, Hind Oudrhiri, Florence Renault-Darsi, Bouchra Salih, Katrin Ströbel, Corinne Troisi, and Syham Weigant.

61. For a discussion of these collections, see Pieprzak, "Nostalgia."

62. Ströbel and La Source du Lion, *De l'espace autre*, 5.

63. Freeman, *Time Binds*, xiii.

64. Richeux, *Climats de France*, 15.

65. Richeux, *Climats de France*, 19.

66. Manthia Diawara translates *pensée du tremblement* as "quakeful thinking" in his essay "Kader Attia: A Poetics of Re-appropriation." Michael Wieborn calls it "the thought of trembling" in "Glissant's *Philosophie de la Relation*." In chapter 2, I explore and develop Glissant's concept of "poetics of relation."

67. Glissant, *Philosophie de la Relation*, 54.

68. Glissant, *Philosophie de la Relation*, 56.

69. Wiedorn, "Glissant's *Philosophie de la Relation*."

70. Rivera, "Poetics Ashore," 242.

71. Rivera, "Poetics Ashore," 242.

72. In my reading of mass housing in Nanterre, I have constrained my analysis to artwork that engages the bidonville, and I do not engage the large body of literature, visual art, film, and music that has been produced since the 1980s on/from/of Parisian mass housing projects called HLM: *habitations de loyer modéré*. Contemporary French studies has addressed much attention to the HLM, and while more work certainly remains to be done from a Maghrebi perspective, this falls beyond the scope of this book and its chronology.

73. I borrow the verbs *endure*, *resist*, *insist*, and *assert* from Kristin Ross's introduction to her book *May '68 and Its Afterlives*. Ross uses the term *afterlife* to articulate that "the events of May '68 cannot now be considered separately from the social memory and forgetting that surround them. That memory and that forgetting have taken material forms, forms whose history I trace in this book" (1). I borrow the verb *live on* from Susan Slyomovics in her work on French Algerian monuments and statues, who like Ross shows how the memory of an event, as well as the object of its memorialization, is deeply embedded in living social memory. See, for example, Slyomovics, "Patrimoine."

CHAPTER 1. SONIC REPAIRS TO THE GRID

1. I will use the name *Carrières Centrales* when writing of the colonial-period bidonvilles and Hay Mohammadi to reference the neighborhood beyond its bidonvilles, and also its history from 1956 to the present.

2. Avermaete and Casciato, *Casablanca Chandigarh*, 8.

3. For further reading on Yto Barrada, see Chubb, "Differential Treatment"; Salti, "Sleepers, Magicians, Smugglers"; Karroum, "Yto Barrada"; Powers, "Yto Barrada'"; Enwezor, "Radiant Conflagration"; Azimi, "Tangerine Dreams."

4. Salti, "Sleepers, Magicians, Smugglers," 99.

5. Berrada, "Yto's Toys," 7.

6. Campt, *Listening to Images*, 4.

7. Souiba's novel was published in France under the title *L'homme qui voulait être comédien*.

8. For an anthropological treatment of daily life in Hay Mohammadi, see Cristiana Strava's 2022 book, *Precarious Modernities: Assembling State, Space and Society on the Urban Margins in Morocco*.

9. De Vroey and Nevens, "Heritage for the Future?," 460.

10. Miller, *History of Modern Morocco*, 150.

11. Sheila Crane's forthcoming book, *In the Shadow of the City*.

12. Cohen and Eleb, *Casablanca*, 246.

13. GAMMA was an official subgroup of the Moroccan CIAM chapter. The group was founded in 1951 by Michel Écochard and at the time included architects who were working with the Service de l'Urbanisme: Elie Azagury, Claude Béraud, Vladimir Bodiansky, Georges Candilis, Georges Godefroy, Bernard Kennedy, Pierre Mas, Shadrach Woods, and Jean-François Zevaco. For an important and nuanced history of the group, see Chaouni, "Depoliticizing Group GAMMA."

14. ATBAT-Afrique was the African branch of ATBAT, founded in 1947 by Le Corbusier, Vladimir Bodiansky, André Wogenscky, and Marcel Py. In 1951, an African branch was established in Tangiers and was led by George Candilis, Shadrach Woods, and Henri Piot.

15. Avermaete and Casciato, *Casablanca Chandigarh*, 120.

16. The Algerian delegation presented a grid of the Mahieddine bidonville in Algiers at the 1953 CIAM as well.

17. Avermaete and Casciato, *Casablanca Chandigarh*, 112.

18. Avermaete and Casciato, *Casablanca Chandigarh*, 94.

19. Von Osten, *In the Making*, 114.

20. One might argue that for some colonial urban planners and architects, these two forms of modernist housing were first and foremost aesthetic objects and then sites for housing. One might further argue that such an aesthetic approach and attraction still holds for contemporary architects (and photographers) like Rem Koolhaus who have abstracted the favelas of Brazil and the shantytowns of Nigeria into sweeping aerial blocks of color.

21. The photographs were reprinted at 60 × 60 cm in subsequent exhibits under the name *Reprendre Casablanca*.

22. Pieprzak, "Whitewash as Affective Platform."

23. Enwezor, "Radiant Conflagration," 24.

24. The grid has been described, analyzed, and debated by architectural historians at great length, including the "conceptual layer woven into the 8 × 8 grid . . . of difference and change." As Avermaete describes, Écochard "realized that urban development was not an equal or gradual process, and made a plea for urban planning approaches that could be differentiated and were open to change." The grid sought to provide a "stable framework" for an otherwise evolving built environment. Avermaete and Casciato, *Casablanca Chandigarh*, 156, 157. For further reading about the Écochard *trame*, see

Cohen, "Moroccan Group," as well as work by Aziza Chaouni, Tom Avermaete, Karim Rouissi, Sascha Roesler, Marion von Osten, Zeynep Çelik, and Monique Eleb.

25. Rouissi, "Housing," 4.

26. Avermaete, Karakayali, and von Osten, *Colonial Modern*, 33.

27. Chaouni, "Depoliticizing Group GAMMA," 76. To read more about evolutionary discourse in relationship to colonial-era mass housing in North Africa, see Demerdash, "Tunisia, 1940–1970."

28. Rouissi, "Housing," 10.

29. Canadian Centre for Architecture, "In Conversation: Yto Barrada & Takashi Homma," November 27, 2013, YouTube video, https://www.youtube.com/watch?v=C-P1uPDm_xY, 52:30.

30. Canadian Centre for Architecture, "In Conversation: Yto Barrada & Takashi Homma."

31. Slyomovics, *Performance of Human Rights*, 108. For more reading on Carrières Centrales in particular, see the work of Jim House and Léopold Lambert on political action in the Casablanca shantytowns in 1952 such as House, "L'impossible contrôle," and Lambert, "Casablanca 1952."

32. Campt, *Listening to Images*, 6.

33. For more about von Osten's capacious artistic, scholarly, and curatorial practice, see Hlavajova and Holert, *Marion von Osten*.

34. For more on the Bauhaus Imaginista project, see von Osten and Watson, *Bauhaus Imaginista*.

35. Hlavajova and Holert, *Marion von Osten*, 282. For more about the practice of Labor k3000, see Peter Spillmann, "Our Relation to All These Places is Operative: Practices Beyond Curating" in Hlavajova and Holert, *Marion von Osten*, 188–217.

36. The online project is no longer accessible due to changing user agreements and copyright related to YouTube.

37. Von Osten, *In the Making*, 92.

38. Von Osten, "From High-Rise," 113.

39. Diawara, "Kader Attia," 7.

40. Von Osten, *In the Making*, 81.

41. Von Osten, *In the Making*, 81.

42. Von Osten, *In the Making*, 83: In addition to dance and music videos, this included amateur crime stories shot on the roofs of the Écochard grid houses, atmospheric films of Casablanca's El Hank neighborhood during sunset, and so on.

43. Von Osten, *In the Making*, 82.

44. Pithouse, "Fidelity to Fanon," 228.

45. Younes Hariri, dir., *Calme-toi*, by Ach Man, 2019, YouTube video, accessed November 24, 2020, https://www.youtube.com/watch?v=gix3A3fESxc.

46. Translation by Zakaria Haterbach.

47. Younes Hariri, dir., *04-HM Psyco-Polini*, 2020, YouTube video, accessed November 24, 2020, https://www.youtube.com/watch?v=8_nIDwTYmcI.

48. Abderrahman Janyen, dir., *Hamza Namira Al Ayta (Cover vidéo)*, Izla Production, 2019, YouTube video, accessed November 24, 2020, https://www.youtube.com/watch?v=uCkJG24UHZg.

49. For a full biography, see Chebbak, *Lahcen Zinoun*. For an analysis of his later film work, see Tissières, "Femme écrite," and also Zaganiaris, "Une 'révolution symbolique'?"

50. Tissières, "Femme écrite," 136.

51. Cohen and Eleb, *Casablanca*, 246.

52. Cohen and Eleb, *Casablanca*, 245.

53. Connect Institute, "Comment Lahcen Zinoun a découvert la danse," April 24, 2018, YouTube video, https://www.youtube.com/watch?v=oCA6QqjQQIg.

54. Zinoun, *Piano*, 3:49–4:15. I am grateful to Zakaria Haterbach and Brahim El Guabli for their assistance in the translation and transliteration of quotes in Moroccan Arabic in this chapter.

55. Zinoun, *Piano*, 5:02.

56. In the film, the piece is performed by the Orchestre Philharmonique du Maroc under the direction of Jean-Charles Biondi, with Nicole Salmon at the piano.

57. Bouchfar, "Le piano."

58. Bouchfar, "Le piano."

59. Sakkouti/Zinoun is described as follows:

> A présent, c'était une violence sans nom, sublimée par ces allers retours à la maison/conservatoire pour accomplir tous les jours son double cursus d'apprenti musicien danseur, en plus la corvée contraignante d'une école trop modérément appréciée. Qu'à cela ne tienne! Sa forme délicatement longiligne, son corps d'athlète finement sculpté à coups d'exercices physiques intenses, lui conférait le statut de playboy de toute une partie de la ville."

> (In the moment, it was an unnamed violence, sublimated by those round-trips to and from the house and the conservatory in order to fulfill his double curriculum of apprentice musician/dancer, in addition to the constraining chores of a moderately appreciated school. But that doesn't matter. His delicately long form, his athletic body, finely sculpted from intense physical exercise, conferred upon him the status of a playboy in one whole part of the city.)

Souiba, *L'homme*, 59. The significance of the name Sakkouti in Arabic is silence—literally, "be quiet!"

60. Souiba, *L'homme*, 57.

61. Souiba, *L'homme*, 96.

62. Khalil Rais, "Hay Mohammadi Story."

63. For more on the relationship between literature, state violence, and Moroccan historiography, see Brahim El Guabli's important book *Moroccan Other-Archives*.

64. Merrahi, "Identité et éclatement."

65. Souiba, *L'homme*, 23, 24.

66. Souiba, *L'homme*, 23.

67. Souiba, *L'homme*, 23–24.

68. Souiba, *L'homme*, 24.

69. Souiba, *L'homme*, 25.

70. Saïd Aïssaoui, "Histoire: Le Noël sanglant du marché central de Casablanca," *Yabiladi*, December 24, 2017, https://www.yabiladi.com/articles/details/59468/histoire-noel-sanglant-marche-central.html.

71. Souiba, *L'homme*, 26.
72. Souiba, *L'homme*, 26.
73. Souiba, *L'homme*, 27.
74. Souiba, *L'homme*, 27.
75. My deep thanks to Jim House for asking Sakib about this episode.
76. Souiba, *L'homme*, 28.
77. Souiba, *L'homme*, 182. Abdelaziz Mouride was a political activist and prisoner detained in Derb Moulay Cherif. His memoir *Ici on affame bien les rats!* is a graphic novel that narrates his imprisonment for his political work.
78. Souiba, *L'homme*, 183.
79. Rouissi, "Housing," 4.
80. Hélène Harder and Karima El Kharraze, dir., *Casamantes*, forthcoming. See the Abel Afam website, https://www.abelaflam.com/film/casamantes/.
81. Souiba, *L'homme*, 24, 95.
82. Musée Collectif de Casablanca, *Radio de mon quartier*, SoundCloud, accessed July 27, 2023, https://soundcloud.com/mahattatradio/sets/radiodemonquartier-haymohammadi.
83. Muhanna and Sayyed, "Folk the Kasbah," 135. See also Sadiq, *Nass El Ghiwane*.
84. Omar Sayyed, Allal Yaala, Boujmii, and Laarbi Batma all grew up on Moulay Sherif Street in Hay Mohammadi. Muhanna and Sayyed, "Folk the Kasbah," 142.
85. Jaouad Mdidech, "Hay Mohammadi, mémoire d'un quartier mythique," *La Vie Eco*, accessed July 27, 2023, https://www.yabiladi.com/article-culture-659.html.
86. Initiative Urbaine, *Cariane central Hay Mohammadi*, 30.
87. Initiative Urbaine, *Cariane central Hay Mohammadi*, 30.
88. Initiative Urbaine, *Cariane central Hay Mohammadi*, 31.
89. Mona Badri, "Nass El Ghiwane: Story of a Moroccan Legend," *Morocco World News*, April 22, 2014, https://www.moroccoworldnews.com/2014/03/126067/nass-el-ghiwane-story-of-a-moroccan-legend.
90. Muhanna and Sayyed, "Folk the Kasbah," 144–45.
91. This translation is my amalgam of official and unofficial translations by Tom Bruce-Mitford and Brahim El Guabli.
92. A 2014 unofficial YouTube video made by a fan presents an interesting set of accompanying images. When the song gets to the verse "High-rise buildings go up / Shanties are buried," the video creator has inserted the movie poster from Nabil Ayouch's 2012 film *Horses of God*, an adaptation of Mahi Binebine's novel *The Stars of Sidi Moumen*, about the 2003 Casablanca suicide bombings. I published an article in *Research in African Literatures* entitled "Zones of Perceptual Enclosure: The Aesthetics of Immobility in Casablanca's Literary Bidonvilles" in which I am critical of the film and novel in its staging of the Moroccan bidonville as a breeding ground for terrorism, a reflection of state security discourses. In the video we see the invocation of negative space that is associated with the bidonville in those dominant discourses, discourses that I would argue do not reflect the sense of Hay Mohammadi espoused by the band. See Sarsari malika, "Nass El Ghiwane—Essemta," December 17, 2014, YouTube video, https://www.youtube.com/watch?v=hAX033iW0sw.

93. Muhanna and Sayyed, "Folk the Kasbah," 143. Omar Sayyed also wrote:

You know, our parents spoke in a dialect, a vernacular that was very poetic. It was creative and complicated, and they had learned it from their parents. That language is almost seductive in its descriptiveness, and it is full of proverbs, which are passed from generation to generation. Anyway, this is the language we sing in, and if it sounds different to you than the ordinary dialect you hear on the street, that's because it is older. Al-Mellih, one of Morocco's greatest writers once said that he loved Nass El Ghiwane because the language we used had a scent, a perfume. I think he meant that this language has the scent of an earlier time, before independence, before colonialism, when our great-great-grandparents were young. Most of our songs are written in that language, and we incorporated a lot of images from old proverbs. Our name, even. We found it in a *melhoun*:

> I ask the jasmine about you
> I asked the rose
> I asked the friends of Ghiwane about you.

Of course, we took proverbs from all over the county, not just the most famous ones—not just Abderrahman al Majdub. And we drew heavily from the poetry of the Amazighen, the Berbers. The creativity of the Amazighen is incredible; you don't find it anywhere else.

Muhanna and Sayyed, "Folk the Kasbah," 143.

94. Sonia Terrab, dir., *L7asla*, 2020, 2M, https://2m.ma/fr/programme/l7asla-hay-mohammadi-les-reves-brisees-dune-jeunesse-effervescente-aigrie-par-la-misere-replay-20201019.

95. *Ultras* is a term that describes soccer fan clubs around the world, not just in Morocco. For further reading about this type of fandom, see Doidge, Mintert, and Kossakowski, *Ultras*, and Close, *Cairo's Ultras*.

96. I thank Zakaria Haterbach for his transcription and translation of these lyrics, and Brahim El Guabli for subsequent transliterations in this section.

97. Terrab, *L7asla*, 2:06.

98. Terrab, *L7asla*, 4:33.

99. Terrab, *L7asla*, 14:53.

100. De Vroey and Nevens describe the continued presence of Dar Chahab as a spatial hinge for memory: "Remarkably then, this building—today quite demoted and underused—still proves to be able to figure as a spatial hinge for stories, persons, and actions to be remembered." De Vroey and Nevens, "Heritage for the Future?," 463.

101. Entertainment GO, "RAJA CASABLANCA FANS song," November 22, 2018, YouTube video, https://www.youtube.com/watch?v=KAdeLpa-Ylk.

102. De Vroey and Nevens, "Heritage for the Future?," 456.

103. De Vroey and Nevens, "Heritage for the Future?," 464.

104. De Vroey and Nevens, "Heritage for the Future?," 464.

105. Simone, *Improvised Lives*, 8.

106. Wylie, "Who We Are," 59.

CHAPTER 2. AFFECTING RELATION IN CLIMAT DE FRANCE, ALGIERS

1. Ghania Khelifi, "Le mal logement: Une plaie algérienne," *Mashallah News*, April 1, 2011, https://www.mashallahnews.com/le-mal-logement-une-plaie-algerienne/; Claire Guillot, "Images d'une utopie en miettes" *Le Monde*, August 4, 2014, https://www.lemonde.fr/culture/article/2014/08/02/images-d-une-utopie-en-miettes_4465868_3246.html; "Climat de France, la plus grande cité d'Alger," *Le Monde*, May 21, 2012, https://www.lemonde.fr/international/portfolio/2012/05/21/climat-de-france-la-plus-grande-cite-d-alger_1704557_3210.html.
2. "Alger, Quartier de Climat de France: Pourquoi l'émeute . . ." *La Montagne*, March 25, 2011, https://www.lematindz.net/news/3999-alger-quartier-de-climat-de-france-pourquoi-lemeute.html.
3. Benchicou, *Le mensonge de Dieu*, 70.
4. Glissant, *Poetics of Relation*, 160, 172.
5. Hamid Rahiche, phone interview with the author, February 2, 2021.
6. Çelik, *Urban Forms*, 154.
7. Pouillon, *Mémoires d'un architecte*, 207–8. Cited in Zeynep Çelik, "Bidonvilles, CIAM et grand ensembles" in Jean-Louis Cohen et al., *Alger: paysage urbain et architectures, 1800–2000*, Collection Tranches de villes (Paris: Imprimeur, 2003), 223.
8. Richeux, *Climats de France*, 15, 17.
9. Richeux, *Climats de France*, 9.
10. Tresfels, "Fear Within."
11. Richeux is also known for being the producer, host, and voice of multiple radio shows on the French radio station France Culture where she currently runs *Par les temps qui courent*.
12. Each chapter title consists of three identifying categories: the name of the character from whose perspective or whose story the chapter engages, a location that identifies the place of the story or where it was heard, and a date that references either when the action took place or when it was narrated (e.g., "Malek, Paris, printemps 1961").
13. Bernard cites the following quote from the novel: "Sur la petite table de la salle de lecture m'attendent . . . les six tomes de réunions de chantier de *Climat de France*. Lourds cahiers aux feuilles jaunies comme la pierre, 1954–1957." Bernard, "Histoire et paysages," 233. While Richeux hasn't talked at length about her research process for the novel in interviews, she does include a short citation page at the end of the novel for the three quoted passages from Pouillon and Chevallier that she inserted into the novel. In my analysis I will resist collapsing the author with the character and will refer to the author as Richeux and to the character as Marie.
14. Richeux, *Climats de France*, 19.
15. Marie Richeux, interview by Librairie Mollat, August 24, 2017, YouTube video, https://www.youtube.com/watch?v=ryEw_Z-YTog.
16. Thanks to Denise Buell for this evocative phrasing.
17. Richeux, *Climats de France*, 48.
18. Richeux, *Climats de France*, 15–16.

19. While French president Emmanuel Macron formally announced and condemned French colonialism and the brutality of the Algerian War, calling it a *war* for the first time, and while French universities are beginning to teach colonialism through the lens of oppression rather than civilization, the question of personal responsibility in and for the continuation of oppressive structures by "ordinary citizens" remains still far from consideration. Furthermore, as Susan Slyomovics articulates in her article on reparations for colonial crimes in Algeria, the legal French definition and practice of reparations still only applies to former settler-colonial populations. In the legal system, the settler is the one seen as having been wronged by Algerian independence. Slyomovics, "Repairing Colonial Symmetry."

20. Richeux, *Climats de France*, 214.

21. Richeux, *Climats de France*, 71.

22. Richeux, *Climats de France*, 72–73.

23. Richeux, *Climats de France*, 73.

24. Pouillon, *Mémoires d'un architecte*. Also see Gruet, Roy, and Pouillon, *Pouillon, une architecture durable*.

25. Richeux, *Climats de France*, 103.

26. There has been more scholarly attention recently to recuperating Chevallier's reputation and legacy. For example, see Fralon, *Jacques Chevallier*; Herbeth, *Jacques Chevallier*; and C. Chevallier, "Jacques Chevallier." Chevallier also wrote his own political account of his time as mayor: *Nous, Algériens*.

27. Richeux, *Climats de France*, 33.

28. Richeux, *Climats de France*, 91.

29. Richeux, *Climats de France*, 79.

30. Richeux, *Climats de France*, 193.

31. The last paragraph of the last chapter (titled "Malek, Meudon-la-Fôret, Fin Novembre 2016") describes Malek and Marie's final conversation before she leaves again for Algiers (the trip described in two preceding chapters). Marie recounts:

> Avant de me raccompagner à la porte, Malek me redit que, dans l'alignement de la fenêtre de la chambre, du couloir et de la fenêtre du salon, la lumière du soleil le perce comme lorsque, enfant, il s'attardait avec sa mère sur l'astre rouge au levant. Sur le palier, il me souhaite un très bon voyage. "N'oublie pas que ce qu'il y a d'incomparable là-bas, mais comme partout en fait, c'est la clarté. Surtout, pense à la clarté."

> (Before accompanying me to the door, Malek tells me again that in the alignment of the bedroom window with the hallway and the living room window, the sun pierces him like when he was a child and he would linger with his mother watching the red star in the east. On the landing, he wishes me a good journey. "Don't forget that there is something that is incomparable over there, well as everywhere really, and that's the clarity. Above all think of the clarity."

The concluding lines are Malek's but the clarity of light, sight lines, and perspective on history and human relations reflect Marie's desired project and its ultimate failure. I would argue that presenting everyone and everything "in their best light" ultimately rendered any hope for clarity incomplete because the very structures undergirding their relationality are not deeply questioned or challenged. Richeux, *Climats de France*, 259.

32. Richeux, *Climats de France*, 252–53.

33. Richeux, *Climats de France*, 254.

34. Richeux, *Climats de France*, 253–54.

35. For further reading on colonial legal classification and rights in Algeria, see Lorcin, *Imperial Identities*. For more on terms of identity classification and housing, also see Samia Henni, "From 'Indigenous' to 'Muslim.'"

36. Richeux, *Climats de France*, 49.

37. Richeux, *Climats de France*, 48.

38. Richeux, *Climats de France*, 58.

39. Richeux, *Climats de France*, 27.

40. Richeux, *Climats de France*, 30.

41. Richeux, *Climats de France*, 65.

42. Glissant, *Poetics of Relation*, 27.

43. Crane, "Housing as Battleground," 207.

44. Crane, "Housing as Battleground," 208.

45. Crane, "Housing as Battleground," 208.

46. Feraoun, *Journal, 1955–1962*, 279.

47. Feraoun, *Journal, 1955–1962*, 282.

48. This poem originally appeared in Sénac, *Matinale de mon peuple*. It can also be accessed in Barrat, *Espoir et parole*, 202–7.

49. Jean Sénac, *Oeuvres poétiques*, 309–404. I thank Sheila Crane for introducing me to this poem. To read more about it, see Ferdjani, "La poésie du métissage."

50. The exact length of the film is fourteen minutes and forty-eight seconds.

51. Menia has produced two versions of the film, one with narration in French and the other in English. Apart from language, the image sequencing and narrative content is the same. I will be citing the English version in this chapter.

52. Written for the 2020 exhibit *Notre monde brûle / Our World Is Burning* curated by Abdellah Karroum in a collaboration between the Palais de Tokyo and Mathaf: Arab Museum of Modern Art. Karroum, Danesi, and Grossi, *Notre monde brûle*, 184.

53. Amina Menia, Facebook interview for the Palais de Toyko exhibit *Notre monde brûle*, April 10, 2020.

54. Coussonnet, "Amina Menia."

55. Amina Menia, interview by author, July 18, 2023.

56. Menia, "Looping the Loop," 8.

57. Shevchenko and Sarkisova, "Album as Performance," 42–53.

58. Shevchenko and Sarkisova, "Album as Performance," 44.

59. Shevchenko and Sarkisova, "Album as Performance," 46.

60. Glissant, *Poetics of Relation*, 32, 27.

61. Amina Menia, "A Peculiar Family Album," https://aminamenia.com/works/un-album-de-famille-bien-particulier/.

62. I thank Sophie Saint-Just for this important observation.

63. I thank one of the press readers for their insightful comment that Pouillon's post-1962 Algerian state-financed housing and hotel projects are quite different from his colonial-era projects. For two recent articles on this work, see Merzelkad-Hallal, "Les complexes touristiques sahariens,"; Maïza and Kacemi, "Fernand Pouillon."

64. Glissant, *Poetics of Relation*, 27.

65. Coussonnet, "Amina Menia."

66. See Slyomovics, "Repairing Colonial Symmetry."

67. Reggad, "Economy of Hope."

68. Winant, "We Found Love."

69. Coussonnet, "Amina Menia."

70. Galerie Christophe Gaillard, "Stéphane Couturier—Biography" https://galeriegaillard.com/en/artists/10672-stephane-couturier/biography/.

71. Sausset, "Image of Reality," 32.

72. Sausset, "Image of Reality," 29, 33.

73. Jordan, "Not Yet Fallen," 182.

74. This story of Couturier's arrival in Climat de France was related to me in an interview with Couturier on February 1, 2021.

75. Hamid Rahiche, phone interview with the author, February 2, 2021.

76. "Alger, Climat de France," accessed February 10, 2021, http://www.thomaslallier.com/alger.

77. "Alger, Climat de France: La cité vue par le photographe Stéphane Couturier," *Paris Art*, July 6, 2017, https://www.paris-art.com/alger-climat-de-france/.

78. The festival transforms the Breton village of La Gallicy into an immense outdoor exhibition space where photography covers building facades as well as other more traditional exhibit venues.

79. "Climat de France," Festival Photo La Gacilly, accessed February 25, 2021, https://www.festivalphoto-lagacilly.com/node/126.

80. Gérard Leménager, "La Gacilly Climat de France Alger," 2018, YouTube video, https://www.youtube.com/watch?v=-4WX10CG71I.

81. "Videos," accessed April 1, 2024, https://www.stephanecouturier.fr/videos.

82. LE BAL, "Rencontre Stéphane Couturier—LE BAL LAB—24.09.2014," 2014, Vimeo video, https://vimeo.com/108119310.

83. LE BAL, "Rencontre Stéphane Couturier."

84. Stéphane Couturier, interview by the author, February 1, 2021.

85. Couturier describes his methodology of making video portraits as a further play on the video/photography loops he creates. The subject is filmed for about forty-five seconds, but afterwards he cuts and recomposes the footage to create longer works. Couturier displayed such eight video portraits in looped format in his 2014 *Hotel des Arts de Toulon* exhibit. See LE BAL, "Rencontre Stéphane Couturier."

86. Other French photographers and filmmakers have taken on Climat de France in recent years as more attention has been given to Pouillon's architectural legacy. See the work of photographers Stéphane Gruet, Franck Gautré, and Milan Neumann, and the documentary film by Marie Claire Rubinstein, *Fernand Pouillon 1912–1986, Une architecture habitée, Alger 1953–1957*.

87. Leica Internet Team, "Bruno Boudjelal: Algeria, Troubling Proximities" *Leica Blog*, February 26, 2013, https://www.leica-camera.blog/2013/02/26/bruno-boudjelal-algeria-troubling-proximities/.

88. Goni, "Bruno Boudjelal."

89. Hamid Rahiche, interview by the author, February 2, 2021.

90. Yasmine.H, "En photographie, l'hommage à Paz."

91. In Rahiche's words, evocative of Richeux's cited text about the inseparability of the history or buildings from the history of people, "Je raconte l'histoire du bâti et aussi l'histoire des gens."(I tell the story of that which is built as well as the story of people.) Rahiche, interview by author, Feb 2, 2021.

92. Hamid Rahiche, phone interview by the author, February 2, 2021.

93. Hamid Rahiche, phone interview by the author, February 2, 2021.

94. Bérengère Chamboissier, "Hamid Rahiche 'Alger, Climat de France,'" *Bérengère Chamboissier*, April 27, 2017, http://berengerechamboissier.fr/index.php/2017/04/27/hamid-rahiche-alger-climat-de-france/nouh0071.

95. nouh0071, "Climat De France, Casbah, Bab El Oued," Aug 21, 2011, YouTube video, https://www.youtube.com/watch?v=-vISZbQ9Fkk.

96. See DJ Snake, "DJ Snake—Disco Maghreb (Official Music Video)," 2022, YouTube video, https://www.youtube.com/watch?v=M7xQEdKHtvo.

CHAPTER 3. REMEMBERING AND REPAIRING WOMEN'S HOMES

1. Hadjadj, *Vol au-dessus des bidonvilles*, 37.

2. While there have been a tremendous number of scholarly works that explore mass housing and immigration in the Parisian suburbs (by Kenny Cupers, Paul Silverstein, Kristin Ross, and others), these studies have focused primarily on the large HLM housing projects and not on life in the bidonvilles. The bidonville is often the beginning of a narrative about high-rise project buildings but not the focus of the work. This has shifted over the past ten years, and there has been more attention afforded to bidonville history.

3. House and MacMaster, *Paris 1961*, 326.

4. Indeed, there are far fewer memoirs written by women from the bidonville. Two notable exceptions are Malika Bellaribi, *Les sandales blanches: L'Histoire vraie de la diva des banlieues*; and Akila Hadjadj, *Vol au-dessus des bidonvilles: Parcours d'un femme des Aurès à Paris*.

5. Mortimer, "Unearthing Hidden History," xvii.

6. Mortimer, "Unearthing Hidden History," xvii–xviii.

7. We can and certainly should argue with Sebbar's wide characterization of gender and space in Algerian culture, for Algerian culture is not one monoculture, and women's spaces certainly differ when approached through class and urban versus rural geographies. This is not the focus of this chapter, however.

8. Mortimer, "Unearthing Hidden History," xix.

9. Brozgal, *Absent the Archive*, 5–6.

10. Feldman, *From a Nation Torn*, 199.

11. Fişek, *Aesthetic Citizenship*, 5.

12. Fişek, *Aesthetic Citizenship*, 21.

13. See Mireille Rosello's 1997 article about the necessity to problematize representations of bidonvilles: "French *Bidonvilles* in the 1960s: Urban and Individual Initiatives."

14. Sebbar, *La Seine était rouge*, 7. Citations of English are from Mortimer's translation: Sebbar, *The Seine Was Red*, 2.

15. Sebbar, *La Seine était rouge*, 23; *The Seine Was Red*, 17.

16. Sebbar, *La Seine était rouge*, 31; *The Seine Was Red*, 26.

17. Brozgal, *Absent the Archive*. See chapter 3, especially 145–57.

18. This figure of a neo-Orientalist white man with knowledge of North Africa or the Algerian experience and harboring a love interest for the central female Beur character is first introduced in Sebbar's *Shérazade, 17 ans* and is a recurring character type in her work.

19. Sebbar, *La Seine était rouge*, 25; *The Seine Was Red*, 19–20.

20. Sebbar, *La Seine était rouge*, 44–45; *The Seine Was Red*, 41–42.

21. Sebbar, *La Seine était rouge*, 28; *The Seine Was Red*, 23.

22. Sebbar, *La Seine était rouge*, 32–33; *The Seine Was Red*, 27.

23. This includes Brozgal, *Absent the Archive*; House and MacMaster, *Paris 1961*; and Rothberg, *Multidirectional Memory*.

24. Hadjadj, *Vol au-dessus des bidonvilles*, 45.

25. Feldman, *From a Nation Torn*, 169.

26. Djebar, *Femme d'Alger*, 149; *Women of Algiers*, 136.

27. Maffre, *Demain, demain: Nanterre*. The graphic novel has no page numbers or chapter headings.

28. McKinney, "Naming the Place," 98.

29. Hervo and Charras, *Bidonvilles: L'enlisement*.

30. *Gourbi* is also a term prevalent in Tunisia, and one of the Tunisian terms for bidonville was *gourbiville*.

31. Hervo, *Nanterre*, 66 (my translation).

32. Hervo and Charras, *Bidonvilles: L'enlisement*, 42 (my translation).

33. Hervo and Charras, *Bidonvilles: L'enlisement*, 43.

34. Sayad and Dupuy, *Un Nanterre Algérien*, 51.

35. Hervo and Charras, *Bidonvilles: L'enlisement*, 163

36. Chevillot and Imache, "Beurette suis et beurette," 633.

37. Imache, *Une fille sans histoire*, 81–82.

38. The title of Malika Bellaribi's 2007 memoir of growing up in the Paquerettes shantytown in Nanterre, *Les sandales blanches: L'histoire vraie de la diva des banlieues*, also points to the distinction of spotless shoes as sign of respectability.

39. Murray-Román, "Hom(e)ing Devices," 1148.

40. Hervo, *Nanterre*, 69.

41. Silverstein, *Algeria in France*, 118.

42. Langston Hughes, "Dream Variations" in *Collected Poems*, and reprinted on Poets.org, American Academy of Poets, https://poets.org/poem/dream-variations.

43. Originally available at www.bidonville-nanterre.arte.tv.fr.

44. Cohen, "Demain, demain."

45. Cohen, "Demain, demain," 158.

46. Cohen, "Demain, demain," 160.

47. Rosello, "French *Bidonvilles*," 109.

48. Feldman, *From a Nation Torn*, 193.

49. Gordon, *Ghostly Matters*, xvi.

50. Maffre, *Demain, demain: Gennevilliers*. The second volume of this graphic novel, like the first, has no page numbers or chapter headings.

51. Police surveillance is constant, and a resident guard is nicknamed Rouge-gorge (Red Robin) by the residents because of his territorial stance. The guard's job is to collect rent, conduct move-ins, do maintenance, distribute the mail, control exterior lighting, and monitor who goes in and out of the site. He takes bribes in order to do any of these things and profits from his position of power. Maffre links the power structure in the *cité* to that of colonial Algeria: the guard is a French ex-military officer from the colonial army; he speaks Arabic.

52. Massumi, "Future Birth," 53.

53. Teenage resident, and perceived troublemaker, Mouloud tells his friends that they need to control their relationship to the mud and earth around them. Under his leadership, they create a soccer field and dig holes in the earth for fire pits to light up their field at night: "On peut compter que sur nous-mêmes. Les promesses qu'on peut nous faire, c'est que dalle. Mettez-vous ça dans le crâne." (We can only count on ourselves. The promises that they can make us, they are just nothing at all. Put that in your heads.)

54. Lallaoui, *Monique H., Nanterre 1961*, 9.

55. Lallaoui, *Monique H., Nanterre 1961*, 11.

56. In one staged production in Rennes on October 19, 2015, the backdrop consisted of a screen upon which Hervo's photographs of La Folie were projected. See "'Monique.H . . . Nanterre 1961' de Mehdi Lallaoui. Extraits," 2015, YouTube video, https://www.youtube.com/watch?v=SMTpZYXOlvI. Actresses are Leila Guérémy in the role of Fryette and Myriem Allal as Monique.

57. Lallaoui, *Du bidonville aux HLM*, 11.

58. "Un témoignage poignant." Djazairess: Un Témoignage Poignant, *Le Midi Libre*, February 19, 2012, https://www.djazairess.com/fr/lemidi/1202191401.

59. In an April 27, 2023, email exchange with me, Mehdi Lallaoui wrote:

Le personnage de Fryette est le condensé d'une militante du FLN ayant vécu dans la clandestinité dans le bidonville de Nanterre. Elle avait usurpé l'identité de sa cousine pour venir rejoindre des proches en France durant la période trés dur de répression en Algérie. Elle était messagère et circulait souvent déguisée en européenne dans tous les bidonvilles de la région parisienne. Elle dépendait directement du responsable de l'OS (l'Organisation Spéciale) de la super Zone Paris-Nord de la Fédération de France du FLN. Elle n'a jamais souhaité que l'on communique sa véritable identité. Elle est décédée en juillet 1995 en Algérie.

(Fryette is a condensed character based on an FLN militant who had lived clandestinely in the Nanterre bidonville. She had taken the identity of her cousin in order to join her relatives in France during the very repressive period in Algeria. She was a messenger, and she moved around all the bidonvilles of the Parisian region, often disguised as a European. She reported directly to the head of the Special Organization of the super zone Paris-North of the FLN French Federation. She never wanted her true identity to be revealed. She died in 1995 in Algeria.)

60. The play's name was also used by Lallaoui for a 2011 thirty-eight-minute documentary with Hervo, "Un témoignage poignant."

61. Lallaoui, *Monique H., Nanterre 1961*, 12.

62. Lallaoui, *Monique H., Nanterre 1961*, 14.

63. Lallaoui, *Monique H., Nanterre 1961*, back cover.

64. Mehdi Lallaoui, email to author, April 27, 2023.

65. "Programme Festival du Livre" 2019, accessed June 2021, http://www.lefestivaldulivre.fr/wp-content/uploads/2020/09/programme-FestivalduLivre2019.pdf; and Nadjila Bouzeghrane, "Monique Hervo: Actrice et témoin du 17 octobre 1961. Une vie dédiée aux plus faibles et aux opprimés," *El Watan*, October 10, 2019, https://www.elwatan.com/pages-hebdo/histoire/monique-hervo-actrice-et-temoin-du-17-octobre-1961-une-vie-dediee-aux-plus-faibles-et-aux-opprimes-17-10-2019.

66. Centre France, "Mémoire—Un bouquet d'animations à Tulle autour du 17 Octobre 1961," *La Montagne*, October 11, 2018, https://www.lamontagne.fr/tulle-19000/loisirs/un-bouquet-danimations-a-tulle-autour-du-17-octobre-1961_13012787/.

67. Taylor, *Archive and Repertoire*, 86.

68. Hadjadj, *Vol au-dessus des bidonvilles*, 121–22.

69. Taylor, *Archive and Repertoire*, 30.

70. Taylor, *Archive and Repertoire*, 20.

71. Cited in Fişek, *Aesthetic Citizenship*, 58.

72. Fişek, *Aesthetic Citizenship*, 59.

73. Fişek, *Aesthetic Citizenship*, 59.

74. Lallaoui, *Monique H., Nanterre 1961*, 17.

75. Lallaoui, *Monique H., Nanterre 1961*, 23–24.

76. Lallaoui, *Monique H., Nanterre 1961*, 17.

77. Lallaoui, *Monique H., Nanterre 1961*, 17.

78. Lallaoui, *Monique H., Nanterre 1961*, 31.

79. Lallaoui, *Monique H., Nanterre 1961*, 31.

80. Lallaoui, *Monique H., Nanterre 1961*, 34.

81. Lallaoui, *Monique H., Nanterre 1961*, 31.

82. Lallaoui, *Monique H., Nanterre 1961*, 36.

83. Lallaoui, *Monique H., Nanterre 1961*, 43–44.

84. Lallaoui, *Monique H., Nanterre 1961*, 36.

85. Lallaoui, *Monique H., Nanterre 1961*, 48.

86. Lallaoui, *Monique H., Nanterre 1961*, 41.

87. Lallaoui, *Monique H., Nanterre 1961*, 48.

88. Lallaoui, *Monique H., Nanterre 1961*, 41.

89. Char, "À***," in *À une sérénité crispée*, 17; "To . . . ," in *This Smoke*, 83.

90. Char, "À***," in *À une sérénité crispée*, 17 ; "To . . . ," in *This Smoke*, 83.

91. Lallaoui, *Monique H., Nanterre 1961*, 66–67.

92. Lallaoui, *Monique H., Nanterre 1961*, 67.

93. See, for example, Katarzyna Falęcka's 2021 exhibit and accompanying essay "Beyond Metaphor: Women and War."

94. Lallaoui, *Monique H., Nanterre 1961*, 72.

95. Lallaoui, *Monique H., Nanterre 1961*, 73.
96. Berlant, "Properly Political Concept," x.
97. Sebbar, *La Seine était rouge*, 10; *The Seine Was Red*, 2.
98. Alexandra Bogaert, "Le quotidien à la Folie mis en bulles," *20 Minutes*, March 29, 2012, https://www.20minutes.fr/paris/906989-20120329-quotidien-folie-mis-bulles.
99. "Come and Celebrate the 40th Anniversary of Parc André-Malraux!—Nanterre Info," Nanterre Info, September 16, 2020, https://m.nanterreinfo.fr/venez-feter-les-40-ans-du-parc-andre-malraux-.
100. "Vision," Yes We Camp website, accessed July 24, 2023, https://yeswecamp.org/vision/.
101. Correspondence with the organization revealed how their knowledge of the land they are working on is limited to the present and how evoking memories of La Folie are not a priority.
102. "Artist Spotlight with Wiame Haddad," ArteEast, November 3, 2022, https://arteeast.org/programs/wiame-haddad/.

CONCLUSION

1. The two-day event was on May 27–28, 2011, and took place in different locations in Hay Mohammedi. Participating artists included Youssef Amine El Alamy, Meryem Koufi, Daniel Barba Moreno, Hassan Darsi, Touria Haddraoui, Youssef Barrada, and Mohamed Elkhadiri.
2. I thank Meryem Jazouli for giving me access to her files and photographs of the event.
3. Noland, introduction, *Migrations of Gesture*.
4. Noland, introduction, *Migrations of Gesture*, 13.
5. Text from the flyer created for Nass SOCICA: Veiller par le geste.
6. Gruzinski, "From Holy Land," 216.
7. Iaione and Van de Velde, "City as a Commons."
8. Oussama Tabti, *Sweethome!*, 2019, Vimeo video, https://vimeo.com/420480380.
9. Llorens, "Oussama Tabti."
10. Azoulay, *Potential History*, 542. Other important passages include: "Worldly reparations are by definition the undoing of imperial structures; they cannot be envisaged in terms of inclusion into existing imperial structures" (540); "Reparations are part of the incessant labor of repair. Asking the question 'what are reparations?' again and again, with others, is not an attempt to find one ultimate answer—to finally be able to pay, in Truth's terms—but to affirm that it is through the potentializing of history that the labor of reparations could yield the recovery of a shared world of common care" (567).
11. This expression is a central concept Simone develops in *The Surrounds* (viii–ix).
12. Sugiuchi, "Traveling South."
13. Azoulay, *Potential History*, 556.
14. "An act of imagination is needed here, one that will allow us to recall that the political realm could be different." Azoulay, *Potential History*, 571.
15. Azoulay, *Potential History*, 567.
16. Sénac, *Matinale de mon peuple*.

BIBLIOGRAPHY

Alessandra, Jacques. *Abdellatif Laâbi: Traversée de l'œuvre*. Paris: Éditions de la Différence, 2008.

Arrif, Abdelmajid. "Fragments d'une enquête dans un bidonville de Casablanca." *Ethnologie française* 31, no.1 (2001): 29–39.

Arrif, Abdelmajid. "Le passage précaire: Du bidonville au lotissement; Anthropologie appliquée d'une mutation résidentielle; Le cas de Hay Moulay Rachid à Casablanca." PhD diss., Université Aix-Marseille 1, 1992.

Attia, Kader. "Accident as Repair." Lecture and discussion. Dartmouth Hood Museum of Art, January 30, 2018. YouTube video. https://www.youtube.com/watch?v=-ybUeLyNb3o.

Avermaete, Tom, and Maristella Casciato. *Casablanca Chandigarh: A Report on Modernization*. Edited by the Canadian Centre for Architecture. Photographic missions by Yto Barrada and Takashi Homma. Montreal: Canadian Centre for Architecture, 2014.

Avermaete, Tom, Serhat Karakayali, and Marion von Osten. *Colonial Modern: Aesthetics of the Past, Rebellions for the Future*. London: Black Dog, 2014.

Azimi, Negar. "Tangerine Dreams and Magic in the City: A Conversation between Negar Azimi and Yto Barrada." In *Riffs: Artist of the Year 2011*, edited by Yto Barrada, 125–31. Frankfurt: Deutsche Bank, 2011.

Azoulay, Ariella. *Potential History: Unlearning Imperialism*. Brooklyn, NY: Verso, 2019.

Barrat, Denise, ed. *Espoir et parole: Poèmes algériens*. Paris: Lierre et Coudrier Editeur, 1992.

Bellaribi, Malika. *Les sandales blanches: L'histoire vraie de la diva des banlieues*. Paris: Calmann-Lévy, 2007.

Benchicou, Mohamed. *Le mensonge de Dieu*. Paris: Michalon, 2011.

Benkirane, Réda. *Bidonville et recasement, modes de vie à Karyan Ben M'Sik*. Geneva: Institut Universitaire d'Études du Développement, 1993.

Berlant, Lauren. "A Properly Political Concept of Love: Three Approaches in Ten Pages." *Cultural Anthropology* 26, no. 4 (2011): 683–91.

Bernard, Isabelle. "Histoire et paysages dans quelques écritures de terrain contemporaines: Jean-Christophe Bailly, François Bon, Patrick Deville et Marie Richeux." *Arcadia* 54, no. 2 (2019): 231–56.

Berrada, Omar. "Yto's Toys." *Orriak* 4 (2016): 3–9.

Best, Susan. "Anger and Repair: The Art and Politics of Judy Watson's *the holes in the land* (2015)." *Third Text* 32, no. 1 (2018): 79–100.

Blanc-Chaléard, Marie-Claude. *En finir avec les bidonvilles: Immigration et politique du logement dans la France des Trente Glorieuses*. Paris: Éditions de la Sorbonne, 2016.

Bouchfar, Yasmine. "'Le piano,' instrument au-delà de l'impossible." *Libération*, May 31, 2017. https://www.libe.ma/_a86926.html?print=1.

Brozgal, Lia Nicole. *Absent the Archive: Cultural Traces of a Massacre in Paris, 17 October 1961*. Contemporary French and Francophone Cultures 73. Liverpool: Liverpool University Press, 2020.

Caillet, Elisabeth. "Le Monument d'Alger et Landowski." In *Archives au présent*, edited by Patrick Nardin, Catherine Perret, Soko Phay, and Anna Seiderer, 113–20. Saint-Denis: Presses universitaires de Vincennes, 2017.

Campt, Tina. *Listening to Images*. Durham, NC: Duke University Press, 2017.

Çelik, Zeynep. *Urban Forms and Colonial Confrontations: Algiers under French Rule*. Berkeley: University of California Press, 1997.

Chaouni, Aziza. "Depoliticizing Group Gamma: Contesting Modernism in Morocco." In *Third World Modernism*, edited by Duanfang Lu, 57–84. London: Routledge, 2011.

Char, René. *This Smoke That Carried Us: Selected Poems*. Translated by Susanne Dubroff. Buffalo, NY: White Pine, 2004.

Char, René. *A une sérénité crispée*. Paris: Gallimard, 1951.

Chebbak, Mostafa. *Lahcen Zinoun ou le corps libéré*. Casablanca: Maha Éditions, 2012.

Chevallier, Corinne. "Jacques Chevallier, l'Algérien." *Confluences en Méditerranée* 90, no. 3 (2014): 175–94.

Chevallier, Jacques. *Nous, Algériens*. Paris: Calmann-Lévy, 1958.

Chevillot, Frédérique, and Tassadit Imache. "Beurette suis et beurette ne veux pas toujours être: Entretien d'été avec Tassadit Imache." *French Review* 71, no. 4 (1998): 632–44.

Chubb, Emma. "Differential Treatment: Migration in the Work of Yto Barrada and Bouchra Khalili." *Journal of Arabic Literature* 46, no. 2/3 (2015): 268–95.

Close, Ronnie. *Cairo's Ultras: Resistance and Revolution in Egypt's Football Culture*. Cairo: American University in Cairo Press, 2019.

Cohen, Jean-Louis. "The Moroccan Group and the Theme of Habitat." *Rassegna* 52, no. 4 (1992): 58–67.

Cohen, Jean-Louis, and Monique Eleb. *Casablanca: Colonial Myths and Architectural Ventures*. New York: Monacelli, 2002.

Cohen, Muriel. "Demain, demain." *Vingtième Siècle: Revue d'histoire*, no. 116 (2012): 157–61.

Cohen, Muriel. *Des familles invisibles: Les Algériens de France entre intégrations et discriminations*. Paris: Editions de la Sorbonne, 2020.

Coussonnet, Clelia. "Amina Menia, Stepping into the Breach, the Polemics of Place." *Another Africa*. Accessed March 25, 2021. https://www.anotherafrica.net/art-culture/amina-menia-stepping-into-the-breach-the-polemics-of-place.

Crane, Sheila. "Housing as Battleground: Targeting the City in the Battles of Algiers." *City and Society* 29, no. 1 (2017): 187–212.

Crane, Sheila. *Mediterranean Crossroads: Marseille and Modern Architecture*. Minneapolis: University of Minnesota Press, 2011.
Cupers, Kenny. *The Social Project: Housing Postwar France*. Minneapolis: University of Minnesota Press, 2014.
Dakhlia, Jocelyne. *L'oubli de la cité*. Paris: Éditions de la découverte, 1990.
Demerdash, Nancy. "Tunisia, 1940–1970: The Spatial Politics of Reconstruction, Decolonization, and Development." *Architecture beyond Europe Journal*, nos. 9–10 (2016). Accessed April 1. 2024, http://journals.openedition.org/abe/10958.
De Vroey, Laure, and Lize Nevens. "Heritage for the Future? Towards an Operational Definition of Heritage in Hay Mohammadi, Morocco." In *Envisioning Architecture: Image, Perception and Communication of Heritage*, edited by Anetta Kępczyńska-Walczak, 456–65. Łodz: Łodz University of Technology, 2015.
Diawara, Mathia. "Kader Attia: A Poetics of Reappropriation." In *The Repair: From Occident to Extra-Occidental Cultures*, edited by Kader Attia, 5–13. Berlin: Green Box, 2014.
Djebar, Assia. *Femmes d'Alger dans leur appartement: Nouvelles*. 3rd ed. Paris: Des femmes, 1983.
Djebar, Assia. *Women of Algiers in Their Apartment*. Translated by Marjolijn De Jager. CARAF Books. Charlottesville: University Press of Virginia, 1992.
Doidge, Mark, Svenja-Maria Mintert, and Radoslaw Kossakowski, eds. *Ultras: The Passion and Performance of Contemporary Football Fandom*. Manchester: Manchester University Press, 2022.
Enwezor, Okwui. "A Radiant Conflagration (*H'reg*): On Burning and the Subjectivity of Photography in Yto Barrada's Work." In *Riffs: Artist of the Year 2011*, edited by Yto Barrada, 21–32. Frankfurt: Deutsche Bank, 2011.
Falęcka, Katarzyna. "Beyond Metaphor: Women and War." apexart, 2021. https://apexart.org/Beyond-Metaphor-essay-ENG.php.
Fanon, Frantz. *Oeuvres*. Edited by Jean Khalfa and Robert Young. New York: Khalfa, 2011.
Fanon, Frantz. *The Wretched of the Earth*. Translated by Constance Farrington. New York: Grove, 1963.
Feldman, Hannah. "As the World Constricts: Kader Attia's Pictures of Spacelessness." *Nka: Journal of Contemporary African Art*, no. 26 (2010): 60–69.
Feldman, Hannah. *From a Nation Torn: Decolonizing Art and Representation in France 1945–1962*. Durham, NC: Duke University Press, 2014.
Feraoun, Mouloud. *Journal, 1955–1962: Reflections on the French-Algerian War*. Translated by James D. Le Sueur. Lincoln: University of Nebraska Press, 2000.
Ferdjani, Youssef. "La poésie du métissage et du rapprochement comme arme contre la politique de l'exclusion: Georges Henein et Jean Sénac." *Babel: Littératures plurielles*, no. 41 (2020): 155–76.
Fişek, Emine. *Aesthetic Citizenship: Immigration and Theater in Twenty-First-Century Paris*. Evanston, IL: Northwestern University Press, 2017.
Fralon, José-Alain. *Jacques Chevallier: L'homme qui voulait empêcher la guerre d'Algérie*. Paris: Fayard, 2012.

Freeman, Elizabeth. *Time Binds: Queer Temporalities, Queer Histories*. Durham, NC: Duke University Press, 2010.

Glissant, Édouard. *Philosophie de la relation*. Paris: Gallimard, 2009.

Glissant, Édouard. *Poetics of Relation*. Translated by Betsy Wing. Ann Arbor: University of Michigan Press, 1997.

Goni, Marian Nur. "Bruno Boudjelal: de la photographie en mouvement . . ." *Africultures*, July 5, 2010. http://africultures.com/bruno-boudjelal-de-la-photographie-en-mouvement-9578.

Gordon, Avery. *Ghostly Matters: Haunting and the Sociological Imagination*. Minneapolis: University of Minnesota Press, 2008.

Gordon, Lewis R. "Through the Hellish Zone of Nonbeing: Thinking through Fanon, Disaster and the Damned of the Earth." *Human Architecture: Journal of the Sociology of Self-Knowledge* 5, special issue (Summer 2007): 5–12.

Gordon, Lewis R. *What Fanon Said: A Philosophical Introduction to His Life and Thought*. New York: Fordham University Press, 2015.

Grabar, Henry S. "Reclaiming the City." *Cultural Geographies* 21, no. 3 (2014): 389–409.

Gruet, Stéphane, Hélène Roy, and Fernand Pouillon. *Pouillon, une architecture durable: Les deux cents colonnes, et autres brefs essais*. Toulouse: Éditions Transversales, 2018.

Gruzinski, Serge. "From Holy Land to Open Your Eyes." Translated by Hoda Fourcade Zeid. In *RepaiR*, edited by Kader Attia and Léa Gauthier, 215–17. Paris: Blackjack Éditions, 2014.

Guabli, Brahim El. *Moroccan Other-Archives: History and Citizenship after State Violence*. New York: Fordham University Press, 2023.

Hadjadj, Akila. *Vol au-dessus des bidonvilles: Parcours d'une femme des Aurès à Paris (1957–2010)*. Paris: Éditions L'Harmattan, 2014.

Haut-Commissariat au Plan, Direction Régionale du Grand Casablanca. *Recensement général de la population et de l'habitat 2014: Région du Grand Casablanca*. 2016. https://www.hcp.ma/reg-casablanca/attachment/673642/.

Henni, Samia. *Architecture of Counterrevolution: The French Army in Northern Algeria*. Zürich: gta Verlag, 2017.

Henni, Samia. "From 'Indigenous' to 'Muslim.'" *E-Flux Architecture*, December 2017. https://www.e-flux.com/architecture/positions/160964/from-indigenous-to-muslim/.

Herbeth, Alain. *Jacques Chevallier: Les fidélités successives du dernier maire d'Alger*. Paris: L'Harmattan, 2018.

Hervo, Monique. *Nanterre en guerre d'Algérie: Chroniques du bidonville, 1959–1962*. Arles: Actes Sud, 2012.

Hervo, Monique, and Marie Ange Charras. *Bidonvilles: L'enlisement*. Paris: F. Maspero, 1971.

Hlavajova, Maria, and Tom Holert, eds. *Marion von Osten: Once We Were Artists*. Amsterdam: Valiz, 2017.

House, Jim. "L'impossible contrôle d'une ville coloniale? Casablanca, décembre 1952." *Genèses* 86, no. 1 (2012): 78–103.

House, Jim. *Shantytowns and the City: Colonial Power Relations in Algiers and Casablanca, 1919–1962*. Oxford: Oxford University Press, forthcoming.

House, Jim. "Shantytowns in the City: Algiers and Casablanca as a (Post)Colonial Archive." *Francosphères* 3, no. 1 (2014): 43–62.

House, Jim, and Neil MacMaster. *Paris 1961: Algerians, State Terror, and Memory.* Oxford: Oxford University Press, 2006.

Hughes, Langston. *The Collected Poems of Langston Hughes.* Edited by Arnold Rampersad and David E. Roessel. New York: Knopf, 1994.

Iaione, Christian, and Kati Van de Velde. "The City as a Commons." *Green European Journal*, November 9, 2016. https://www.greeneuropeanjournal.eu/the-city-as-a-commons/.

Imache, Tassadit. *Une fille sans histoire: Roman.* Paris: Calmann-Levy, 1990.

Initiative Urbaine. *Cariane central Hay Mohammadi: Mémoire et dignité.* Moroccan Conseil National des Droits de l'Homme, 2011. Accessed April 1, 2024. https://www.cndh.ma/fr/ouvrages/cariane-central-hay-mohammadi-memoire-et-dignite.

Jackson, Steven J. "Rethinking Repair." In *Media Technologies: Essays on Communication, Materiality, and Society*, edited by Tarleton Gillespie, Rablo J. Boczkowski, and Kirsten A. Foot, 221–39. Cambridge, MA: MIT Press, 2014.

Jordan, Shirley. "Not Yet Fallen: Memory, Trace and Time in Stéphane Couturier's City Photography." *Nottingham French Studies* 53, no. 2 (July 2014): 169–85.

Joris, Pierre, and Habib Tengour, eds. *Poems for the Millennium: The University of California Book of North African Literature.* Berkeley: University of California Press, 2012.

Jouder, Dana Al. *Enfilade.* 2013. Vimeo video. https://vimeo.com/user12174799.

Jouder, Dana Al. "Poetics of Mass Housing: 'Enfilade.'" Omnibus Urban Research Platform, December 5, 2013. http://omnibus-lab.com/blog/poetics-of-mass-housing-enfilade/.

Jouder, Dana Al. *Tiles.* July 28, 2013. Vimeo video. https://vimeo.com/71201586.

Karroum, Abdellah. "Yto Barrada: 'A Modest Proposal.'" Translated by Emma Chubb. *Nafas Art Magazine*, February 2010. http://universes-in-universe.org/eng/nafas/articles/2010/yto_barrada.

Karroum, Abdellah, Fabien Danesi, and Frédéric Grossi, eds. *Notre monde brûle = Our world is burning.* Paris: Palais de Tokyo, 2020.

Kılınç, Kıvanç, and Mohammad Gharipour, eds. *Social Housing in the Middle East: Architecture, Urban Development, and Transnational Modernity.* Bloomington: Indiana University Press, 2019.

Kraftl, Peter, and Peter Adey. "Architecture/Affect/Inhabitation: Geographies of Being-In Buildings." *Annals of the Association of American Geographers* 98, no. 1 (2018): 213–31.

Lallaoui, Mehdi. *Du bidonville aux HLM.* Collection Au nom de la mémoire. Bezons: Au nom de la mémoire, 1993.

Lallaoui, Mehdi. *Monique H., Nanterre 1961: Théâtre.* Montigny-lès-Cormeilles: Au nom de la mémoire, 2014.

Lambert, Léopold. "Casablanca 1952: Architecture for the Anti-Colonial Struggle or the Counter-Revolution." *Funambulist Magazine*, August 9, 2018.

Lambert, Léopold. *Etats d'urgence: Une histoire spatiale du continuum colonial français.* Toulouse: Premiers matins de novembre éditions, 2021.

Llorens, Natasha Marie. "Oussama Tabti." *ElaineAlain*, 2020. https://elainealain.fr/artists/oussama-tabti.

Lorcin, Patricia M. E.. *Imperial Identities: Stereotyping, Prejudice, and Race in Colonial Algeria*. Lincoln: University of Nebraska Press, 2014.

Maffi, Irene. *Pratiques du patrimoine et politiques de la mémoire en Jordanie*. Lausanne: Editions Payot, 2004.

Maffre, Laurent. *Demain, demain: Gennevilliers, cité de transit 51*. Actes Sud BD. Arles: Actes Sud, 2019.

Maffre, Laurent. *Demain, demain: Nanterre, bidonville de la Folie, 1962–1966*. In consultation with Monique Hervo. Actes Sud BD. Arles: Actes Sud, 2012.

Maïza, Myriam Maachi, and Malika Kacemi. "Fernand Pouillon en Algérie ou quand la composition devient pittoresque." *Méditerranée* 132 (2021): 75–82.

Massumi, Brian. "The Future Birth of the Affective Fact: The Political Ontology of Threat." In *The Affect Theory Reader*, edited by Melissa Gregg and Gregory J. Seigworth, 52–70. Durham, NC: Duke University Press, 2009.

Massumi, Brian, Jacob Ferrington, Alina Hechler, and Jannell Parsons. "Affect and Immediation: An Interview with Brian Massumi." *disClosure: A Journal of Social Theory* 28, no. 13 (2019): 110–21.

Mbembe, Achille. *Necropolitics*. Translated by Steven Corcoran. Durham, NC: Duke University Press, 2019.

McKinney, Mark. "Naming the Place and Telling the Story in *Demain, demain: Nanterre, bidonville de La Folie, 1962–1966* by Laurent Maffre." In *Immigrants and Comics: Graphic Spaces of Remembrance, Transaction, and Mimesis*, edited by Nhora Lucía Serrano, 89–102. Routledge Advances in Comics Studies. New York: Routledge, 2021.

Menia, Amina. "Enclosed @Mosaic Rooms." Accessed April 2, 2024. https://aminamenia.com/works/enclosed-at-mosaic-rooms/.

Menia, Amina. "Looping the Loop: A Conversation between Amina Menia and Laura Allsop." Interview by Laura Allsop. *Ibraaz* (2012): 1–10.

Merrahi, Mohamed El. "Identité et éclatement des genres: Vers une esthétique romanesque de Fouad Souiba." *L'Opinion*, January 25, 2016.

Merzelkad-Hallal, Rym. "Les complexes touristiques sahariens de Fernand Pouillon en Algérie, entre conception et analogie." *Bulletin de la Société Géographique de Liège* 77 (2021/22): 105–18.

Miller, Susan Gilson. *A History of Modern Morocco*. Cambridge: Cambridge University Press, 2013.

Mortimer, Mildred P. "Unearthing Hidden History." Introduction to *The Seine Was Red: Paris, October 1961*, by Leïla Sebbar. Bloomington: Indiana University Press, 2008.

Muhanna, Elias, and Omar Sayyed. "Folk the Kasbah." *Transition* 94 (2003): 132–49.

Murray-Román, Jeannine. "Hom(e)ing Devices: Locating Identity in the Work of Tassadit Imache." *French Review* 77, no. 6 (2004): 1140–50.

Noland, Carrie. Introduction to *Migrations of Gesture*, edited by Noland and Sally Ann Ness, 17–22. Minneapolis: University of Minnesota Press, 2008.

O'Sullivan, Simon. "The Aesthetics of Affect: Thinking Art beyond Representation." *Angelaki: Journal of the Theoretical Humanities* 6, no. 3 (2001): 125–34.

Pieprzak, Katarzyna. "A Beautiful Grave: Innocent Objects, Museums and the Modern Self in Driss Chraïbi's La Civilisation, ma Mère! . . . and the Ben M'Sik Community Museum." *Studies in Twentieth and Twenty-First Century Literature* 38, no. 2 (2014): 1–17.

Pieprzak, Katarzyna. "Nostalgia and the New Cosmopolitan: Literary and Artistic Interventions in the City of Casablanca." *Studies in Twentieth and Twenty-First Century Literature* 33, no. 1 (2009): 47–69.

Pieprzak, Katarzyna. "Participation as Patrimony: The Ben M'Sik Community Museum and the Importance of the Small Museum in Morocco." In *Ben M'Sik Community Museum: Building Bridges*, edited by Samir El Azhar, 11–15. Casablanca: Université Hassan II, 2012.

Pieprzak, Katarzyna. "Whitewash as Affective Platform: Art and Politics of Surface in the Work of Yto Barrada and Hassan Darsi." *ARTMargins* 8, no. 3 (2019): 29–54.

Pieprzak, Katarzyna. "Zones of Perceptual Enclosure: The Aesthetics of Immobility in Casablanca's Literary Bidonvilles." *Research in African Literatures* 47, no. 3 (2016): 32–49.

Pithouse, Richard. "Fidelity to Fanon." In *Living Fanon: Global Perspectives*, edited by Nigel Gibson, 225–34. New York: Palgrave Macmillan, 2011.

Popescu, Carmen. "Three Tenses: Mass-Housing in Contemporary Art." *Architektúra a urbanizmus* 46, nos. 3–4 (2012): 302–21.

Pouillon, Fernand. *Mémoires d'un architecte*. Paris: Éditions du Seuil, 1968.

Powers, Holiday. "Yto Barrada: Tangier's Changing Cosmopolitanisms." *Nka: Journal of Contemporary African Art*, no. 28 (2011): 130–39.

Rais, Khalil. "Hay Mohammadi Story: Rencontre avec l'auteur et cinéaste Fouad Souiba." *L'Opinion*, September 14, 2012.

Reed, Mike. "Bureaucratic Theory and Intellectual Renewal in Contemporary Organization Studies." In *The Oxford Handbook of Sociology and Organizational Studies*, edited by Paul Adler, 559–84. Oxford: Oxford University Press, 2009.

Reeves-Evison, Theo, and Mark Justin Rainey. "Ethico-Aesthetic Repairs." *Third Text* 32, no. 1 (2018): 1–15.

Reggad, Yasmina. "The Economy of Hope." *Arte East* (blog), June 20, 2013. http://arteeast.org/quarterly/the-economy-of-hope-working-title/.

Richeux, Marie. *Climats de France*. Paris: Sabine Wespieser, 2017.

Rivera, Mayra. "Poetics Ashore." *Literature & Theology* 33, no. 3 (2019): 241–47.

Rosello, Mireille. "French *Bidonvilles* in the 1960s: Urban and Individual Initiatives." *Culture, Theory and Critique* 40, no. 1 (1997): 97–110.

Ross, Kristin. *May '68 and Its Afterlives*. Chicago: University of Chicago Press, 2002.

Rothberg, Michael. *Multidirectional Memory: Remembering the Holocaust in the Age of Decolonization*. Stanford, CA: Stanford University Press, 2009.

Rouissi, Karim. "Housing for the Greatest Number: Casablanca's Under-appreciated Public Housing Developments." *Journal of North African Studies* 26, no. 3 (2021): 439–64.

Sadiq, Abdelhai. *Nass El Ghiwane: Protest song au Maroc*. Marrakech: Editions Chatr, 2001.

Salti, Rasha. "Shall We Dance?" *Cinema Journal* 52, no. 1 (2012): 166–71.

Salti, Rasha. "Sleepers, Magicians, Smugglers: Yto Barrada and the Other Archive of the Strait." *Afterall: A Journal of Art, Context and Enquiry* 16 (2007): 98–106.

Sausset, Damien. "An Image of Reality." In *Melting Point (Continued): Stéphane Couturier*, edited by Martin Hochleitner, 29–34. Fotohof edition 147. Salzburg: Fotohof, 2010.

Sayad, Abdelmalek, and Eliane Dupuy. *Un Nanterre Algérien, terre de bidonvilles*. Français d'ailleurs, peuple d'ici. Paris: Autrement, 1995.

Sebbar, Leïla. *La Seine était rouge: Paris, Octobre 1961*. Paris: Babel, Editions Thierry Magnier, 2003.

Sebbar, Leïla. *The Seine Was Red: Paris, October 1961*. Translated by Mildred P. Mortimer. Bloomington: Indiana University Press, 2008.

Sebbar, Leïla. *Shérazade, 17 ans, brune, frisée, les yeux verts*. Paris: Stock, 1982.

Sekyi-Otu, Ato. "Fanon and the Possibility of Postcolonial Critical Imagination." In *Living Fanon: Global Perspectives*, edited by Nigel Gibson, 45–60. New York: Palgrave Macmillan, 2011.

Sénac, Jean. *Matinale de mon peuple: Poèmes*. Rodez: Subervie, 1961.

Sénac, Jean. *Œuvres poétiques*. Arles: Actes Sud, 2019.

Shevchenko, Olga, and Oksana Sarkisova. "The Album as Performance: Notes on the Limits of the Visible." In *Russian Performances: Word, Object, Action*, edited by Julie A. Buckler, Julie A. Cassiday, and Boris Wolfson, 42–53. Madison: University of Wisconsin Press, 2018.

Shouse, Eric. "Feeling, Emotion, Affect." *M/C Journal* 8, no. 6 (2005). http://journal.media-culture.org.au/0512/03-shouse.php.

Silverstein, Paul A. *Algeria in France: Transpolitics, Race, and Nation*. Bloomington: Indiana University Press, 2004.

Simone, AbdouMaliq. *Improvised Lives: Rhythms of Endurance in an Urban South (After the Postcolonial)*. Cambridge: Polity, 2019.

Simone, AbdouMaliq. *The Surrounds: Urban Life within and beyond Capture*. Durham, NC: Duke University Press, 2022.

Slyomovics, Susan. "Is Patrimoine 'Good to Think with'?" *Journal of North African Studies* 25, no. 5 (2020): 689–96.

Slyomovics, Susan. *The Performance of Human Rights in Morocco*. Philadelphia: University of Pennsylvania Press, 2005.

Slyomovics, Susan. "Repairing Colonial Symmetry: Algerian Archive Restitution as Reparation for Crimes of Colonialism?" In *Time for Reparations: A Global Perspective*, edited by Jacqueline Bhabha, Margareta Matache, and Caroline Elkins, 201–18. Philadelphia: University of Pennsylvania Press, 2021.

Souiba, Fouad. *L'homme qui voulait être comédien*. Saint-Denis: Édilivre, 2016.

Source du Lion. *La Source du Lion de 1 à Z: de l'art au Maroc, 1995–2022*. Casablanca: Editions La Source du Lion, 2022.

Strava, Cristiana. *Precarious Modernities: Assembling State, Space and Society on the Urban Margins in Morocco*. London: Zed Books, 2022.

Ströbel, Katrin, and La Source du Lion, eds. *De l'espace autre*. Casablanca: Editions La Source du Lion, 2016.

Sugiuchi, Deirdre. "Traveling South to Understand the Soul of America." Interview with Imani Perry. *Electric Literature*, June 7, 2022. https://electricliterature.com/south-to-america-a-journey-below-the-mason-dixon-to-understand-the-soul-of-a-nation-book-imani-perry/.

Talbayev, Edwige Tamalet. *The Transcontinental Maghreb: Francophone Literature across the Mediterranean*. New York: Fordham University Press, 2017.

Taylor, Diana. *The Archive and the Repertoire: Performing Cultural Memory in the Americas*. Durham, NC: Duke University Press, 2003.

Terrab, Sonia, dir. *L7Asla*. TV 2M and Ali'N production, 2020. 60 min.

Tissières, Hélène. "Femme écrite du cinéaste Lahcen Zinoun: Corps à corps dansé de l'écrit et de l'image." *International Journal of Francophone Studies* 20, nos. 1–2 (2017): 135–48.

Toufic, Jalal. *The Withdrawal of Tradition Past a Surpassing Disaster*. Jalatoufic.com, 2009.

Tresfels, Cécile Marie Amelie. "The Fear Within: Apprehension in Sixteenth-Century French Literature." PhD diss., Stanford University, 2019.

Von Osten, Marion. "From High-Rise to High-Rise." In *Colonial Modern: Aesthetics of the Past, Rebellions for the Future*, edited by Tom Avermaete, Serhat Karakayali, and Marion von Osten, 112–15. London: Black Dog, 2014.

Von Osten, Marion. "In the Making: Traversing the Project Exhibition in the Desert of Modernity: Colonial Planning and After." PhD diss., Malmö Faculty of Fine and Performing Arts, Lund University, 2018.

Von Osten, Marion, and Grant Watson, eds. *Bauhaus Imaginista: A School in the World*. London: Thames and Hudson, 2019.

West, Kim. "Repair as Redemption or Montage: Speculations on Kader Attia's Ladder of Light." In *Continuum of Repair: The Light of Jacob's Ladder*, edited by Kader Attia, 55–69. London: Whitechapel Gallery, 2014.

Wieborn, Michael. "Glissant's *Philosophie de la Relation*: 'I Have Spoken the Chaos of Writing in the Ardor of the Poem.'" *Callaloo* 36, no. 4 (2013): 902–15.

Winant, Gabriel. "We Found Love in a Hopeless Place." *N+1*, no. 22 (2015). http://nplusonemag.com/issue-22/essays/we-found-love-in-a-hopeless-place/.

Wylie, Diana. "'Part of Who We Are': Using Old Buildings to Foster Citizenship in North Africa (Oran, Algeria, and Casablanca, Morocco)." *Buildings and Landscapes: Journal of the Vernacular Architecture Forum* 25, no. 1 (2018): 44–63.

Yasmine.H. "En photographie, l'hommage à Paz." Maghreb Info, November 3, 2020. https://www.maghrebinfo.dz/2020/11/03/en-photographie-lhommage-a-paz.

Zaganiaris, Jean. "Une 'révolution symbolique' dans le champ artistique marocain?" *SociologieS [En ligne]*, June 19, 2018. http://journals.openedition.org/sociologies/8247.

Zaki, Lamia. "Après le bidonville. Les relogés de Lahjajma (Casablanca): Entre déni et nostalgie." In *L'enseignement supérieur dans la mondialisation libérale: Une comparaison libérale (Maghreb, Afrique, Canada, France)*, edited by Sylvie Mazzella, 277–94. Rabat: Institut de recherche sur le Maghreb contemporain, 2007.

Zaki, Lamia. "Transforming the City from Below: Shantytown Dwellers and the Fight for Electricity in Casablanca." In *Subalterns and Social Protest: History from Below in *the Middle East and North Africa*, edited by Stephanie Cronin, 116–37. New York: Routledge, 2008.

Zinoun, Lahcen, dir. *Piano*. La Cité en Fête et Lahcen Zinoun, 2002. 16 min.

Zrika, Abdallah. *Rires de l'arbre à palabre*. Translated by Abdellatif Laâbi. Paris: L'Harmattan, 1982.

INDEX

absence, 1–2, 34–37, 41–42, 147–49, 159, 161–63, 168–69; archival, 118–20; women and, 107, 118–19

abstraction, 28–29, 34–36, 101–2, 168–69, 180n20

accompaniment, 8, 171

Ach Man, 46

adaptation. *See* appropriation

Aday, Peter, 15

aesthetics: agency and, 1–2, 45–46; belonging and, 120, 128; of built environment, 1–2, 4, 15–16, 19–20, 28, 31–32, 34, 38–39, 44–45, 108–9, 120–21, 136–37, 139–43; colonialism and, 38–39, 44–45, 139–43; gender and, 1–2, 120–21, 136–37; of poverty, 45–46; repair and, 18, 136–37, 139–43. *See also* art

affect, 18, 178n59; art and, 13–17, 22–25, 35–36, 170–71; body and, 22–23, 168–69; encounter and, 70–76, 83–86; epistemology of, 21–25, 73–74, 83–85, 157–58, 165–66; history and, 89–90, 95, place and, 47; politics of, 84; relationality and, 23–25, 84–86, 88–90, 159, 165–67, 170–71; repair and, 21–25, 165–71; representation and, 139–40, 143, 170; sound and, 57–58. *See also* incipience; individual affects by name

afterlives, 69–70, 94, 98, 176n17, 179n73

Agamben, Giorgio, 7

agency, 1–2, 4, 45, 87–88, 140–42, 159, 170

Ain' Diab bidonville, 38–39

album, family, 91–95, 112, 145–48

Algeria, 87–88, 187n35; civil war, 104–5, 121–23; colonial history, 10–13; Memorial to the Liberation of Algeria (Le Pavois), 10–13; War of Independence, 71–72, 74–75, 79–87, 104–5, 117–18, 140–41, 159, 170–71, 186n19

Al Jouder, Dana, 1–2, 27, 47

Allouche, Merzak, 104–5

Amarouchène, Myriam, 149–50

anthropology, 9, 18, 31–32, 35, 166, 180n8

anticolonialism, 53–60; gender and, 115–17, 149, 155–57; heroism and, 57–58; mass housing and, 40–41, 91–93, 115–17, 177n44. *See also* liberation; resistance

apprehension, 73–78, 81–85, 88–89

appropriation, 18; art and, 28, 108; of built environment, 32–35, 37–38, 47, 104–7, 115–16, 135–39, 168–69; gender and, 115–16, 169; repair and, 92–94, 97, 104–7

Arab Spring, 7–8

architecture, 177n34: agency and, 6–8, 37–38, 84–88, 167–71; affect and, 15–17, 22–25, 72–74; art and, xii–xiii, 1–2, 15–16, 98–102, 108–11; colonialism and, 4–9, 14–16, 19–20, 28, 44–45, 75–80, 88–89, 91–93; form and, 31–42, 66–67, 97–111; sound and, 75–76

archive, 8–9, 11, 74–75, 81–82, 87–92, 95–96, 106–7; colonial, 11–13, 95; marginalization in, 118–23, 139–39, 147, 150–52. *See also* history

Arrif, Abdelmajid, xi–xii

art, 1–2, 9–10; affect and, 13–17, 22–25, 35–36, 170–71; architecture and, xii–xiii, 1–2, 15–16, 98–102, 108–11; class and, 51–52; colonialism and, 9–14, 19; form and, 120–21; future and, 170–71; history and, 2–3, 115–16, 119–20; mass housing and, xii–xviii, 1–3, 6, 8–10, 19–20, 25–26, 44–45, 48–54, 170–71, 179n72; mediation and, 9, 16–18, 120–21; relationality and, xii–xiii; repair and, xii–xiii, 9–10, 13–14, 17–19, 21–22, 29, 51–52, 67, 120–21, 165–71; relationality and, 70–72, 170–71; universality and, 51–54
ATBAT. *See* Atelier des Bâtisseurs
Atelier de l'Observatoire, 58–59
Atelier des Bâtisseurs (ATBAT) Afrique, 31, 180n20
Attia, Kader, 17–20, 41, 178n49
autofiction, 88–91
Avermaete, Tom, 5, 7–8, 27–28, 32–35, 180n24
Azoulay, Ariella Aïsha, 8–9, 70–71, 169

Bab El Oued neighborhood (Algiers), 112
Badri, Mona, 62–63
bare life, 7
Barette, Michèle, 47–48
Barrada, Yto, 27–29, 32–38, 43–44, 53–54, 115–16, 179n3; exhibit for Centre for Canadian Architecture, 34–35, 37, 41; *Gran Royal Turismo*, 35–36; *A Guide to Trees for Governors and Gardeners*, 35–36; *Marks Left by a Football*, 35–36; *Reprendre Casa* (Taking back Casa), 38
Batma, Laarbi, 61–62
Bauhaus, 42–43. *See also* von Osten, Marion
Belcourt neighborhood (Algiers), 112
belonging, 16–17, 21–22, 120, 128–29, 147–48, 165–66, 169–70
Ben M'Sik neighborhood (Casablanca), xi–xvi, 175n1, 175n3; anticolonial resistance in, 41; Community Museum, xii; photographs of, 34, 38–39
Benchicou, Mohamed, 69–70
Benkirane, Reda, 5–7
Berlant, Lauren, 159
Berlioz, Hector, 49
Bernard, Isabelle, 74–75, 185n11, 185n13
Berrada, Omar, 28

Best, Susan, 10–11
bidonville (worker settlement), xi, xiii–xvi, 4–7, 19–20, 30–32, 34, 38–39, 45, 115–17, 189n2
Bidonville de la Folie (Nanterre), 25–26, 115–18, 121–61
Binebine, Mahi, 45, 183n92
Blanc-Chaléard, Marie-Claude, 117
body, xvi–xvii, 1–2, 21–22, 47, 137–38, 142–43, 147–52, 165; absence and, 37; affect and, 22–23, 168–69; architecture and, 1–2, 15–16; encounters and, 70–76, 83–86; gender and, 115–16, 165–66, 169; meaning and, 165–66; memory and, 150; repair and, 18, 165–69; resistance and, 56–57; visual and, 97–98. *See also* affect; touch
Bouchfar, Yasmine, 51–52
Boudjelal, Bruno, 108–9
Bouih, Fatna El, 58–59
Boujmii, 61–62. *See also* Nass El Ghiwane
Boussaa, Youssef, 150–52
Brion, Edmond, 31, 48
Brozgal, Lia, 119–20
built environment, 4; affect and, 13–14; agency and, 8, 35–37; art and, xii–xiii, xvi–xvii, 2–3, 170; body and, xvi–xvii; colonialism and, 55–56; gender and, 115–17, 161, 169; materiality of, xvi–xvii; repair and, 2–3, 9–10, 66–67, 169–70; space of, 102–3, 109–11, 128–38, 161. *See also* architecture; mass housing

Campt, Tina, 29, 42
Camus, Albert, 111
Canadian Centre for Architecture, 27–28, 34–35, 37, 41
Candilis, Georges, 31, 37–38, 40–41, 180n20
Cantor, Mircea, xviii
capture, captivity, 3, 7–9, 70–71, 97–98, 169. *See also* containment
care, xviii, 20, 105, 154–56, 169–70
Cariane Central, Hay Mohammadi: Mémoire et dignité, 58–59, 61–62
Carrières Centrales shantytown (Casablanca), xiii–xvi, 25–26, 30–44, 179n1, 181n31; anticolonial resistance and, 41, 58–60; Nid D'Abeille building, 31; Semiramis building, 31. *See also* Hay Mohammadi

206 INDEX

Casablanca, 7–8, 21–22, 177n44; bread riots, xiii–xvi; Legal Frères building, 14–17; L'Hermitage park, 14, 16–17; Raja soccer team, 63–65; Sidi Moumen shantytown, 7–8. See also Carrières Centrales; Hay Mohammadi
Casamantes (dir. Harder and El Kharraze), 58–59
Casbah (Algiers), 108, 112
Casciato, Maristella, 27–28, 32–35
Çelik, Zeynep, 5, 72, 176n12
Chamboissier, Bérengère, 109–11
Chaouni, Aziza, 5, 37–38
Char, René, 155–58
Charras, Marie-Ange, 118
Chevallier, Jacques, 72, 74–75, 80–81, 83–84, 88–90, 95–96, 105–6, 186n26
Chopin, Frederic, 50–51
choreography. *See* dance
Chouaki, Yasmine, 108–9
CIAM. *See* Congrès International d'Architectures Modernes
cité, 4, 6–7, 86–87; *horizontale*, 27, 29, 31, 39–40; *de transit* (transitory housing), 143–45; *vérticale*, 27, 29, 31
Cité de Transit 51 (Gennevilliers), 143–45
citizenship, xii–xiii, 82–83
class: art and, 51–52; mass housing projects and, 47–48, 63; stigmatization and, 5–6
"Climat DeFrance, Cassbah, Bab El Oued," 112
Climat de France housing project (Algiers), 6, 22–23, 25–26, 60–86, 89–92, 94, 97–102, 104–12, 168–69, 188n74, 188n86; Deux Cents Colonnes, 72, 102–3
CNDH. *See* Conseil National des Droits de L'Homme
Cohen, Jean-Louis, 48, 176n12
Cohen, Muriel, 117–18, 139–40
collaboration, 42–43, 58–59, 98–100, 107–8
collage, 19
collectives (art), 42–43
collectivity, xvi, 86–87, 169; future and, 160–61; knowledge and, 21–22, 95–96; repair and, 21–25, 90–91
colonialism, 4–22, 25–26, 29, 42–43, 155–57, 169, 178n55, 187n35; architecture and, 32–34, 40–42, 44, 47; archives and, 11–13, 95;

citizenship and, 82–83; gender and, 107, 152–53; history and, 41–42, 75–77, 81–83, 87–89, 92–95, 162–63, 169–71, 176n17, 182n63, 186n19; relationality and, 71–72, 75–77; repair and, 10–11, 13–14; resistance and, 53–54, 57–60; sound and, 57–58, 60–61; urban planning and, 34–35, 37–41, 44–45, 80–81, 86–87, 97–98, 117, 180n20; violence of, 54–61, 125, 141–43, 154
community, 20, 128–29, 137–39, 150–53
concrete, 1–2, 4, 10–11, 17–20, 115–16. *See also* material, materiality
Congrès International d'Architectures Modernes (CIAM), 31–34, 180n13
Connect Institute (Agadir), 48
Conseil National des Droits de L'Homme (CNDH), 58–59
containment, 1–3, 6–8, 25, 44–45, 47–52, 70–71, 104–5, 128–29, 137–39, 143–44. *See also* capture, captivity
control, 37–41, 79–82, 87–88
Coussonnet, Clelia, 90–91
Couturier, Stéphane, 71–72, 188n74, 188n85; *Alger—Cité "Climat de France,"* 97–98, 100–108, 168–69; *Alger—Cité "Climat de France"—Travelling latéral—Place des deux cents colonnes*, 102–3; *Melting Point* and *Melting Point (continued)*, 98–99; relationship with Abdelhamid Rahiche, 99–100, 107–8, 11; *Seoul—Tanji*, 102
COVID-19 pandemic, 46, 111
Crane, Sheila, 4–5, 41, 85–86, 176n12, 178n55
creativity, 21–22, 25, 37, 44–46, 49–51, 67, 115–16, 169–70
Crozier, Jean, 15
Culturgest Fundação Caixa Geral de Depòsitos, 19–20

dance, xiii–xvii, 1–2, 15–16, 43–48, 137–38; examples, 46–48, 165–67
Daoud, Kamel, 111
darkness, 6–7, 74
Darsi, Florence Renault, xii–xiii
Darsi, Hassan, xii–xiii, 14–17
death, xvi, 7–8, 57–58, 62–63, 84, 143, 154–59
Debussy, Claude, 60–61
decolonialism, 7–8, 42–43, 71–72, 87–88, 137–38, 141–42, 170–71. *See also* resistance

INDEX 207

Delacroix, Eugène, 128–29
Demerdash, Nancy, 5
depth, 102–3
De Vroey, Laurie, 29, 66–67
Diar el-Kef housing project (Algiers), 112–13
Diar el-Mahçoul housing project (Algiers), 89–92, 94
Diar es-Saada housing project (Algiers), 89–90, 92
Diawara, Manthia, 44, 178n49, 179n66
dignity, xvii, 27–28, 57, 63, 66, 71–72, 106–7, 155–57
Djebar, Assia, 128–29
DJ Snake, 112–13
dOCUMENTA (13), 18
documentary, 10, 35–38, 46, 58–59, 63–66, 89–90, 119, 123–17. *See also* film
domesticity, 91–92, 115–21, 129–40, 144–45. *See also* home

Écochard, Michel, 19–20, 31–32, 34, 37–41, 180n13, 180n24
Ecole Ballet Théâtre Zinoun, 47–48
Eleb, Monique, 48, 176n12
embodiment. *See* body
enchantment, 139–40, 147–48
enclosure, 6–7, 9, 20
encounter, 28, 71–76, 83–84, 167
Enwezor, Okui, 35–36
epistemology: affect and, 22–25, 73–74, 83–85, 157–58, 165–66; art and, 25, 35, 42, 82–83, 168–69; colonialism and, 87–88, 155–57; history and, 67, 76–77, 82–83, 90–91, 121–23, 125–27; instability and, 23–25; liberation and, 155–57; relationality and, 105; of repair, 21–26, 76–77, 169–70
equality, 63, 80–81
erasure, 11–12, 17–18, 32–34, 103, 115–16, 121–23, 133–34, 143, 169
ethnography, xi–xii, 58–59
exclusion, xii–xvi, 6–7, 16–17, 20, 69–72, 93–94, 134–40, 144–45, 169–71. *See also* marginality
experimentation, 3, 5, 165–67

family. *See* kinship
Fanon, Frantz, 5–8, 137–38, 152–57, 159

Feldman, Hannah, 5, 18, 120, 128, 141–42, 178n49
Feraoun, Mouloud, 86–87
"Fī blādī ẓlmūnī" (In my country, they've done me wrong), 65–66
film, xviii, 9, 87–95, 97–98; archival, 106–7; examples, 1–2, 14–17, 19–20, 47–52, 61, 63–66, 87–98, 102–8, 165–69; form and, 102–6; narrative and, 102–4. *See also* documentary; video
Fişek, Emine, 120, 150–52
flatness, 102–3
Flood, Finbarr Barry, 16–17
form, 28–29, 34–36, 38–40, 42, 97–98; film and, 102–6; of graphic novel, 138–39; meaning and, 168–69; mediation and, 120–21; photography and, 98–102, 108–9
fragmentation, 19, 88, 102–3
freedom, 50–51, 53–54, 80–81, 137–38
Freeman, Elizabeth, 21–22
friendship, 147–48, 152–59
Front de Libération Nationale (FLN), 117–18, 125–26, 146–47, 153–54
future: affect and, 139–40; architecture and, 78–80; art and, xii–xiii, xvii–xviii, 2–3, 13–14, 18, 93–94, 120–21, 170–71; collective, 95–96, 154, 160–61, 163; gender and, 21–22, 115–16, 126–27; relationality and, 71–72; repair and, 10–11, 29, 66–67, 115–16

Gallicy Photography Festival, 100–102
GAMMA. *See* Groupe d'Architectes Modernes Marocains
gender, 1–2, 10, 90–91, 189n7; agency and, 159; body and, 115–16, 149–50, 165–66, 169; built environment and, 115–17, 161, 169; colonialism and, 107, 152–53; friendship and, 152–59; history and, 21–22, 115–16, 118–21, 126–29, 150, 159, 161–63; immigration and, 117; inheritance and, 106–7; mass housing and, 117–18, 121–40, 144–45, 162–63; memory and, 150; political activism and, 117, 125–27, 153–59, 162–63; repair and, 107–8, 150–52, 159, 162–63; representation and, 128–29, 152–53; silence and, 118–29, 159, 161–63
genealogy, 19
gesture, 165–67, 170–71

Gharipour, Mohammad, 4
Glissant, Édouard, 23–25, 70–71, 84–85, 93–94
Gordon, Avery, 142–43
Gordon, Lewis R., 6–7
gourbi (hut), 130–33
graphic novels, xiii, 9, 120–21, 163, 183n77; examples, 127–45. See also novels
grid, 31–35, 37–44, 47–48, 53–54, 66–67, 112, 180n24
Groupe d'Architectes Modernes Marocains (GAMMA), 31, 35, 37–38, 42–44, 180n13; "Habitat for the Greatest Number Grid," 31–34
Gruzinski, Serge, 167
Guabli, Brahim El, 54

habitations de loyer modéré (HLM), 133–34, 179n72, 189n2
Hached, Ferhat, 41
Haddad, Wiame, 161–63
Hadjdaj, Akila, 115–16, 127, 150–52
halqa (storytelling), 66–67
Hamma neighborhood (Algiers), 112
happiness, 81–82
Harder, Hélène, 58–59
Hassan II University, xii–xiii
Hay Mohammadi neighborhood (Casablanca), 45–48, 53–56, 63–64, 66–67, 179n1, 180n8, 183n92; Dar Chabab community arts center, 61, 64–65; Derb Moulay Cherif police station, 56, 58–59, 61, 183n77; sounds of, 60–66. See also Carrières Centrales
Henni, Samia, 5
Hentsch, Jean, 39–40
Hervo, Monique, 115–16, 118, 128–40, 146–49
history, 16–17, 34, 170–71; affect and, 89–90, 95; art and, 2–3, 115–16, 119–20; belonging and, 128–29; colonialism and, 41–42, 75–77, 81–83, 88–89, 92–95, 162–63, 169–71, 176n17, 182n63, 186n19; gender and, 118–21, 128–29, 150, 159, 161–63; images of, 11–13, 41; knowledge and, 67, 76–77, 82–83, 90–91, 121–23, 125–27; relationality and, 91–95; repair and, 18–19, 66–67, 95, 119–20, 169–70; silence and, xii, xviii, 75–77, 81, 85, 115–16, 118–29, 159, 161–63, 169–70; writing, 54–60

HLM. See *habitations de loyer modéré*
home, 26, 112–13, 115–16, 135–37, 140–41, 168–70
Homma, Takashi, 27–28, 37
House, Jim, 41, 117, 176n17, 177n30, 177n34
Hughes, Langston, 137–38
humanism, 80–81
human rights, 58–59

Imache, Tassadit, 134–35
imagination, xvi–xvii, 2, 25–26, 37, 70–71, 147–48, 163, 169–70. See also creativity
immigration, 19, 147; mass housing and, 5–7, 117, 151–52, 189n2; racism and, 7, 128–30
incipience, 2–3, 13–15, 22–23, 72–74, 112–13, 166, 170–71. See also affect
inheritance, 71, 105–7
Initiative Urbaine, 58–59, 67
innocence, 54–55, 59–60, 75–77, 80–83
installation, xiii, 41, 88–89; examples, 10, 17–20, 167–69
intermediality. See mediation
intimacy, 38, 41, 84–85, 89–92, 104–5, 108–13, 121–23, 128–29, 145–48, 157–59, 165–67. See also affect
Issiakhem, M'hamed, 10

Jackson, Steven J., 21
Janyen, Abderrahman, 46
Jazouli, Meryem, *Nass SOCICA: Veiller par le geste* (People of SOCICA: Watching/caring through gesture), 165–71
Jordan, Shirley, 99
Josic, Alexis, 31
joy, xv–xvi, 6, 27, 44, 46–47, 51, 64–65, 127, 137–38, 169. See also affect
justice, 57, 63, 126, 128–29, 140–42; injustice, xvii, 60–61, 143. See also dignity

Kaci, Nadia, 149–50
Kahina (theater troupe), 150–52
Kameli, Katia, *Trou de mémoire* (Memory gap, or hole), 10–13
Karakayali, Serhat, 7–8
karian (worker settlement), xi, 4–7
Kharraze, Karima El, 58–59
kinship, 71–72, 82–83, 91–94, 105–6, 112–13, 145–46

INDEX 209

Kılınç, Kıvanç, 4
Kraftl, Peter, 15

Laâbi, Abdellatif, xiii–xvii
Labor k3000, 42–44, 47, 181n35. *See also* von Osten, Marion
Lallaoui, Mehdi, *Du bidonville aux HLM* (From the shantytown to low-income housing), 146–47; *Monique H., Nanterre 1961*, 120–21, 145–59
Lallier, Thomas, 99–100, 103–4
Lambert, Léopold, 41, 176n17
Landowski, Paul, 10
Le Corbusier, 4, 19–20, 31–32, 87–88, 180n20
Lemchaheb, 29, 60–61; "L7asla" (Impasse or Dead-End), 63–64
lghis. *See* mud
liberalism, 80–81
liberation: 6–8, 10–11, 154–59
listening, xi–xii, 29, 42, 120–21, 126–27, 171. *See also* sound
looking, 2, 91–92, 102–5
loss, 19, 60–64, 143, 145–47. *See also* affect
love, 10–11, 91–92, 97, 128–29, 147–48, 154–59. *See also* affect

Maanouni, Ahmed El, 61
MacMaster, Neil, 117
Maffre, Laurent, *Demain, demain* (Tomorrow, tomorrow), 120–21, 127–43, 160; *Demain, demain: Gennevilliers, cité de transit 51*, 143–45
Maghreb, 4–6; art and, xvii, 2–3, 9–10, 60–61
makzhen (structures of royal power), 5–6
Malraux, André, 160
mapping, 43–44
Marché Central bombing, 56–58
marginality, xi–xiii, 5–7, 117–23
Maspero, François, 118
mass housing, xi–xiii, 4, 176n12; art and, xii–xviii, 1–3, 6, 8–10, 19–20, 25–26, 34, 44–45, 48–54, 170, 179n72; colonialism and, 4–9, 19, 25–26, 41, 44–45, 53–60, 92–93, 117, 169–71, 178n55; containment and, 45, 47–52, 104–5, 128–29, 137–39, 144; exclusion and, 5–7, 134–40, 144–45; gender and, 115–18, 121–40, 144–45, 162–63; history and, 170–71; nonbeing and, 7, 170; political activism and, 7–8, 41, 53–59, 69–70, 85–87, 117, 159, 162–63, 177n30; relationality and, 4–6, 8, 19–20, 44–45, 47, 60–72, 75–80, 84–88, 97–100, 104–7, 112–13, 166–67, 170–71; repair and, 19, 25–26, 165, 169–70; sound and, 60–67. *See also* architecture; built environment
Massumi, Brian, 13–14, 144–45, 178n59
material, materiality, xiii–xvii, 4–7, 16–20, 30–31, 38–39, 85–86, 95–96, 127–37, 162–63. *See also* concrete; mud
Mbembe, Achille, xvi, 7, 178n49
McKinney, Mark, 130
Mdidech, Jaouad, 61
mediation, 9, 19, 102, 119–21, 128–29
memorial, memorialization, 10–13
memory, 175n14, 179n73; activism and, 117, 126–27; affect and, 21–22; built environment and, xiii–xvii, 19, 28–29, 58–59; gender and, 149–51, 159; history and, 16–17, 19, 140–41; repair and, 90–92, 117–21, 126–27
Menia, Amina, 88–89, 115–16; *Africaines*, 95–96; *Enclosed*, 10–13; *Extra Muros*, 95–96; *Iconoclastes*, 95–96; *Notre monde brûle* exhibit, 88–89; *A Peculiar Family Album / Un Album de famille bien particulier*, 71–72, 87–96
Meskoud, Abdelmadjid, 112
migration, rural, 4–7, 19, 27–28, 30–31, 60–61, 63, 112
modernism, 1, 4–5, 19, 27–28, 31–34, 42–44, 47, 115–16; colonialism and, 29, 42–45, 47. *See also* grid
Mohamed V (king), 41, 57
monster, 73–74
monument, monumentality, 10–11, 42, 71–72, 100–103, 121–23, 160
Morocco, 41–42, 47–48; Beni Aïssi village, 14; Benslimane area, 14; French Protectorate and, 5–6, 30–31; Law 09-09, 65–66
Mortimer, Mildred, 118–19, 123–25
Mouride, Abdelaziz, 58, 183n77
movement, xiii–xviii, 1–2, 15–16, 21–22, 46, 108–9, 133–34, 165–66. *See also* dance
mud, 7, 127–45, 152–53. *See also* material, materiality

Muhanna, Elias, 60–61
multiplicity, 109–11, 120–21
Murray-Román, Jeannine, 134–35
Musée Collectif de Casablanca, 58–59; *Radio de mon quartier—Hay Mohammadi*, 60–61
museum, xii–xiii, 16–17
music, 44–51, 60–66; politics and, 53–54, 62–63, 65–66; repair and, 51–53
mutual aid. *See* solidarity

Nanterre, Nanterrology, 5, 117. *See also* Bidonville de la Folie
narrative: built environment and, 97–98, 139–43; film and, 102–4; visual and, 90–94, 106–7
Nass El Ghiwane, 29, 60–64, 66
nation, nationalism, 7–8, 11, 86–87, 92, 120, 149; anticolonialism and, 40–41, 56–58; exclusion and, 70–71; relationality and, 80–81
necropolitics, xvi, 7–8
neglect, 7–8
neocolonialism, 14, 16–17
neoliberalism, 16–17, 160–61
Nevens, Lize, 29, 66–67
Noland, Carrie, 166
nonbeing, 6–7, 170
nonviolence, 118, 153–54
nostalgia, 63–64, 112, 123–25. *See also* affect
novels, 9, 29, 45, 71–72, 120–21, 150, 163, 185n13; examples, 22–23, 38–41, 52–60, 69–70, 72–86, 118–19, 121–27, 160. *See also* graphic novels

October 17 massacre, 83–84, 117–20, 123–28, 140–43, 146–50, 158–59, 161–63
Office de Radiodiffusion-Télévision Française (ORTF), 107–8
opposition, xi, 7, 52–54, 57–60. *See also* resistance
order, disorder, 38–40
Orientalism, 128–29
ORTF. *See* Office de Radiodiffusion-Télévision Française
O'Sullivan, Simon, 13–14
ownership, xvi–xvii, 1–2, 29, 71–72, 105–6, 128, 168–69

Panijel, Jacques, 158–59
Parc André Malraux (Nanterre), 160
pensée du tremblement. *See* quakeful thinking
performance, 16–17, 91–92, 107–8, 119–20, 149–53, 166. *See also* theater
Perry, Imani, 169–70
photography, xiii, 6, 8–9, 91–92, 128–29, 135–39, 141, 188n78, 188nn85–86, 191n56; absence and, 35–38, 41–42; architecture and, 98–102, 108–11; colonialism and, 11–13, 42; examples, xviii, 10–14, 18–19, 21–22, 27–29, 32–42, 71–72, 98–102, 108–11, 112, 115, 118, 145–48, 160–63, 165–66; form and, 32–40, 42, 98–102, 108–9; intimacy and, 109–11; knowledge and, 35, 42; repair and, 42; taking, 38, 42. *See also* album
Pithouse, Richard, 45
plurality, 71–72, 81–82, 93–94, 109–11
poetry, poetics, 6, 9, 25, 175n14; examples, xiii–xvii, 63–64, 86–88, 107–8, 137–38, 155–59, 170–71; relation and, 70–72, 84–88, 95–96, 103–4, 112; repair and, xii–xiii, xvi–xviii, 2–3, 25–26, 107–8, 157–58; revolution and, 86–87; urban planning and, 87–88
police, policing, 117, 141–43, 152–53, 158–59, 191n51
politics: affect and, 84; of art and, 2–3, 28, 42, 62–63, 65–66, 170; of care, xviii; exclusion and, xiii–xvi, 6–7; materiality of, 6–7
Popescu, Carmen, 2
portraiture, 104–8
positionality, 21–22, 80–85, 88–91, 107–8, 128–29, 153–54
possibility, 2–3, 13–14, 45, 51–52, 70–71, 109–11, 155–57, 170–71. *See also* future
Pouillon, Fernand, 71–72, 74–76, 78–82, 86–90, 92–96, 102–3, 105–6, 188n86
poverty, xvi, 7, 55–56, 130–37, 141–42; aesthetics of, 38–39, 45, 48; shame and, xiii–xvi
power, 5–6, 15–16, 21–22, 35–36, 42
precarity, xi–xii, 15–16, 20, 69–70, 90–91, 159
presence, 1–2, 16–17, 35–38, 58–59, 107, 133–34, 168–69. *See also* absence
privacy, private, 27–28, 91–92, 118–19, 148–49
protest. *See* resistance
"Psyco-9—ZÉRO 4-HAY MOHEMADI ft Polini," 46

quakeful thinking, 23–25, 179n66
quiet, 29, 41–42

race, racism: discriminatory structures of, 5, 121–23, 140–44, 155–57; mud and, 127–40, 144–45, 152–53; relationality and, 78–80; representation and, 82–86, 128–40, 152–53; urban planning and, 160, 169
Rahiche, Abdelhamid, 6, 71–72, 97–100, 103–7; photographic practice, 108–11
Rainey, Mark Justin, 10–11
Rais, Khalil, 54
rap, 46. *See also* music
reciprocity, xi–xii, 71–72, 82–83, 103–4, 108–9
recognition, xvii, 20, 71–74, 84–85, 97, 103–5, 107–8, 140–41, 152–53
Reeves-Evison, Theo, 10–11
Reggad, Yasmina, 95
relation, relationality, xii–xiii, xviii, 71–72, 104–5, 150–52; accompaniment and, 8; affect and, 23–25, 84–85, 88–90, 159, 165–67, 170–71; art and, 35, 170–71; built environment and, 92–96, 99–100, 102–3, 109–11; colonialism and, 71–72, 75–77; expansiveness and, 77–78, 92; history and, 91–95; kinship and, 71–72, 82–83, 91–94, 105–6; mass housing and, 4–6, 8, 19–20, 44–45, 47, 60–72, 75–80, 84–88, 97–100, 104–7, 112–13, 166–67, 170–71; nation and, 80–81; poetics of, 70–72, 84–88, 95–96, 103–4, 112; repair and, 2–3, 10–11, 19, 23–25, 44, 71–72, 90–91, 93–94, 112–13, 168–70; representation and, 95, 108–9; of visual, 94, 104–5
Renault-Darsi, Florence, 21–22
repair, xvi–xviii, 2–3, 8–11, 37–38, 59–60, 76–77, 176n5, 178n49; affect and, 21–25, 71–72, 165–71; appropriation and, 105–7; art and, 42, 47–48, 51–53, 66, 120–21, 150–52, 165–71; body and, 165–69; colonialism and, 10–14, 186n19; epistemologies of, 21–26, 76–77, 120–21, 169–70; future and, 170–71; gender and, 107–8, 150–52, 159, 162–63; history and, 66–67, 95, 119–20, 169–70; home and, 135–40; immateriality and, 17–18; mass housing and, 19, 25–26, 165, 169–70; mediation and, 120–21; poetics of, xii–xiii, xvi–xviii, 2–3, 25–26, 107–8, 157–58; relationality and, 10–11, 19, 23–25, 44, 71–72, 90–91, 93–94, 112–13, 168–70; representation and, 169–70; scar of, 17–19; silence and, 85; sound and, 29, 47, 66–67; space of, 161, 167, 169
repetition, 34–35, 42, 63–64, 98, 100–103
representation: affect and, 139–40, 143, 170; agency and, 140–41; fixed, 9, 12–13, 70–71, 170; historical, 54–60; knowledge and, 82–83; positionality and, 128–30, 134, 139–40, 149; race and, 82–86, 152–53; relationality and, 95, 108–9, 169–70; repair and, 169–70; of self, 71–72, 112, 128–29; of space, 135–37, 139–40; transformation and, 109–11
repression, 42, 54–58, 117, 120, 141–43
resettlement campaigns, xi–xvi
resistance, xvi–xvii, 29, 41, 53–56, 69–70, 86–87, 176n17, 177n44
restructuralization, xiii–xvi
revolution, 50–51, 86–87, 141–42
Richeux, Marie, 115–16, 185n11, 185n13; *Achille*, 74–75; *Climats de France*, 22–25, 71–86; *Polaroids*, 74–75
Rivera, Mayra, 25
Roesler, Sascha, 28
Rose, Gillian, 91–92
Rosello, Mireille, 140
Rouissi, Karim, 37–38, 40–41, 58–59

Saddiki, Tayeb, 52–53, 61
Sakib, Mohamed, 57, 66–67
Salti, Rasha, xvi–xvii, 27–28
Sarkisova, Oksana, 91–92
Sausset, Damien, 98–99
Sayad, Abdelmalek, 134
Sayyed, Omar, 62–63
scaffolding, 95–96, 109–11, 115–16
scar, 2–3, 17–19
Sebbar, Leïla, *La Seine était rouge* (*The Seine Was Red*), 118–29, 160; *Shérazade, 17 ans, brune, frisée, les yeux verts*, 119, 128–29
Sekyi-Out, Ato, 7
self-constitution, 6–8, 20, 45–48, 60–70, 97, 135–37, 169. *See also* agency
self-representation, 20, 43–45, 47, 112, 128

Sénac, Jean, "Istiqlal El Djezair" (Algerian independence), 86–87, 170–71
Sgard, Jacques, 160
shame, xiii–xvi, 5–6
shantytown, 6–8. *See also* mass housing
Sharjah Art Foundation Biennale II, 10
Shevchenko, Olga, 91–92
Sidi Othman, 39–40
silence, 29, 34, 42, 47, 75–77, 81, 85–86, 107, 115–29, 159, 161–63, 169–70. *See also* sound
Silverstein, Paul, 135–37
Simone, AbdouMaliq, xviii, 8–9, 66–67, 70–71, 169
Simounet, Roland, 19–20
Slyomovics, Susan, 11–13, 41, 179n73, 186n19
Société pour la Construction de la Cité des Industriels de Casablanca (SOCICA) housing project, 29, 31, 46–49, 165–69
sociology, xii–xiii, 9, 15, 94
solidarity, 20, 63, 105, 128–29, 139–40, 147–48, 153–54, 158–59
Sons of the Hay and Proud of It (documentary), 46
Soual, Mohammed, 58–59
Souiba, Fouad, 29, 52–61
sound, 41, 75–76; colonialism and, 57–58, 60–61; film and, 104; knowledge and, 42; mass housing and, 60–67; politics of, 42; quakeful, 57–58; repair and, 29, 47, 66–67; resistance and, 53–54, 57–58; spatial dynamic of, 29, 66–67; of violence, 54–56, 60–61. *See also* listening
Source du Lion, xii–xiii, 14, 16–17, 21–22
space: appropriation of, 135–39; body and, 47; boundless, 51–52; of built environment, 1–2, 29, 102–3, 129–38; captive, 7–9; containment and, 48, 51–52; control and, 37–38, 40–41; disruption of, 21–25; memory and, 119; relationality and, 155–58, 166–67; repair and, 161, 167, 169; representation and, 128–29, 135–3, 139–40; sound and, 29, 66–67; urban, 10, 87–90, 92–96
Spillmann, Peter, 43–45
sports, 63–66
Ströbel, Katrin, 21–22
Studer, André, 39–40
surface, 35–36, 41, 97–99, 102–3. *See also* depth

Tabti, Oussama, *Sweethome!*, 167–71
Taki, Najib, 58–59
Talbayev, Edwige Tamalet, 4–5
Taylor, Diana, 150–52
Terrab, Sonia, *L7asla* (Lḥaṣla), 29, 63–66
testimony, 58–59, 128–29, 139–40, 159
theater, xvii, 67, 120–21, 163; examples, 145–59
Tillion, Germaine, 74–75
time: of built environment, 1, 102–3; contemplation and, 2; disruption of, 21–25; narrative and, 90–92, 94; visual and, 90–92, 94. *See also* future; possibility
Tiong Bahru Estate HDB (Singapore), 1
Tissières, Hélène, 47–48
totality, 23–25
touch, 11, 15–16, 22–23, 49–50, 58–59, 73–74, 165–69
Toufic, Jalal, 16–17
trace, 34–38, 53–54, 66–67, 115–16, 121–23, 126–27
trame Écochard, 31, 34, 38, 180n24. *See also* grid
trauma, 118–20, 123–24, 127, 146–47, 154, 158–59
Tresfels, Cécile, 73–74
trompe l'oeil, 100–102
Troux, Manon, 58–59

uncertainty, 13–15, 20, 23–25
universalism, 51–54, 80–81, 155–57
urban planning, 5–7, 10, 16–17, 19–20, 31–32, 177n34; colonial, 34–35, 37–41, 44–45, 80–81, 86–87, 97–98, 117, 180n20; gender and, 115–16; grid and, 32–34, 39–41; poetry and, 87–88; race and, 160, 169

video, xiii, 9, 10; amateur, 42–47, 112–13; examples, 1–2, 29, 42–47, 65–66, 71–72, 89–98, 102–8, 112–13, 165–69; grid and, 43–44, 47. *See also* film
violence: colonial, 80–81, 92, 125, 141–43, 154; police and military, 54–61, 158–59; race and, 121–23; state and, 140–45, 182n63
visibility, 25, 90–92, 102–3, 117, 140–44
visual, 29, 32–35, 37–38, 42–47, 89–90; embodiment and, 97–98; narrative and, 90–94; relationality of, 94, 104–5, 107–8; temporality of, 90–92, 94
Vive les Groues, 160–61

voice, xii, xvi–xvii, 29, 32–33, 42–44, 54, 61–62, 82–86, 89–92, 104, 106–7, 138–40, 146–50

von Osten, Marion, 5, 7–8, 32–34, 37–38, 115–16, 181n33; *Bauhaus Imaginista*, 42–43, 181n33; *Colonial Modern: Aesthetics of the Past, Rebellions of the Future*, 42–43; *In the Desert of Modernity: Colonial Planning and After*, 42–43; *This Was Tomorrow!*, 29, 42–47, 112

whiteness, 76–77, 82–83, 128–29, 190n18. *See also* race, racism

Wiedorn, Michael, 25, 179n66

Winant, Gabriel, 21, 95

Woods, Shadrach, 31, 180n20

world: art and, xvii–xviii, 2; belonging to, 169–70; broken-world thinking, 21–22; possibility and, 109–11, 156–58; repair and, xvii–xviii, 25; world making, 98–99, 120–21, 156–58, 169–71

wound, 17–18, 170. *See also* scar

Wylie, Diana, 67

xenophobia, 112

Yaala, Allal, 61

Yacine, Kateb, 159

Years of Lead, 56, 59–60

Yes We Camp (NGO), 160–61

Zaki, Lamia, xvi, 5–6

Zidi, Myriam, 67

Zinoun, Lahcen, *Le piano*, 29, 47–53, 167

Zrika, Abdallah, xiii–xvii, 6